T0305048

Public Expenditure Control in Europe

Public Expenditure Control in Europe

Coordinating Audit Functions in the European Union

Edited by

Milagros García Crespo

Professor of Applied Economics, University of the Basque Country, Spain

Edward Elgar

Cheltenham, UK • Northampton, MA, USA

Published by
Edward Elgar Publishing Limited
Glensanda House
Montpellier Parade
Cheltenham
Glos GL50 1UA
UK

Edward Elgar Publishing, Inc.
136 West Street
Suite 202
Northampton
Massachusetts 01060
USA

A catalogue record for this book
is available from the British Library

ISBN 1 84376 837 2

Printed and bound in Great Britain by MPG Books Ltd, Bodmin, Cornwall

Contents

List of figures and tables   vii
List of boxes   viii
List of contributors   ix
Foreword   xi
Acknowledgements   xiv
List of abbreviations   xv

PART I   DIFFERENT FORMS OF PUBLIC CONTROL

1   Public control: a general view   3
    Milagros García Crespo

2   Public audit in the United Kingdom   30
    Sir John Bourn

3   Public expenditure control in the Netherlands   55
    Saskia J. Stuiveling and Rudi W. Turksema

4   Public financial control in Europe: the example of the Federal   79
    Republic of Germany
    Hedda von Wedel

5   The system of public control in Spain   99
    Milagros García Crespo

6   External audit institutions: the European Court of Auditors   127
    and its relationship with the national audit institutions of the
    Member States
    Antoni Castells

PART II   TOWARDS COORDINATION STRATEGIES

7   A policy to fight financial fraud in the European Union   151
    Alfredo José de Sousa

8   The coordination of internal controls: the single audit – towards   184
    a European Union internal control framework
    Vítor Caldeira

9   Towards the coordination of financial reporting at the different   211
    levels of public administration in Europe
    Vicente Montesinos Julve

Index   243

Figures and tables

FIGURES

3.1	Causal policy model	60
3.2	The new budget structure	62
3.3	The NCA strategy 2004–09	69
9.1	Public sector financial information systems	212
9.2	The new governmental accounting	214
9.3	International Public Sector Accounting Standards (IPSASs)	217
9.4	Phases and dates of accrual accounting reform	222
9.5	Norm and rule setting for national governments in Europe	224
9.6	The main principles and objectives of budgetary and financial reporting	228
9.7	Overview of principal controls	234

TABLE

2.1	Some of the studies in 2002 and 2003	48

Boxes

2.1 Financial audit reports by the Controller and Auditor General 31

2.2 Reports in the public interest by auditors appointed by the
Audit Commission 32

2.3 Reports on criminal cases by the Comptroller and Auditor
General 33

2.4 Reports by the Comptroller and Auditor General leading to
significant financial savings 33

2.5 Reports by the Comptroller and Auditor General leading to
improvements in the quality of public services 34

2.6 Reports by the Auditor General for Scotland 34

2.7 Reports by the Auditor General for Wales 35

3.1 Illustration of the three W questions 63

Contributors

Bourn, Sir John, Comptroller and Auditor General of the United Kingdom

Caldeira, Vítor, Member of the European Court of Auditors

Castells, Antoni, Professor of Public Finance, University of Barcelona. Former Member of the European Court of Auditors

García Crespo, Milagros, Professor of Applied Economics, University of the Basque Country. Former President of the Tribunal de Cuentas of Spain

Montesinos Julve, Vicente, Professor of Accounting, University of Valencia. President of the Sindicatura de Cuentas of Valencia

Sousa, Alfredo José de, Member of OLAF's Supervisory Committee. President of Tribunal de Contas of Portugal

Stuiveling, Saskia J., President of the Netherlands Algemene Rekenkamer

Turksema, Rudi W., Senior Auditor of the Netherlands Algemene Rekenkamer

Wedel, Hedda von, Member of the European Court of Auditors. Former President of the German Bundesrechnungshof

Foreword

As economic and social development have progressed, financial control and political scrutiny of the budget have become essential components of the democratic legitimisation of public expenditure.

Supreme Audit Institutions should contribute decisively to the quality and effectiveness of this process. Audit reports identify shortcomings and recommend measures to improve the management. They thereby help the executive to make the best possible use of public funds; in other words to ensure that the political objectives of the expenditure are achieved at minimum cost and that the accounts drawn up are transparent. Lastly, the publication of audit findings enables citizens to become familiar with and to legitimise the actions of their government and representatives.

Public expenditure in a democratic society should rely on an effective financial management and control system.

These types of statements could be quoted very easily from any Public Finances student's manual or from any specialized publication in government audit. They are taken as a kind of *axiom*, easily assumed and undisputed in any analysis of public finances systems. But are these assertions also valid in the European Union context, or do they remain commonplaces, closer to our wishes than to political reality?

Today, we could already speak of the consolidation of a 'European public sector' in which European, national, regional and local funds jointly finance all kinds of projects to improve people's quality of life. The EU budget has dramatically increased from the 20 billion euro in the 1970s to more than 100 billion euro in 2004. Common rules govern the working of public administrations and European companies in increasingly varied domains such as agriculture, regional development, finance, the environment and transport. Our common currency, the euro, is part of the everyday life of millions of people.

Thus the European Union involves social, economic and fiscal policy integration, including a strong common budgetary instrument. However, this trend has not been followed by the development of an adequate financial management and control system able to provide the assurance that European public funds are soundly expended.

Over the last few years, with the encouragement of the European

Parliament and the Commission, this topic has been brought to the political agenda of the Union. The Commission has undertaken an in-depth administrative reform: a new financial regulation was adopted in 2002; internal control has been decentralized and assigned to line managers (Directors-General); internal control standards have been introduced and a strong internal audit function has been put in place.

These measures have certainly had a positive effect in terms of improving the quality of Commission management; nevertheless, they have a very limited impact on the areas of the budget directly administered and controlled by national administrations. These areas represent more than 80 per cent of expenditure and include the agriculture subsidies and the structural funds which are transferred into national budgets and pulled together with national resources.

In this way, common financial resources and rules serve to integrate the European, national, regional and local public sectors. But what about the control systems? Have they been integrated to the same degree?

Control systems involve several institutions and bodies: the European Court of Auditors, the Commission's Internal Audit Service, the National Supreme Audit Institutions, Regional Audit Offices, national internal auditors, inspectorate bodies, certifying accounts and paying agencies, and so on. Are all these bodies working in an efficient and cost-effective way? I think they are not. The audit field is not properly covered, there is too much overlapping and duplication; moreover, they are not able to rely sufficiently on the work carried out by the other bodies.

In the case of the Supreme Audit Institutions (SAIs), and despite the evident interest of all concerned and the resources that have been provided by them, we should not be content with the results of the existing collaboration. Coordinating structures, such as the Contact Committee of Presidents and the liaison officers' meetings, have been created; procedures for mutual assistance and the exchange of information have also been established. But the decisive step of establishing effective, operational coordination still has to be taken (thereby avoiding unnecessary repetition or shortcomings in our audit work). Our work programmes should be coordinated, and we should be able swiftly to exchange our audit findings and to use this information in our own work.

The enlargement of the Union will no doubt bring other difficulties, such as more languages, a larger population and territory, weak financial control systems and young institutions which need our support to improve their administrative practices. Incoming countries will be important beneficiaries of the structural funds and of the common agricultural policy subsidies. There is no doubt that this trend will be justified, *vis à vis* European public opinion, but only if the sound utilization of these funds is rigorously accounted for. The success of the enlargement process will partly depend on the vigilance of the control and on the relevance of the corrective measures that will be envisaged and proposed.

However, we must not be pessimistic, rather the opposite. The history of the European project has shown that with political will and the resolve born of sound ideas, we have been able to solve greater organizational problems. As already mentioned, the main problem concerns the areas of shared management, where national authorities administer and control European Union budget funds. Shared management should also involve shared control; cooperation and the application of the subsidiarity principle are, in my view, the keys elements in this process.

We have now reached a critical stage in the construction of the European public sector. It is necessary to redefine the responsibilities and prerogatives of Member States and European Institutions, and it is essential to determine the resources and powers that are necessary for the control of the Community funds. This is not an easy task. It calls for increased collaboration between all the bodies involved in this matter. Effective cooperation between SAIs is one of the starting points for any rational system of external control of Europe's finances. Cooperation must be founded on respect for the independence and operating mandate of each SAI and for their different organizational and operational approaches. At the same time, cooperation must be strengthened through each institution's commitment to developing concrete actions aimed at improving the system of control of Europe's finances. Above all, however, there is a need for willingness and openness so that agreements can be reached which, while perhaps not always entirely satisfactory for all sides, are globally beneficial.

This book presents a very thorough analysis of the public expenditure control in Europe and the coordination strategies available: strategies that should aim at strengthening collaboration between the different levels of financial control – internal and external; European Union, national and regional. I am convinced that by respecting the independence of each control body and its own style of organization and work, we can create a system for the control of European funds which is more effective and which guarantees greater democratic legitimization of European public expenditure. The creation of such a system is without doubt a sound idea which will help to improve the lives of our fellow citizens.

Juan Manuel Fabra Vallés
President of European Court of Auditors

Acknowledgements

This book is essentially a collective work. All the contributors hold, or have held, posts of responsibility in various Supreme Audit Institutions in different European countries. They translate into these pages their direct and irreplaceable experience on public expenditure control. But their contribution is also indirectly indebted to the experience and knowledge of a large number of auditors and experts who work in those same institutions.

I must personally express my gratitude to all the professors in the Department of Applied Economics of the University of the Basque Country, particularly to Felipe Serrano, Roberto Velasco, Marisol Esteban and Jaime del Castillo, who encouraged me to use my experience as President of the Spanish Tribunal de Cuentas and of the Tribunal Vasco de Cuentas Públicas as the basis for this book.

I also want to express my gratitude to the team of auditors with which I worked for nearly ten years, and whose opinions have helped me to form my own views on the subject of this book, particularly to Gregorio Cuñado, María Luz Martín, Mercedes Martín and Domingo Fidalgo, without forgetting the decisive and enthusiastic input of the late Gloria Muruaga.

The other members of the Tribunal de Cuentas have also contributed, through heated and mostly friendly discussions in the course of the Full Sessions, to give shape to my personal views. Numerous meetings with representatives from all Spanish regional audit bodies have also proved fruitful.

I also had the opportunity, through the Contact Committee that gathers representatives from European SAIs and the European Court of Auditors, as well as through EUROSAI, to meet my colleagues from other European countries, and to become familiar with the diverse European control institutions that they represent. I want to thank them all for their invaluable contribution.

Finally, I must of course point out that all errors and omissions that may be found in this book are my own responsibility.

Abbreviations

CAP	Common Agricultural Policy
CNMV	Comisión Nacional del Mercado de Valores
COB	Commission des Opérations de Bourse
CONSOB	Commissione Nazionale per le Società e la Borsa
EAGGF	European Agricultural Guidance and Guarantee Fund
ECA	European Court of Auditors
EMU	Economic and Monetary Union
ESA	European System of National Accounts
EU	European Union
EURORAI	European Organization of Regional Audit Institutions
EUROSAI	European Organization of Supreme Audit Institutions
FEE	European Federation of Accountants
GFS	Government Finance Statistics
IACS	Integrated Administration and Control System
IAS	International Accounting Standard
IASB	International Accounting Standards Board
IBRD	International Bank for Reconstruction and Development
IDA	International Development Association
IFAC	International Federation of Accountants
IFAC-PSC	Public Sector Committee of the International Federation of Accountants
IFRS	International Financial Reporting Standard
IMF	International Monetary Fund
INTOSAI	International Organization of Supreme Audit Institutions
IPSASs	International Public Sector Accounting Standards
MERCOSUR	Mercado Común del Sur (Common Market of the Southern Cone)
NPM	New Public Management
OECD	Organization for Economic Co-operation and Development
OLAF	European Anti-Fraud Office
SAI	Supreme Audit Institution

SGP	Stability and Growth Pact
SNA	System of National Accounts
UCLAF	Anti-Fraud Co-ordination Unit

PART I

Different Forms of Public Control

1. Public control: a general view

Milagros García Crespo

EFFECTIVENESS AND EFFICIENCY IN ECONOMIC THEORY

The study of the economic activity of the State is one of the classic fields of reflection in economic theory. This reflection has known different historical phases according to the economic paradigm prevalent at the time. Authors following the neoclassical approach have explained the origin of the State functions taking as a starting point the solution offered by the theorems of welfare economy. Thus the theory of market failures became the main reference in the study of the economic activity of the State. This theory has subsequently seen its analysis enriched with the incorporation of new concepts derived from the observed information difficulties encountered by economic agents when they try to optimize their decisions. The hypothesis of perfect information has been nuanced in response to the existence of information asymmetries and thus an important new field of reflection has been opened up, described by Stiglitz (1994) as a new paradigm, the 'paradigm of information', as opposed to the 'neoclassical paradigm' represented by the welfare economy.

Accepted or not as a new paradigm, acknowledgement of the existence of information deficiencies has enlarged in new directions the neoclassical field of research on the State functions. Nevertheless, the novelty is not as radical as the words of Stiglitz would make us believe. During the first third of the last century, institutional economics had already explored some of the areas of study that follow from the assumption of an asymmetry of information. The real novelty lies in the integration of this old line of economic thought within the neoclassical paradigm, dominated by the principle of instrumental rationality and maximization of individual utility.

In any case the New Institutional Economy has rediscovered the importance of institutions – and among them, public institutions – for the correct functioning of market economies. Imperfect information in the hands of economic agents prevents the market from achieving a state of equilibrium; that is, it prevents the market from making efficient allocations. State intervention can correct those information failures in order to ensure that free interaction between agents through the market ends up in equilibrium solutions. The reduction of transaction costs thus becames a measurement of the effectiveness of State intervention.

The public choice school of thought underlines the need to analyse the political process of decision-making. The theory of bureaucracy and political parties, as well as the theory of constitutions, proposes an analytical body with a clear objective: to provide information about the existence of asymmetries between the potential need for intervention required by the market and the response – in the form of functions – offered by the State. The theory of political failures represents the mirror image, in the sphere of the political market, of the theory of market failures, thus contributing to close the neoclassical paradigm in the study area of public activity.

These analyses ignore one dimension of public activity that is at present attracting more and more attention: the achievement of efficiency in the internal allocation of public resources. The design of optimal administrative structures, partially studied by the theory of constitutions, must receive all the attention it deserves. Administration is efficient when it provides all necessary services at a minimal cost, assuring that those services respond to social demand that is revealed through, among other channels, political elections.

The search for efficiency, or indeed sound government, is not only a desirable objective in itself. A sound economy of public resources allows for more goods and services to be provided without substantially increasing taxes. In the same way that a sound institutional design can contribute to reduce transaction costs, a sound administrative design should help reduce the costs of supplying goods and services. In order to clarify our position, it is useful to establish a comparison with other proposals for administrative reform that have been made in the economic literature.

The problem of temporal inconsistencies of economic policies had opened, by the end of the 1970s, a strong debate about the optimal way of reaching the objectives of economic policy. The debate centred around a straight choice: rules versus discretionary powers. One of the central elements of the debate was the optimal institutional design to be adopted in the context of an economic policy based on regulation. In order to avoid the problems of strategic re-adaptation to which economic agents are subjected when administrations operate along the principle of non-restriction, the best option was considered to be the setting-up of independent agencies, the clearest example being the choice of independent Central Banks.

The search for the best institutional design has found economic efficiency to be the key criterion when it is necessary to discriminate between alternative institutional designs. In the last analysis, it is a question of building institutions that keep away from the political tensions of the moment in order to respond to the real needs of the economic process. In theoretical terms, we could say that the only optimal institutions are those that contribute towards reaching economic equilibrium, as traditionally understood in neoclassical theory.

The research on institutional design that we undertake in the present book does not aim at those theoretical aspects. Our reflection is guided by the search for administrative structures providing a service at a minimal cost. From our perspective, therefore, every administrative design must be subjected to the prerequisite of efficiency. It is not essential to our aim that institutions are conceived to be run according to rules or in a discretionary way. And although this is a very important debate, for our purposes it is only secondary. We are not saying that the two perspectives cannot be related, they obviously can, we are only saying that at present this relationship will not be the object of our attention.

Public control institutions are key elements that can help in achieving efficient administrative structures. These institutions exercise several functions, two of them of particular relevance: (1) they carry out the essential function of audit, and (2) they can be used as potential sources of information for policy makers.

The activity of public control responds to the social demand for sound government. Control of public decisions cannot be restricted to political elections, in which there are other issues at stake apart from the efficient allocation of public resources – such as social demands dealing with the general orientation of public expenditure, the amount of taxes that society is prepared to endure, or the institutional design demanded by the people. In the same way that we expect to find transparent administration in a private enterprise, we also require from the public administrations an efficient allocation of those resources that society considers must be managed collectively.

In the achievement of this objective, control institutions generate information relevant to the knowledge of inefficiencies in administrative structures; this information must be used by governments in order to improve efficiency.

We face at present the task of further reflecting on a new design of control organisms inspired, at least within the European Union, by the need for coordination. And the need for coordination is imposed on us by the administrative changes taking place as a result of the European integration process, as the Member States delegate more powers to the European Commission. On the other hand, another factor demanding the need for a redesign of control bodies is the process of decentralization affecting many States, where powers are being transferred to regional, federal and local administrations.

This gradual transformation from a centralized administration towards a decentralized administration in which different expenditure and income units enjoy exclusive powers, has not been accompanied by a parallel transformation of control bodies. On the contrary, there has been a proliferation of control units at every level of administration that generates overlapping of procedures and, eventually, an efficiency deficit of control institutions.

A SYSTEMATIZATION OF THE DIFFERENT ASPECTS OF PUBLIC CONTROL

Considering the body that exercises it, control can be external or internal. Internal control is carried out by specialized organisms that belong to the structure of the audited institution. It is within the administration itself that the legality and efficiency of its organ's actions are inspected and checked. Reports coming from this kind of control remain within the internal domain of the institution and are rarely made public.

In the case of external control, the inspection and assessment of the controlled entity or action are carried out by organisms outside the public administration. The institution in charge of control is independent from the controlled entity. External audit reports, usually made public, are destined for parliaments and governments.

As the external auditor, the Supreme Audit Institution (SAI) has the task of examining the effectiveness of internal audit. If internal audit is judged effective, efforts shall be made to achieve the most appropriate division or assignment of tasks and cooperation between the SAI and internal audit, without prejudice to the right of the former to carry out an overall audit (INTOSAI, 1977).

According to the timing, control can be before the fact (pre-audit), concomitant (continuous), or after the fact (post-audit). Pre-audit can be carried out either by internal control bodies or by SAIs. In either case, the procedure is similar.

The task of pre-audit involves the authorizing of public expenditure, essentially as part of the financial control process. Typically the control body receives all payment orders and supporting documentation, checks that the transaction has been authorized, that it is legal and regular and that there is sufficient provision for it in the budget. It then either sanctions the payment or, where the transaction does not meet these criteria, returns it to the auditee for amendment.

Pre-audit is carried out by the SAI in five European countries (Belgium, Greece, Italy, Luxembourg and Portugal) although the number of transactions subject to such scrutiny varies. Although it is true that the

SAIs carrying out pre-audits consider that this type of audit has a number of advantages, there is nevertheless a tendency to minimize its scope and content. On the other hand, a form of high level pre-audit is found in Ireland and the United Kingdom, where the Auditor General has an additional comptroller function and is responsible for ensuring that funds are only issued to the executive for purposes approved by Parliament.

Post-audit is not an exclusive of SAIs, as there are in some cases internal control institutions belonging to public administrations that have the attributions to perform it. That said, all European Union SAIs undertake some form of post-audit, and in countries where they do not carry out pre-audit control, the SAIs rely on it when examining the government accounts. Here, we already encounter the need for coordination between internal and external control in order to avoid duplications. The quality of internal control is a fundamental issue that SAIs must take into consideration when planning the scope of their subsequent intervention. Some SAIs rely to a significant extent on the assessment of internal controls or on the work of internal auditors. The need for SAIs to have access to the documentation necessary to carry out their duties is acknowledged in all EU countries. SAIs carrying out pre-audits have all the documents relating to financial transactions sent to their headquarters.

Finally, according to the content of control, we can distinguish between legality, financial or efficiency controls.

For decades, before the management of public resources was considered one of the objectives of control, the activity of SAIs was restricted to the assessment of formal, procedural and financial legality of public expenditure. However, a good legality audit – either pre-audit or post-audit – can contribute to the improvement of management in public administrations. Thus pre-audit of public works contracts and acquisition of goods and services usually has an important preventive effect.

The information that public managers must provide to the control body contains both financial and management components. In this respect, there are two criteria when presenting accounts: the criterion of authorization to allocate resources and the criterion of property control (IFAC, 1996). According to the first criterion, the accounts only take into consideration those resources in the form of liquid funds, and the audited entities are those financed mainly through the budget; that is, the budgetary sector. According to the criterion of property, all resources under the responsibility of the government are included in the accounts; the audited entities are those belonging to or controlled by the government, including therefore both the budgetary and non-budgetary sectors (Montesinos, 2000).

When dealing with management control, three basic principles (the so-called 'three E's') are usually mentioned: effectiveness, efficiency and economy. To these, some authors add the principles of fairness and environment. All these principles are integrated in the doctrine of control and, either totally or partially, recognized in law; however, they are not always given the same meaning.

Without pretending to arrive at a final conceptual definition, we will limit ourselves to giving their most widely accepted meaning. Thus effectiveness control ascertains the degree of achievement of objectives and the relation between established objectives and results (effectiveness in relation to objectives). Efficiency control (also known as performance or productivity control) checks the relation between provided goods and services and the resources employed to do this. Finally, economy control examines cost minimization of acquired or allocated resources in terms of quality, quantity, price and opportunity of its acquisition.

Control, and particularly management control, is dynamic by nature and therefore feedback becomes a key element. The sequence of the control process is as follows: analysis of public management – carrying out of audit – evaluation of audit findings – effects on public management – changes in management. In order to make feedback work, it is evident that the SAI must have a remit to make recommendations, either to Parliament or to government.

When information coming from public managers is taken as a basis for decision-making the accounts must include, besides conventional financial information, specific management components.[1]

EVOLUTION OF THE CONTENT OF CONTROL

The final innovation in public control took place when management control was added to legality and financial controls.

Historically, business organizations were the pioneers of management control. Taking as a model the evolution of businesses, we can ascertain that for decades they have undergone a process of increase in volume and complexity in their activity, together with a process of internationalization that has obliged them to work in open and heterogeneous scenarios. This new situation necessarily affects management systems. The most significant change resides in the fact that management generally lies in the hands of professionals that do not hold the property of the organization. It is precisely when ownership and management do not coincide in the same individuals that the task of control becomes so important.

This explains why the activity of control has been developed significantly in private enterprise, and why an auxiliary management tool used for supervising and ensuring that the management approach is properly followed has become also a professional and independent tool for the evaluation of the right allocation of resources and the degree of achievement of programmed objectives. Its main function is at present to cooperate in the improvement of management by making specific proposals.

The same evolutionary phenomenon has taken place in the economic and financial activity of the public sector, whose control, without relinquishing its traditional function of ensuring the compliance with the law, now focuses mainly on the supervision of public management.

The traditional organization of public administration allowed the development of a culture of bureaucratic management where innovation and initiative were uncommon features. Logically, this is an untenable situation when the public sector represents between 40 per cent and 60 per cent of GDP in EU countries and must have efficient administrative structures.

This fact has led to the need for an urgent reform of public management in the context of a new culture of management. The reform, introduced in virtually all countries, relies on the theory of public choice, and has resulted in what is known as New Public Management (NPM). The fundamental principles of NPM are as follows.

- Deregulation, aimed at reducing the excessive number of regulations and stressing the establishment of objectives.
- At the same time, NPM emphasizes management responsibilities and motivates management improvements through evaluation methods and management techniques. Evaluation must take place in all layers of management, either in the assessment of policies, in the performance of systems or in the efficient allocation of resources.
- It views the citizen as a customer of public services, and takes into consideration above all the citizen's satisfaction with public services.
- Schemes for the improvement of the public function lead to management decentralization, establishing smaller units that are run according to market and competition mechanisms.[2]

With the above-mentioned modifications, in every democratic system public managers must justify the results of their performance to the citizens, as these are the ones who finance, through taxes, the activity of the public sector. In some cases, the sensitivity of the public in relation to certain issues leads to the carrying out of audits outside the strict content of public accounts. Such is the case, for instance, of environmental audits.

Professional public managers have an executive responsibility, as they receive orders from the government and must in turn deliver a set of results, giving information about their performance and being answerable for it. We are thus in the presence of a chain of relations, beginning with the citizens and leading to those holding political posts, the government and the executive managers whose main task is to provide public goods and services. Along this chain, external contracts and the privatization of services open up an additional line, as third parties carrying out public services must also face public responsibility.

The concept of social, political and financial responsibility of public managers reinforces and widens the content of public accountability. Public audit must also verify the compliance of public managers in relation to their responsibilities and the justification of their performance. The features of this accountability are currently being thoroughly revised in order to ensure its effectiveness, with transparency of information being one of the basic parameters in this reform of public management.

In harmony with this evolution, and with the exception of the SAIs of Greece and Luxembourg, all EU audit institutions have some powers to audit the performance of government departments and other public bodies. Although it is generally agreed that performance audit involves the examination of economy, efficiency and effectiveness, different interpretations are followed in particular countries. There are also differences as to what SAIs can examine in the course of performance audit and at what stage they can start their work.

These changes in the management of public entities have a notable influence on public audit, for different reasons: (1) the scope of control is enlarged; (2) there is a stronger interest in knowing the results of public performance, which in turn leads to deeper analyses of these entities, especially with regard to the effectiveness of their internal controls; (3) priority is given to the investigation of fraud and corruption; and (4) audit reports are expected to be clearer and more timely.

Information on performance goes beyond the limits of financial information, and if it is going to respond to the objectives of control it is necessary to define a set of indicators in order to evaluate the effectiveness, efficiency and economy of the entity's performance as part of its analytical accounting.[3] However, control must follow the increase in desired information, it must never precede it. Sometimes, legislation in different countries affirms the need to carry out effectiveness, efficiency and economy controls before the public administration has developed the corresponding information tools, rendering the task of auditors more difficult (Montesinos, 2000).

The introduction of the culture of total quality in the public sector has been mostly developed in the last decade, much later than in the private sector. The international quality standards (particularly ISO 9000) are applied to public entities in order to verify their compliance with the basic quality requisites, their internal processes, documentation and control. It is advisable that these aspects be supervised by the control bodies. Another field into which control bodies must enter is benchmarking; that is, the practice of permanently comparing the products, services and performance of one entity against those of its more serious competitors. This comparison demands the measurement of results, with customer satisfaction being one of the most important references.[4]

The evaluation of policies adopted by public entities, the accomplishment of established objectives and foreseen management patterns are important aspects to be dealt with in audit, if audit is to become a tool for the efficient allocation of resources and the sound management of public entities. Audit programmes must emphasize, together with the control of legality, the consistency of results with established objectives. It is not easy for the auditor to give an opinion about strategic objectives, but he or she can easily evaluate policies as well as the economic and social consequences, not only of non-compliance with legality, but also of inefficiencies in the designed procedures and the management of resources.

There is in the world of public control a certain controversy about the convenience of taking business audit as a referent for public audit. The fact is that in the EU we find a constant concern for the definition of the functions, scope and objectives of business audit, whereas in the sphere of public audit there are few similar initiatives. The EU has even published a set of conclusions in a Green Book of Audit (that is, private audit),[5] but there is no strategic vision of public management and, consequently, of public audit, capable of establishing a hierarchy of objectives. In the field of public audit, one possible obstacle to moving forward in this direction could be the variation of practices between different countries and, indeed, within the same country.

As the President of the European Court of Auditors pointed out (Fabra, 2003), the European public sector still suffers from a lack of expenditure control mechanisms adjusted to its size and features (federal character, co-financing and co-management). In this sense, none of the multiple control bodies is in a position to ensure the good global use of all resources employed in a given public action or policy. He also asked himself how efficient control of financial resources could be achieved in an enlarged EU.

In our opinion, it is an urgent requirement to draw up a document on the meaning, objectives and scope of public audit in the EU in the context of the Stability Plan, taking into account some of the following points.

- The notion of control does not have a univocal meaning capable of avoiding multiple senses in its application. The definitive meaning is reached through a process of standardization. In the case of public control, standardization begins with its ordering, with the help of adequate guidelines, but we cannot say that there is an organ that has defined the basic concepts of control before the juridical articulation of these guidelines. Decentralization is a phenomenon that also affects control, and new institutions are created that obey their own norms, established by the nearest legislative power, not allowing for comparisons between them.

- It is not unusual to find different norms that regulate the same matter and make use of identical terms, but that give those terms different scope and meanings. This source of confusion, not uncommon within the borders of the same country, is almost impossible to avoid when trying to approach different public control procedures internationally. It is, for example, extremely difficult to agree on a single definition of the terms effectiveness, efficacy and economy; or the terms audit, financial control or performance evaluation.

- When different control institutions give a divergent terminological definition of the various types of control, the possibility of conflicts – not always resolved in a conciliatory way – arises. In practice, conflict situations are usually avoided by means of safeguard clauses allowing for the existence and application of other possible controls. When, as a result of integration processes, problems become internationalized, the main task is trying to reach, as far as possible, a unified system of control, given that the implementation of the greater part of the community budget by EU countries demands a multiplicity of controls beyond the capabilities of the European Court of Auditors. Internal control is carried out in the country receiving a financial transfer, but there is a plurality of centres of expenditure; in the case of Spain, for instance, three different administrative layers are involved. The same thing happens in relation to external control in cases of co-financing between the EU and Member States. This complicated pattern of controls has originated, paradoxically, in those control institutions that must watch over compliance with the principles of effectiveness and efficiency.

INSTITUTIONS

Organizations for Cooperation

There are supranational organizations acting at different levels and aiming at increasing cooperation between public control institutions. The most important one, open to SAIs of all UN countries, is the International

Organization of Supreme Audit Institutions (INTOSAI), an organization that cooperates with the United Nations. Regional working groups were also created, among them the European Organization of Supreme Audit Institutions (EUROSAI). Finally, there is another international organization in the field of European public control: the European Organization of Regional Audit Institutions (EURORAI).

INTOSAI

From the time of its creation in Havana in 1953, INTOSAI has provided the institutional framework for cooperation in the area of public sector control, according to its motto: 'Experientia mutua omnibus prodest'. As a professional organization of SAIs, it helps its members by providing them with the opportunity of sharing information and experiences in the field of public audit. INTOSAI also puts into the public domain international guidelines for financial management.

INTOSAI holds a congress every three years with the objective of sharing experiences, debating issues and approving recommendations in order to improve the public accountability of all governments. We can get an idea of the importance of INTOSAI in the world institutional framework if we consider that representatives of the United Nations and the World Bank, among other organisms, come to these congresses. On top of that, the conclusions and recommendations of annual congresses constitute an internationally respected source of legislative and organic reforms of SAIs, as has been the case in newly constituted African States or Eastern European countries.

There are work groups that promote at the regional level the objectives of INTOSAI, thus allowing Member States to focus on the specific problems of their region. There are seven of these regional groups; the first one to be created, in 1965, was the Latin American and Caribbean Organization of Supreme Audit Institutions; the most recent one was EUROSAI, created in 1990. Simultaneously, a great deal of technical work is done by commissions and work groups focusing on the improvement of public audit by means of the definition of professional standards and methodology, and the issuing of bibliography and other reference information.

One of the first tasks of INTOSAI is the training of public sector auditors. Its biennial seminaries, sponsored jointly with the UN, are particularly important for the training of professionals in developing countries.

The Lima Declaration, adopted in the IX Congress of INTOSAI in 1977, formulates the basic principles to be followed in public control:

- The defence of independence in the area of public control, sanctioned in legislation. This thus expresses the need for the functional, organic and financial independence of SAIs, guaranteed by the Constitution, or by other legislation, in the face of possible interference coming from other State organisms.

- SAIs, apart from fulfilling the traditional tasks of the control of legality and regularity of State financial transactions, must also inspect the effectiveness, efficacy and economy of these transactions, both individually and as part of a global activity, in accordance with the audit programme drawn up by the SAIs themselves.
- The need to cooperate with parliaments, the main beneficiaries of audit reports.
- The need to cooperate with governments that want to introduce administrative reforms, assessing legislative proposals having a financial character and making recommendations aimed at the improvement of financial performance.[6]

EUROSAI

EUROSAI is the European regional group of INTOSAI, and its objectives do not differ from those of INTOSAI. Thus it tries to promote professional cooperation between SAIs and Member States, as well as exchange of information and documentation; it undertakes the study of public audit and encourages the creation of university chairs in this field; it also ensures the unification of public audit terminology. The first constituent Congress was held in Madrid in 1990, subsequently it has held another four triennial Congresses, the last one in Moscow in 2002. At present, the SAIs of 46 countries are members of EUROSAI.

In the constituent Congress, the creation of a Training Committee composed of the SAIs of nine countries was approved; in the IV Congress, held in Paris in 1999, a work group on Environmental Audit was created, presided over by the Polish Supreme Chamber of Control; finally, in Moscow, the creation of another work group on Information Technologies was approved, this time presided over by the Dutch SAI.

All these initiatives respond to the central idea of the organization and the concerns of its members, and are guided by a strong conviction that it is necessary to have official tools in order to coordinate the activity of external control in Europe. The vital support and advice given by EUROSAI members and the European Court of Auditors to Eastern European countries deserves also to be mentioned.

EURORAI

EURORAI is the European Organization of Regional External Public Finance Audit Institutions. It has the same objectives as INTOSAI and EUROSAI: promotion of cooperation, exchange of information and knowledge, the study of matters related to audit and the organization of advanced training courses. Congresses are also held every three years.

Created in 1992, the organization is at present composed of 45 members. Most of its members are regional control bodies belonging to federal States (nine German, two Austrian, three Swiss), quasi-federal or 'devolved' States (ten Spanish regional audit bodies) and Regional Chambers (nine French). There are also local bodies like Rotterdam's Rekenkamer or the Control Chamber of Moscow.

As an indicator of the kind of issues in which the group is mostly interested, we can mention some questions dealt with in the last Congress, held in Graz (Austria) in 2001: 'The function of advice of regional external control bodies' and 'The consequences for the audit function of the transposition of EU directives on public contracts'.

State Audit Institutions in Europe

Different models of SAIs
All European States have an organ that carries out the economical and financial control of the public sector. It generally enjoys constitutional rank and therefore is part of the State structure. That said, its composition, organization and attributions vary considerably from country to country, for historical, cultural and political reasons. However, they are linked by common membership of the EU and by their shared democracy, even though the democratic processes and systems vary in many ways. It is against this background of distinct parliamentary, constitutional and administrative systems that each SAI operates (NAO, 1996).

According to their composition, SAIs can be collegiate or constituted by a single person. In virtue of the contents of their attributions, they can either perform only audit tasks, or perform advice and jurisdictional tasks as well.

The combination of these elements allows us to systematize the different models of European SAIs in the following way:

- *Anglo-Saxon model.* The SAI is a one-person institution, independent from the executive. It exercises audit functions and also gives advice to Parliament. On the assumption that irregularities are detected in the course of an audit, the attributions of imposing a penalty are in the hands of the law courts. Countries following this model outside Europe are the USA, Canada and Israel and, within EU borders, the UK, Ireland and Denmark.
- *German model.* SAIs are collegiate, independent from the executive, performing audit functions and advisory functions to both Parliament and the government. Irregularities are taken to ordinary

law courts. Countries following this model are Germany and the Netherlands.

- *Latin model.* SAIs are collegiate and independent from the executive. They perform audit, advisory and also judicial functions in the case of detected irregularities. This model is followed by countries like France, Italy, Belgium, Greece, Portugal and Spain. In general, Eastern European countries that had to adapt their institutions along democratic lines were interested in following either this model or the German model.

Up to July 2003, when a new law was passed, the Swedish Audit Office was headed by an Auditor General, but it had a subordinated position in relation to the executive, as it was an integral part the government structure. Thus we could speak of a Nordic model of SAI. At present, the Swedish Court of Audit is dependent on Parliament and is run by three Auditors.

The European Court of Auditors stands as a unique model in its own right within the constellation of European SAIs, functioning in a way similar to that of the German model, although on a supranational level, because, despite its name, it has no judicial role.

With the aim of offering a panoramic view of the different models of SAIs within the EU and the configuration of their respective systems of public control, we have selected the following, particularly relevant systems:

- Public audit in the United Kingdom;
- The Netherlands Court of Audit;
- The model of the Federal Republic of Germany;
- The Spanish system of public control;
- The European Court of Auditors.

This selection enables us to study in more depth the one-person model in the case of the Auditor General (UK), a single collegiate model that has introduced interesting control methods (Holland), a collegiate decentralized model with regional control bodies (Germany) and, finally, a collegiate, decentralized model with jurisdictional attributions (Spain).

Public audit in the United Kingdom

There are six public sector auditors in the UK: (1) the National Audit Office responsible for the audit of UK functions like defence and for central government services in England; (2) the Auditor General for Scotland; (3) the Auditor General for Wales; and (4) the Comptroller and Auditor General for Northern Ireland responsible for central government services in those countries; (5) the Audit Commission responsible for the audit of local government in England and Wales; and (6) the Accounts Commission responsible for the audit of local government in Scotland; with the Comptroller and Auditor General of Northern Ireland also being responsible for the audit of local government in Northern Ireland.

Each institution has its own jurisdiction and none is subordinate to any other, although there is cooperation between them; for example, they rely on each other's work for the audit of accounts that contain material from more than one jurisdiction, such as in grants from central to local government.

None of the audit authorities is a court; none has the power to declare expenditure illegal or to punish public servants. But recommendations to take such action are made to executive authorities when required who are expected, in potential criminal cases for example, to put the case into the hands of the police who report to the public prosecutor, who in turn will decide if the case should go to court.

Reports from the public sector audit authorities are mainly to provide assurance that money has been spent according to the law and that accounts give a true and fair view of the transactions of the authority to which they relate – this is financial audit – and to make recommendations for the more economic, efficient and effective provision of public services – this is performance or value for money audit.

Two of the public sector audit authorities in the UK are Commissions – the Audit Commission and the Accounts Commission. In these cases the Commissioners, who are appointed by the UK government for the Audit Commission and the Scottish Executive for the Accounts Commission, have a collective responsibility for the work of their Commissions and their staff.

The other public sector audit authorities report to legislative authorities and are headed by single individuals, in whose name all the work is carried out, and who is alone responsible for its quality and effectiveness. This is very different from public audit authorities in many other countries, though the British model is to be found in the countries of the British Commonwealth and in the USA.

Vesting responsibility in a single individual may be a recipe for the clear and immediate attribution of responsibility, for quick action and ease of management coordination. But a single person may not have the standing, authority and range of experience that a court or commission of several prominent and distinguished individuals may command.

The Netherlands Court of Audit
The Kingdom of the Netherlands, as the country is officially known, is a constitutional monarchy. Responsibility for the government's actions is

borne entirely by the ministers. Parliament is responsible for overseeing government policy.

In addition to Parliament, three independent government bodies play a part in the operation of Dutch democracy: the Council of State, the National Ombudsman and the Netherlands Court of Audit.

The Court of Audit has a Board with three members, including the President, each of whom is appointed by the government on the recommendation of the House of Representatives. Each member is appointed for life or until the retirement age of 70.

The Court of Audit has a very broad mandate to audit central government. The Constitution states that it 'is responsible for auditing state receipts and expenditure'. The Court of Audit has complete independence in its choice of work although it must approve the State Accounts every year.

The Court of Audit's tasks and responsibilities with respect to public expenditure and internal control are laid down in the Government Accounts Act 2001.

Under the Government Accounts Act 2001 each minister is responsible for the regularity, orderliness and accountability of his or her ministry's operational management. The Court of Audit's audit approach is systems based and for its regularity audits it relies heavily on the work of the Ministry Audit Departments.

Performance audits form an important part of the Court of Audit's work.

The Court of Audit can examine the efficiency and effectiveness of government policy but not the policy itself. It interprets its *a posteriori* audit mandate as a means to examine a subject as soon as a minister takes a decision that has financial consequences.

In 1999 a change process in the budgeting system was launched by the government, named 'From Policy Budget to Policy Accountability' (Dutch abbreviation: VBTB). The overriding principle of this outcome-based budgeting system is that budgets and accounts should contain related and consistent information on policy objectives and on budget execution and financial resources.

With the adoption of outcome-based budgeting, policy information has entered the field of regularity auditing. To this end, Ministry Audit Departments are being reorganized into audit departments that also will be able to audit non-financial information.

The Netherlands Court of Audit is in favour of a more transparent auditing structure within Europe. In the opinion of the Netherlands Court of Audit the European Court of Auditors should function as the external auditor of the European Commission, whereas the Member States' SAIs should audit the European grants spent in the Member States.

The Netherlands Court of Audit employs around 340 people, of which 54 per cent are auditors.

The model of the Federal Republic of Germany

The Constitution states that the Federal Republic of Germany is a Federal State. Its main feature is the division of governmental functions between the Federation and the Länder. Financial responsibilities are allocated in accordance with this division. The separation of responsibilities, expenditure and revenue affects the budget system because the Federal government and the Länder are autonomous and independent in terms of their budgets. Nevertheless the principle of budgetary autonomy does not apply without reservation. The law on the Principles of the Budgetary Laws (1969) contains the basic principles necessary to ensure legal uniformity. In accordance with the law, the entire budgetary and financial management of the Federal government and the Länder must be audited by public audit institutions.

Federal external financial control is carried out by the Bundesrechnungshof, which is organized according to the collegiate principle and is currently composed of 61 members. The President and the Vice-President are elected by the Parliament on the recommendation of the Federal government and the other 59 members are appointed by the Federal President on the recommendation of the President of the SAI. All members enjoy judicial independence and a status similar to that of judges.

The Bundesrechnungshof is divided into nine Audit Divisions and 50 Audit Units. Apart from legality, the main audit criteria are the efficiency and regularity of administrative activity. The contradictory procedure is provided by law.

In addition to its audit task, the SAI exercises an independent advisory function in relation to Parliament, the Federal government or an individual ministry. The SAI has no power to give its auditees instructions or to impose penalties.

The Regional Constitutions contain each individual Länder's regulations for external financial control. The regulations largely correspond to those of the Federation, and the 16 Landersrechnunghöfe are responsible for the audit of the budgetary and financial management of their respective Regions.

The financial control of the SAIs is referred to as external control. Institutionalized internal control, as normally carried out via an internal or administrative audit, is traditionally unknown in the public administration of the Federal Republic and Länder. Instead, there is a kind of 'internal supervision', as well as Budget Officers who are in charge of certain supervisory functions.

Up to the re-organization of 1998 and the introduction of nine Regional Audit Offices, the SAI's work was supported by pre-audit units. The purpose of the pre-audit was to prepare for the audit of the Bundesrechnungshof, and to supplement it. Pre-audit units were organizationally integrated in the administrations to be audited.

The Federal government and the Länder are autonomous and independent from each other in terms of their budgets. Nevertheless, the financial systems are closely intertwined, and activities and expenditure responsibilities overlap considerably. The exceptions to the rule on the separation of expenditure brought about by co-financing have consequences for the distribution of tasks among the SAIs. There are a number of legal provisions to avoid conflicts over the implementation of audit tasks. In addition to this, there is the Conference of the Heads of the German SAIs. This body contributes, among other things, to the resolution of any conflicts by means of agreements. Decisions can only be passed unanimously, and at the same time they are not binding for the SAIs.

In all cases of co-financing and other exceptions to the rule on the separation of expenditure from the revenue side, the SAIs' problems can only be solved through cooperation. Technical cooperation is facilitated by the fact that, so far, they have all worked in the governmental field on the basis of almost identical legal backgrounds and very similar budget structure and accounting methods.

The system of public control in Spain
The Spanish Constitution of 1978 set up a parliamentary monarchy as State model. The issue of political and administrative decentralization of the State was openly dealt with, and after a relatively prolonged process, 17 autonomous communities enjoying a high level of self-government were established.

The control of public expenditure is entrusted to two different institutions. Internal control is the responsibility of the State General Intervention (Intervención General del Estado, or IGAE). Among the tasks of the IGAE we find the function of intervention and financial control, the direction and management of public accounting and the drawing up of the State Accounts. External control is the responsibility of the Tribunal de Cuentas. The Constitution characterizes the Tribunal as the 'supreme audit organ controlling the accounts and economic performance of the State, as well as those of the public sector' (art.136). It is directly dependent on the Parliament and its members enjoy the same independence as ordinary judges. As specified in the Constitution, the Tribunal enjoys jurisdictional powers of its own.

Present legislation regulating the activity of the Tribunal de Cuentas is constituted by the Organic Act of 1982 (Ley Orgánica del Tribunal de Cuentas) and the Law of Procedure of 1988 (Ley de Funcionamiento). The Tribunal is made up of 12 Counsellors, six appointed by each of the lower and upper houses of the Cortes Generales by a qualified majority of three-fifths. They are elected for a nine-year period. The President of the Tribunal is appointed by the monarch for a three-year period, on the recommendation of the Counsellors. The Full Session is the supreme decision-making organ of the Tribunal. It approves the audit reports and makes recommendations for the improvement of the public sector management.

The Tribunal exercises two kinds of functions:

- The *audit function*, which consists in the audit of economic and financial activity of the public sector – is defined as the State administration, the administrations of the autonomous communities, local entities, social security, autonomous organisms and public enterprises. The aim of audit is the compliance of all economic and financial transactions of the public sector with the principles of legality, efficiency and economy. Apart from audits specified in the annual programme drawn up by the Tribunal itself, it has the duty to produce a report on the State Accounts. Reports are subjected to contradictory procedure. The audit cycle ends with the presentation in Parliament of proposals for the improvement of public performance and of motions on specific issues that can lead to changes in legislation.
- The *judicial function*, whose existence explains why the institution is named 'tribunal' (that is, a 'court'), consists in the judgment of accounting responsibility issues of those in charge of managing public resources, in cases of misuse.

The Tribunal acts as an auxiliary technical organ of Parliament in the exercise of its functions of financial control of the government's transactions. Parliamentary consideration of the reports of the Tribunal, except the Annual Report, is delegated to the Joint Committee for the relationship with the Tribunal de Cuentas. Parliament takes the report of the Tribunal as a basis for the political control of the Administration, puts forward resolution proposals founded on the report's recommendations and urges the government to comply with them.

Within the context of State decentralization, there has been a phenomenon of emulation of the State by the new autonomous communities, leading to the establishment of regional internal control bodies dependent on the regional governments in all 17 autonomous communities.

Regional external control bodies have also been gradually created. The process of decentralization was not totally free of tensions, and even today there is in some instances an overlap of competences, as in the case of financial control of the autonomous communities. This overlap is a result of the Organic Act of 1982, that created two superimposed layers of public control, conferring on the Tribunal de Cuentas the supremacy of public control, while at the same time claiming a possible exception in favour of the devolved audit bodies according to the Estatuto de Autonomía of each autonomous community. Devolved audit bodies are created by a law passed in the regional parliaments. There are at present 11 regional audit bodies in Spain. All of them reproduce at the regional level the audit function of the Tribunal de Cuentas, but do not enjoy jurisdictional powers. When in the course of an audit they detect situations of accounting responsibility, the Tribunal de Cuentas must immediately take charge.

The structure of public control in Spain, both internal and external, also reveals the specific difficulties of coordination with the European Court of Auditors in relation to EU public resources.

The European Court of Auditors
There are three phenomena that strongly determine the present context in which external control institutions develop their activity. The analysis of these phenomena contributes to place the European Court of Auditors in relation to SAIs. The first is the impact of the current parallel processes of supranational integration and State decentralization taking place in Europe. The second is the growing demand for transparency, accountability and external control both in the private and the public sectors. The third is the existence of more complex situations due to the loss of a clear distinction between private and public sectors.

The European Court of Auditors is one of the five EU institutions. It supports the European Parliament in its task of controlling the way in which the European Commission manages the EU budget. Although not so well known by the public, it plays a crucial role as the external control body of the EU executive power.

Established in 1977 by the Treaty of Brussels, the European Court of Auditors began its activity the same year. In the Treaty of Amsterdam of 1999 it received the status of an EU institution and as a consequence enlarged its sphere of action to the three EU pillars. It was also given the possibility of appealing to the European Court of Justice in defence of its prerogatives.

At present it is composed of 15 members, one for each Member State.[7] They are appointed by the European Council by unanimity at the proposal of Member States, after having heard the opinion of the European Parliament.

A collegiate organ, it approves the reports and adopts all decisions regarding its organization and procedures. It is organized in audit sectors; each sector being the direct responsibility of one of the members of the Court.

The mission of the Court of Auditors consists in carrying out the controls of legality, regularity and sound financial management of the EU budget. In the exercise of its functions, its staff travel to the seat of the EU institutions, the Commission included, and of the rest of audited entities; they also travel to the Member States in missions organized jointly with the respective SAI. The contradictory procedure is used in virtue of the auditee's right to make allegations.

The Annual Report on the management of the EU budget is perhaps the most important piece of work by the Court of Auditors. This Report, together with a series of special reports, enables the procedure of budget discharge by Parliament. As a rule, Parliament puts forward a resolution in which it makes recommendations to the Commission.

Because of the uniqueness of the EU framework, the Court of Auditors has some distinctive features that set it apart from other control institutions, such as:

- the peculiar character of the EU institutional architecture;
- the confluence within the Court of Auditors of different control traditions;
- the complexity of the task of controlling the EU budget due to its specific features.

On the other hand, the fact that a high percentage of the EU budget is managed by the Member States, means that control must also take place jointly with the States' own administrative services. On top of that, part of the expenditure is co-financed with the national administrations (central, regional and local); this leads to an overlap of two or more controls carried out by different institutions on a single object.

In the chapter in this volume devoted to the Court of Auditors (Chapter 6) we study the articulation of the tasks carried out by this EU institution with those carried out by the external control institutions of Member States. It is a complex articulation, probably insufficiently regulated, that will become even more intricate after the enlargement to include ten new EU members.

COORDINATION STRATEGIES

The Need for Coordination

The second part of this volume points out some of the indispensable steps towards a real coordination of the various tasks involved in public audit, taking into account the present situation in the EU, where so many public agents and control bodies co-exist.

The coherence of the control system must be established with the help of a few basic principles: subsidiarity, proportionality and the sound management of control institutions themselves. It is necessary, therefore, to support the improvement of the institutionalized cooperation mechanisms already in place at different levels. Such coordination mechanisms must be put into action at different phases in the audit process, mainly in the establishment of audit programmes and during their implementation, they must also facilitate access to audit findings and reports at all levels.

We study here three lines of action for the strengthening of public control coordination:

- The fight against fraud. The opinion that audit is not oriented towards the repression of fraud, but only towards its detection, had to be revised as a result of a series of important cases of corruption within the public sector. It was made clear that control mechanisms had to be improved in order to reduce the risk of fraud. However, the solution to this problem in the EU is to be found in the adoption of a real anti-fraud policy through the European Anti-Fraud Office (OLAF).
- The establishment of an internal control framework. This must be put in relation to the issue of economy and efficiency in the allocation of public resources. This framework would involve adopting the principles of coordination and simplification of control actions, seeking maximum effectiveness in the organization of controls at different levels. In order to the make the 'single audit' work it is necessary to adopt a framework of common concepts, technical standards of control, standards of relations between auditors and standards for the articulation of coordination systems.
- The adoption of identical accounting criteria. This is necessary in order to avoid the same facts being evaluated differently. Before reaching this ideal goal, it would be at least advisable to minimize present discrepancies given the need to use the same economic and financial information.

The Policy Against Financial Fraud in the European Union

The fight against fraud and corruption is an effective instrument of control of European Union public budget expenditure. We will analyse the origin and grounds for the adoption of a policy to fight fraud while tracing the evolution of the budget regime of the Communities.

The role that Member States can play in the struggle against fraud was reinforced with the signing of the Maastricht Treaty (1992). Member States were endowed with responsibility for fighting fraud prejudicial to the interests of the Communities and for cooperation between them, with the aid of the Commission, in order to achieve this objective. To that end a penal juridical framework was created within the scope of the third pillar by means of the PFI Convention and respective agreements. The effectiveness of the Anti-Fraud Co-ordination Unit (UCLAF), the instrument set up by the Commission, was the subject of an audit report by the European Court of Auditors and of a European Parliament Resolution. Both institutions made profound criticisms and pointed out insufficiencies in the Commission's anti-fraud policy.

The absence of mechanisms for fighting corruption is above all a result of various cases that have not been the object of appropriate procedures. On the initiative of the European Parliament at the outset of 1999, an Independent Expert Committee was established. The report issued by this Committee was the basis of the creation of the European Anti-Fraud Office and the adoption of a new anti-fraud and anti-corruption strategy. The main innovation was the endowment of OLAF with the competency for the internal investigation of community employees and agents and the application of disciplinary and penal sanctions.

The creation of the figure of a European Public Prosecutor had always been foreseen within the scope of the anti-fraud and anti-corruption strategy. This figure would enable the direct prosecution of criminality in this area in the light of Member State jurisdictions. The introduction into the Treaties of a regulatory norm making this possible was not approved in Nice. Nevertheless the Commission once again took the initiative and launched a Green Paper to be publicly debated, thus reformulating the *Corpus Juris* as a basis for the scope of action of the European Public Prosecutor.

Since its creation in 1999, the work of OLAF has revealed both the fragility and ambiguity of its statute. This statute had foreseen the assessment of OLAF at the end of a three-year operation period. The assessment was strongly influenced by the Eurostat surveys and the crisis that the actions of OLAF provoked within the Commission. As a consequence of the crisis, and on the initiative of the European Parliament, a legislative revision procedure on the OLAF statute was initiated.

Coordination of Internal Controls: the Single Audit – Towards an EU Internal Control Framework

This chapter aims to discuss what is meant by single audit in the European Union's particular environment, based on the current EU control and audit arrangements and on the best known 'single audit' experiences. It takes account of the potential impact of the Commission's administrative reform on internal controls and proposes key attributes for the development of a more efficient and effective system of internal controls for European Union revenue and expenditure, as the basis to evolve towards an EU internal control framework.

This framework should provide reasonable assurance on the legality and regularity of transactions, and compliance with the principles of economy, efficiency and effectiveness. The cost of the controls should be in proportion to the benefits they bring. The system should comprise a logical chain structure where controls are undertaken, recorded and reported to a common standard allowing reliance to be placed on them by all in the chain. Many of the building blocks for implementing such a framework are fully or partially in place in the current systems, whereas others would need to be introduced.

To establish and implement a coherent and comprehensive system of internal controls will require the active participation of all parties involved in the financial control of the EU budget. Both improved legislation and work practices are also needed to give a level of openness and transparency over the management and control of the EU budget. This will demand considerable commitment from both the Institutions and the Member States of the European Union.

Coordination of Financial Reporting at Different Levels of Public Administration in Europe

The existence of different political, economic and administrative traditions in Europe has resulted in a wide diversity of public accounting and reporting practices, much greater in the public sector than in the field of business accounting. These differences are found not only between national governments, but also between regions and local authorities in the same country.

Even though a process of reform has being going on for many years, and significant reforms have been adopted in many European public accounting systems, comparability is not yet guaranteed, as old-fashioned and inappropriate accounting systems are still being used. Significant examples can be found, for instance, of public accounting systems where reforms for adopting accrual-based models have not yet been put into practice.

The efforts made by the International Federation of Accountants (IFAC) in order to agree a set of International Public Sector Accounting Standards (IPSASs) constitute an exceptional opportunity to achieve a real harmonization of public reporting practices in Europe, but this harmonization still requires serious discussions on how the process must be carried out and what concrete steps and timetable could be adopted for its implementation.

Taking into account the current state and characteristics of public accounting systems in Europe, as well as the process of convergence between them, we will trace their foreseeable evolution and point out different possible paths towards harmonization. We propose four main topics for reflection, as they constitute key elements in the process of harmonization and the evaluation of alternative policies and decision-making mechanisms.

(a) *Scope and pace of harmonization*. European public accounting systems may evolve in different ways, varying between a lack of harmonization and full development of accounting standards.

(b) *Budgetary information*. A decision must be taken regarding whether or not to include budgetary reporting rules in international public accounting standards. The least contentious solution is to limit the impact of standards in financial reporting, as has been IFAC's policy to date, when a clear policy in this field is not yet designed. If budgetary reporting regulation is finally excluded from accounting standards, only financial information will be taken into consideration, while budgetary accounting and reporting, as well as their links with financial accounting, will carry on being the responsibility of national governments.

(c) *Process management*. It is also to be decided whether or not a European supranational authority must intervene in the process of elaborating and/or introducing new common accounting standards. Either EU authorities lead (or at least support) the process of harmonization, or national governments agree to join it voluntarily.

(e) *European involvement in the elaboration of international standards*. Europe could play a more active and influential role in the process of elaboration and approval of IPSASs, while giving up issuing accounting standards of its own, except for concrete adaptations of international standards. If active involvement is not achieved, European authorities should evaluate *ex post* the convenience of adopting IPSASs, even if the EU has taken no part in the process. Moreover, this policy would be the most consistent one with the Commission's position in relation to business accounting, where it has also renounced the idea of developing its own Accounting Directives model.

The process of setting standards affects particularly the accounting of the European institutions. These institutions could therefore foster the process and even play a leading role in it, for in the European context the position of the EU institutions is quite relevant, especially in the case of the Commission, which essentially represents the executive power in the Union. Given that adaptation of the European institutional accounting system to IPSASs requirements is under way, this reform could constitute an important incentive for Member States to follow suit.

A serious debate and careful reflection are required in order to arrive at the most effective policy for public accounting harmonization in Europe and to ensure the support and leadership of the European institutions. This process is needed in order to clarify the European approach to public comparability and transparency of public financial reports. If the process is negotiated and gradually implemented, political opposition would probably be weak and the possibility of reaching an agreement among governments and institutions would be realistic. The first step could be the adaptation of the European Commission accounting system to the requirements of international accounting standards and generally accepted accounting principles. This step is now under way. Once this adaptation has taken place, it should be easier for the Commission to foster in a decisive way a real harmonization in the field of public accounting.

In fact, as has repeatedly been recommended by the European Court of Auditors, the European Communities are immersed in a process of deep reform of their accounting and budgetary information systems, with the aim of adapting them to internationally accepted accounting principles. This experience offers the opportunity for European institutions to become a reference for Member States, stimulating the reform of their national accounting systems, and adapting them to international standards. On the other hand, and given the fact that around 85 per cent of the European budget is implemented and co-managed by Member States, harmonization of national reporting cultures and practices becomes a key element for achieving sound accountability and transparency in public sector management, as well as effective control of public financial policies and allocation of resources.

It would not be reasonable, thus, to renounce public harmonization in Europe; doing so would mean renouncing a transparent and financially safe European public sector. On the contrary, the European institutions should implement an active policy in this area, or at least urge national governments actively to cooperate, getting involved in a joint project of financial reporting harmonization. The concrete reforms and their gradual introduction would have to be agreed; however, a deadline should be set for the different phases, in order to assure real and effective achievements.

NOTES

1. The position of the Government Accounting Standard Board of the Financial Accounting Foundations (GASB) considers that information of this nature should always be included in the general external information of public entities, although it recognizes the absence of regulatory standards on this matter in the USA (GASB, 1987, 1994).
2. Market and competition mechanisms (MCMs) are based on external contracts with the private sector for the delivery of public goods and services. One of the features of MCMs is that they do not aim at the suppression of public financing or provision, but at a less bureaucratic management. They allow the introduction of competition between public and private services and even between different public units (Albi, 1999). One example of an MCM in the UK is the establishment of Next Steps.
3. According to the GASB (1994) the main indicators are the well-known efficiency indicators, or accomplishment measures, differentiating between results corresponding to product or service units (output) and results corresponding to the entity's actions (outcome), economy indicators and efficiency indicators.
4. There are important examples of benchmarking in the follow-up done in England and Wales by the Audit Commission, as well as in the city of Quebec since 1988.
5. The Green Book of Audit (1996) deals with such important issues as the definition of legal audit, the report, and the auditor's qualifications or his or her independence.
6. The conclusions of the XVII Congress of INTOSAI, held in Seoul in 2001, insist on this point: SAIs have the task of presenting to Parliament, and eventually to the government and the public, their remarks on the economic and financial activities of public administrations; they also have the task of making suggestions in order to improve legislation, regulation and procedures in financial and administrative matters.
7. From 1 May 2004, when ten new countries joined the EU, the number of Member States is 25.

REFERENCES

Albi Ibáñez, Emilio (1999), 'Nuevos esquemas de gestión pública (Mecanismos cuasi-competitivos y de mercado y privatizaciones)', *Revista española de Control Externo*, January.

Fabra Vallés, J.M. (2003), 'Articulación organizativa de la actividad de los diferentes niveles de control en la UE', Ponencia presentada en El Escorial.

Governmental Accounting Standard Board of the Financial Accounting Foundation (GASB) (1987), 'Objectives of Financial Reporting', Stamford.

Governmental Accounting Standard Board of the Financial Accounting Foundation (GASB) (1994), 'On Concepts Related to Service Efforts and Accomplishments Reporting', Norwalk.

International Federation of Accountants (IFAC), Public Sector Committee (1996), 'The Government Financial Reporting Entity', Study 8.

INTOSAI (1977), *Declaración de Lima*.

Montesinos Julve, V. (2000), 'Nuevos ámbitos de la fiscalización de las entidades públicas', *Revista de Control Externo*, **4**, January.

National Audit Office (1996), *State Audit in the European Union*, London: NAO.

Stiglitz, J. (1994), *Whither Socialism?*, Cambridge, MA: MIT Press.

2. Public audit in the United Kingdom

Sir John Bourn

THE CHARACTERISTICS OF THE BRITISH SYSTEM

The modern system of public audit in the UK is a creature of the nine-teenth century, even though early manifestations of financial oversight arrangements can be traced back at least to 1314.

Nineteenth-century developments began with the idea that public authorities – government departments, local government authorities and other public authorities – needed to keep accounts showing the sources of their funds and what they had been spent on. And if accounts were to be kept, they needed to be independently audited to see that they gave a true and fair view of the financial transactions of the authority and that the money had been spent in accordance with the law and appropriate admin-istrative regulations. These developments paralleled the development of accountancy and audit in the private sector, which was necessary for the functioning of industry, commerce and capital markets.

By the start of the twentieth century, as noted below, auditors began to point out cases where money might have been spent lawfully, but still wastefully, such as when goods and services had been purchased of defective quality even though for a legal purpose. Under the impetus of the development of the economics of cost–benefit analysis, by the latter half of the twentieth century auditors began to develop their concern with wasteful expenditure into systems of performance audit, whereby they not only audited accounts but also examined the economy, efficiency and effectiveness with which programmes and projects were executed. Where this concern with performance demanded new legal powers, they were often granted, as in the case of the Comptroller and Auditor General of the United Kingdom in the National Audit Act of 1983.

As the boxes showing examples of their work make clear, there are several public sector audit bodies in the United Kingdom.

The powers and duties of the various bodies vary, and reflect the division in the political structure between the following entities.

- The UK as a whole, for whose functions the Comptroller and Auditor General of the United Kingdom is the auditor, e.g. defence, the collection of income tax and foreign affairs.
- The devolved administrations in:
  - Scotland, for which the Auditor General for Scotland is the auditor, e.g. health service in Scotland;
  - Wales, for which the Auditor General for Wales is the auditor, e.g. parts of the health service in Wales;
  - Northern Ireland, for which the Comptroller and Auditor General for Northern Ireland is the auditor, e.g. the health service in Northern Ireland; and
- The Comptroller and Auditor General of the United Kingdom, which is the auditor for such functions in England.
- Local government authorities within England, Scotland, Wales and Northern Ireland, where:
  - the Audit Commission audits local authorities and some health authorities in England and Wales (although there is a proposal before the UK Parliament to transfer the audit of local authorities and all health bodies in Wales to the Auditor General for Wales);
  - the Accounts Commission audits local authorities in Scotland, employing staff who are administered by the Auditor General for Scotland;
  - the Comptroller and Auditor General for Northern Ireland is responsible for the oversight of the audit of local authorities in Northern Ireland.

The Range of Audit Reports in the UK

Boxes 2.1 to 2.7 list a number of examples of the reports issued by the various public audit authorities in the UK.

BOX 2.1 FINANCIAL AUDIT REPORTS BY THE COMPTROLLER AND AUDITOR GENERAL

The Child Support Agency is the government organization responsible for assessing, collecting and paying child support maintenance. The Comptroller and Auditor General qualified his opinion on the 2002–03 accounts of the Agency on the basis of material misstatement. In his report on these accounts he estimated that, of the £586 million receipts from non-resident parents, there were overpayments of £4.5 million and underpayments of £21.9 million. He further estimated that the amount of £686 million shown in the account as due from non-resident parents for maintenance assessments at 31 March 2003 contained overstatement errors of £21.7 million and understatement errors of £390.9 million in debts arising from full maintenance assessment; and overstatement errors of £2.7 million and understatement errors of £6.8 million in debts arising from interim maintenance assessments. He found that the error rate was mainly the result of errors over a number of years in underlying maintenance assessments and incorrect adjustments to customers' accounts.

BOX 2.2   REPORTS IN THE PUBLIC INTEREST BY AUDITORS APPOINTED BY THE AUDIT COMMISSION

Where Audit Commission-appointed auditors conclude that a matter concerning the conduct of a body is significant enough to be brought to wider public attention, they have the statutory power to issue a 'report in the public interest'. In 2003, and again in 2004, the Audit Commission issued a report in the public interest on Lancaster City Council, in relation to expenditure incurred by the Council in 1994 on the Crinkley Bottom Theme Park in Happy Mount Park, Morecambe. The theme park opened on 30 July 1994, and closed 13 weeks later at the beginning of November 1994. The Council and local taxpayers suffered losses of over £2 million.

The auditor decided that none of the Councillors and Council officers he investigated was guilty of wilful misconduct. However, he found two Council officers guilty of misconduct leading to a financial loss and he was critical of Councillors for being insufficiently challenging of the reports presented to them by officers. The auditor therefore decided to make his findings known in reports in the public interest. His 2004 report acknowledged the lessons which had already been learned by the Council, but made a number of recommendations, to which the Council has responded. Ongoing audit work will monitor the Council's future actions to ensure compliance with the Council's response to the recommendations made.

BOX 2.3   REPORTS ON CRIMINAL CASES BY THE COMPTROLLER AND AUDITOR GENERAL

In 1997 Michael Allcock, a former senior tax inspector in the Inland Revenue, was convicted on six counts of corruption. The total potential tax loss arising from his corruption could not be established, but there had been a tax loss of £130,000 in one of Mr Allcock's investigations. The Comptroller and Auditor General reported in 1998 on the action taken by the Inland Revenue in response to these corrupt activities. Among his recommendations were that the Inland Revenue should consider undertaking periodic staff surveys to assess the impact of its initiatives to improve awareness of expected standards, alerting managers to the warning signals in an employee's behaviour associated with the risk of corruption, and extending vetting arrangements for staff most exposed to this risk.

BOX 2.4   REPORTS BY THE COMPTROLLER AND AUDITOR GENERAL LEADING TO SIGNIFICANT FINANCIAL SAVINGS

Following a report by the Comptroller and Auditor General on vacant family quarters owned by the Ministry of Defence, the Ministry carried out a significant disposal programme to reduce the level of vacant properties. During 2002, the Ministry disposed of 2365 properties, resulting in a saving in maintenance costs of some £6.6 million per annum.

BOX 2.5   REPORTS BY THE COMPTROLLER AND AUDITOR GENERAL LEADING TO IMPROVEMENTS IN THE QUALITY OF PUBLIC SERVICES

In 2000 the Comptroller and Auditor General reported on operations for hip replacements in the National Health Service. He found significant variations in the quality of performance across the country, noted the need to spread good practice more widely for the benefit of patients, and made 20 recommendations for improving the service provided to patients. These included a recommendation to establish a National Joint Registry, which would help to improve the monitoring of the effectiveness of different types of prosthesis, identify problems at an early stage, and track patients who might suffer problems.

In 2003 the Comptroller and Auditor General published a follow-up report. He found that the NHS had improved its procedures, and thereby provided better quality of care for patients. For example, a National Joint Registry had been launched in 2003, and progress had been made on reducing lengths of stay for patients.

BOX 2.6   REPORTS BY THE AUDITOR GENERAL FOR SCOTLAND

In 2003 the Auditor General for Scotland reported on standards of hospital cleanliness. His report found that only half of the hospitals in Scotland had high levels of cleanliness in their wards. Twenty per cent of those inspected showed a clear need for improvement, with a total of 21 hospitals being named as giving cause for concern. Among his recommendations were that trusts should ensure that operational policies specify responsibility for cleaning clinical equipment; that all staff are made aware of their responsibilities; and that an ongoing programme of peer review of standards of cleanliness or a similar quality assurance mechanism should be introduced. As a result, local reports were produced for all hospitals reviewed, identifying action plans and agreeing timescales, and a number of improvements in services were put into place. The

Scottish Executive Health Department also plans to review progress against these action plans; and further follow-up of hospital cleaning will be carried out by NHS Quality Improvement Scotland.

BOX 2.7   REPORTS BY THE AUDITOR GENERAL FOR WALES

The Auditor General for Wales reported in 2003 on a fundamental breakdown in the financial management and controls that should have been operated by the National Council for Education and Training for Wales. This was a newly established body, which had been unable to set up and implement proper arrangements for financial management and control, and the letting of contracts. These failings were particularly evident in an imaginative new project designed to encourage young people to take better advantage of educational opportunities. The Auditor General drew attention to the value of the basic idea of the project, but noted in his report defects in the process of approving and funding, especially the unnecessary advance funding of a project in a converted soft-drinks factory – the 'Pop Centre MP3 Café'. His report recognized that the Council raised the initial concerns over the progress of the Pop Centre project, and noted that over £1.9 million of the £4 million grant had been repaid by 21 May 2003, at the Council's request.

It is possible to enumerate certain features of the variegated system of public audit in the United Kingdom.

- Since there is no written constitution for the UK, its public sector auditors have no special constitutional status, as they have in many countries with a written constitution.
- As distinct from many other countries, the public sector auditor in the UK has no judicial powers. The audit authorities cannot declare expenditure illegal or punish public servants directly. They do not hold public hearings as do courts. They can, however, make recommendations to the responsible legislative and executive authorities that expenditure is illegal or wasteful and that public servants have

acted illegally or wastefully. It is for those authorities to recommend or to decide to take action, depending on their powers, for example to refer the auditor's evidence to the police in the cases of suspected fraud, theft or corruption, or for a government department to implement a programme more economically, efficiently or effectively in cases of wasteful or defective performance.

- In four out of the six public sector auditors, the power of the office is vested in a single person – the Comptroller and Auditor General of the United Kingdom, the Auditor General for Scotland, the Auditor General for Wales and the Comptroller and Auditor General for Northern Ireland. In many countries, especially if the audit authority is a court, there is a collective responsibility shared among the members of the tribunal or court concerned. The reason for vesting responsibility in single individuals in the UK is not clear. The common feature of all four offices is that they make their reports to a legislative assembly – the powers of these Parliaments and assemblies differ, and Northern Ireland's is currently in abeyance. And legislative assemblies in the UK are used to dealing with individual Ministers who are personally responsible to them. By extension, this has perhaps seemed the appropriate arrangement for Auditors General – and for the Parliamentary Ombudsman in the UK, where the office has many similarities to that of the Comptroller and Auditor General. Vesting responsibility in a single individual may be a recipe for the clear and immediate attribution of responsibility, for quick action and ease of management coordination. But a single person may not have the standing, authority and range of experience that a court or commission of several prominent and distinguished individuals may command. Another possibly relevant circumstance is that the UK has no tradition of a separate jurisdiction for administrative law. Cases concerning administrative law are dealt with by the ordinary courts. The audit of accounts may have seemed too far from the usual business of courts to justify the idea of a separate court of accounts in the UK.

- The various public sector audit institutions in the UK have their own jurisdictions and none is subordinate to any other, but there is cooperation between them in many ways. For example, the National Audit Office relies on the work of the Audit Commission in auditing the expenditure by local authorities of certain grants by central government departments whose accounts are audited by the National Audit Office. The National Audit Office and the Audit Commission have worked together to produce complementary reports on subjects where central and local government each have responsibilities, such as some social security payments and the arrangements for providing criminal justice and support programmes for young offenders. All six public sector audit institutions cooperate in such ways as joint training and staff secondments, and in benchmarking and comparing the performance of their auditors across the various jurisdictions. The audit institutions work together in the Public Audit Forum, which is described below.

• The six public sector audit institutions are responsible for the external audit of public accounts in the UK. But external audit is only one aspect of the framework of internal and external financial control of the British system of government. Other aspects are as follows:
  – laying down the standards by which accounts must be prepared;
  – setting rules for the financial management of public authorities;
  – providing for each authority to have a system of internal audit, responsible to the official head of the authority, for investigating such matters as arrangements for safeguarding against corruption and theft. Internal and external audit complement each other, and the external auditor may take account of internal audit's work rather than repeat and duplicate it;
  – voting the money to be made available to each government department for each financial year for the purposes specified in the estimates presented by Ministers to the House of Commons, the lower house of the legislature; and government departments distributing to local authorities and a wide range of grant recipients, such as national museums and art galleries, the money to conduct their services for each financial year. Most aspects of this system work by administrative regulation; but the voting of money to departments and its distribution where appropriate to local and other authorities are matters of law and prescribed in statutes and orders made under their authority. Reference is made in the sections of this chapter below to the main UK legislation.

• The European Court of Audit has the right to audit the expenditure by the UK authorities of grants received from the European Commission. The Court's jurisdiction is separate from those of the UK's audit institutions, but there is cooperation between them. For example, the National Audit Office will advise the Court on the location of the recipients of European money and thus where to begin its investigations. And the National Audit Office may accompany staff from the Court on their audit work. But the Court's reports are its own responsibility. In addition, the UK's public audit authorities have good relations with the European Court; for example, there are staff secondments to the Court and every year the National Audit

Different forms of public control

Office produces for the British Parliament a conspectus of those issues in the Court's annual report which are of special interest to the United Kingdom. This may be examined by the Committee of Public Accounts of the lower house, whose activities are described below.

- The main characteristics of the British system of public sector audit have been outlined in this first section of this chapter. The description and analysis of these characteristics are developed in the rest of the chapter.

THE NATIONAL AUDIT OFFICE OF THE UNITED KINGDOM

Historical Development of the National Audit Office

As noted, the public audit function in the UK dates back to the fourteenth century, but was established in its present form in the mid-nineteenth century as part of a reform of central administration. In 1857 the Select Committee on Public Monies recommended that accounts comparing expenditure with the monies voted by Parliament be produced for all government departments and submitted annually to a committee of the House of Commons. In 1861 the House of Commons, on a motion moved by the then Chancellor of the Exchequer, William Gladstone, created the Committee of Public Accounts. This was followed five years later by the Exchequer and Audit Departments Act 1866, which required all government departments to produce accounts for independent audit.

The 1866 Act also created the position of Comptroller and Auditor General by combining the functions of the Comptroller of the Exchequer, who had authorized the issue of public monies to departments since 1834, with those of the Commissioners of Audit, who had traditionally presented the government accounts to the Treasury. Under the terms of the 1866 Act the Comptroller and Auditor General continued to authorize the issue of money to departments (the Comptroller function) and was given the new task of examining every account and reporting the results to Parliament. He was supported in this task by the Exchequer and Audit Department, staffed with civil servants.

From 1866 onwards parliamentary control over public money was complete. The House of Commons authorized expenditure and the Comptroller and Auditor General controlled the issue of funds, and audited accounts produced by departments. The results were considered by a dedicated parliamentary committee and its conclusions reported to the House of Commons. The requirement for the Comptroller and Auditor

General to report to Parliament on the audited accounts provided an opportunity for him to consider wider issues of financial management. The Committee of Public Accounts actively encouraged such examinations, the results of which formed part of the Comptroller and Auditor General's report on the relevant appropriation account.

The 1866 Act required the Comptroller and Auditor General and his staff to examine every transaction, a task which became less realistic as government activity expanded, especially during the 1914–18 war. The Exchequer and Audit Departments Act 1921 addressed this by allowing the Comptroller and Auditor General to rely in part on departmental systems of control and thus examine a sample of transactions.

Subsequently the most significant alteration in the status of the Comptroller and Auditor General and his staff occurred with the passing of the National Audit Act 1983. The Act followed increasing parliamentary and academic concern about the influence that the executive, in particular the Treasury, retained over public audit. Under the terms of the 1983 Act the Comptroller and Auditor General formally became an Officer of the House of Commons. The Act also established the National Audit Office to assist the Comptroller and Auditor General in the performance of his duties. All statutory powers and rights governing the audit of central government finances are vested in the Comptroller and Auditor General personally rather than the National Audit Office, and the staff of the Office carry out the audit work on his behalf. The staff of the National Audit Office are not therefore civil servants, and their pay and conditions of service differ from those of civil servants. In addition, the 1983 Act provided the Comptroller and Auditor General with express powers to carry out examinations of the economy, efficiency and effectiveness with which departments and certain other public bodies have used their resources (value for money studies).

The Government Resources and Accounts Act 2000 brought further important developments, in particular the change from a cash-based to an accruals-based accounting system for government departments.

The Structure of the National Audit Office

The Comptroller and Auditor General is appointed by the monarch on an address presented by the House of Commons. The motion for this address is made by the Prime Minister acting in agreement with the Chairman of the Committee of Public Accounts (by convention a member of the main opposition party in Parliament). In this way the person appointed must be acceptable to both the main political parties in the legislature. The appointment has no fixed term or age limit and dismissal is by the monarch on a resolution of both Houses of Parliament. This is the same procedure as for the dismissal of judges. A Deputy Comptroller and Auditor General is appointed by the Comptroller and Auditor General.

The Office employs around 800 staff, including some 500 professionally qualified accountants or trainees. It is divided into six audit units, which cover the range of government departments and between them they carry out both financial and value for money audit of all departments, executive agencies and other bodies. Assistant Auditors General, who are appointed by the Comptroller and Auditor General, are responsible for the day-to-day management of units.

The Recruitment, Remuneration and Qualifications of Staff and Other Resources

As noted, before the National Audit Office was established in 1983 the staff employed by its predecessor, the Exchequer and Audit Department, were civil servants. The 1983 Act gave the Comptroller and Auditor General the power to appoint to the National Audit Office such staff as he (or she) considers necessary to discharge his (or her) functions. The Comptroller and Auditor General is also responsible for determining appropriate remuneration for these staff, although statute provides that when setting salary levels he or she should bear in mind the desirability of keeping them broadly in line with the remuneration paid to civil servants. The Comptroller and Auditor General's own salary is set by Parliament and has been linked by statute to that of senior civil servants and High Court judges.

The National Audit Office's audit staff are recruited as university graduates and trained to acquire professional accountancy qualifications, which are as relevant to private sector work as to public sector audit. In recent years the National Audit Office has begun to draw on a wider pool of skills, particularly for value for money work, and now employs specialists on short-term contracts for particular pieces of work. The National Audit Office also subcontracts between 15 and 20 per cent of its financial audit work to professional firms in the private sector. A small number of value for money studies have also been contracted out. The use of specialists and contractors allows the National Audit Office to draw on best practice in the private sector. Indeed, almost all the value for money reports are produced by joint teams of NAO staff and outside experts.

The Scope, Role and Rights of Access of the Comptroller and Auditor General and the National Audit Office

The Comptroller and Auditor General's Comptroller function makes him or her responsible for control of the Consolidated Fund and the National

Loans Fund. The Consolidated Fund is the overall account of government originally set up in 1787 as 'one fund into which shall flow every stream of public revenue and from which shall come the supply for every service'. The Comptroller and Auditor General is required to give authority for Treasury requisitions for issues from this and from the National Loans Fund which covers government borrowing and lending. When authorizing issues the Comptroller and Auditor General (in practice National Audit Office staff acting on his or her behalf) must be sure that credits are requested for purposes having proper statutory authority and within amounts authorized by Parliament.

The audit function of the Comptroller and Auditor General is in two parts: the annual certification audit of the accounts of a wide range of public bodies; and specific examinations of the economy, efficiency and effectiveness with which departments and other public bodies have used their resources. The Comptroller and Auditor General is responsible for the financial audit of almost all central government expenditure, over 600 accounts in total. Many of these accounts fall into the following groups:

- departmental resource accounts (audited by statute under the terms of the Government Resources and Accounts Act 2000);
- accounts of executive agencies (audited by statute under either the terms of the Government Trading Funds Act 1973 or the Government Resources and Accounts Act 2000);
- the accounts of other public bodies (audited either under the terms of the specific statute establishing the body or by agreement). Unlike many countries, the state auditor does not audit the central bank – the Bank of England. The auditor is a private sector firm.

The Comptroller and Auditor General also has inspection rights to some 3000 other bodies that receive public funds to provide public services such as housing, education and training. These rights enable the Comptroller and Auditor General to provide assurance to Parliament that the public money has been spent properly and for the purposes intended by Parliament. The Comptroller and Auditor General's rights to carry out examinations of economy, efficiency and effectiveness extend to most of the bodies that fall within his or her audit and inspection remit. In addition, the Comptroller and Auditor General is the appointed auditor for a number of international bodies.

The terms of the Comptroller and Auditor General's access for financial audit are set out in the Government Resources and Accounts Act 2000 and for value for money examinations in the National Audit Act 1983. In summary, the Comptroller and Auditor General can have such access at all reasonable times to the books of account, other documents and electronic records, and explanations as he or she may reasonably require to carry out statutory functions.

Other Public Sector Audit Institutions

The audit of local government and health authority accounts in England and Wales is the responsibility of the Audit Commission, a public body established in 1982 and now operating under the 1998 Audit Commission Act. It oversees the work of the District Audit Agency and appoints the auditors – who can be from either the Agency or private sector firms – for each local authority and a range of health authorities. In addition, the Audit Commission examines aspects of value for money across local government and publishes the results. It is funded by fees charged to local and health authorities for audit services.

There is a clear distinction between the roles of the National Audit Office and the Audit Commission in most fields. However, in the health area the National Audit Office audits the summarized and summary accounts of health service bodies that are produced by the Department of Health, while the Audit Commission is responsible for appointing the external auditors for all individual National Health Service bodies. The National Audit Office and the Audit Commission cooperate wherever possible to ensure that there is no duplication of effort.

In Scotland a body known as the Accounts Commission performs a broadly similar role to the Audit Commission.

THE DEVOLVED AUDIT INSTITUTIONS

Separate audit arrangements for Northern Ireland have been in place since 1921. And, following devolution, there has been further revision of audit responsibilities within the UK.

The Northern Ireland Audit Office

A separate post of Comptroller and Auditor General for Northern Ireland, established in 1921, is responsible for auditing all expenditure on devolved functions by Northern Ireland departments and agencies, as well as a number of other bodies. He or she also has the power to conduct value for money investigations.

Between 1921 and 1972, the Comptroller and Auditor General for Northern Ireland reported to the Northern Ireland Parliament. Following the suspension of the Parliament, he reported to the UK Parliament and his reports were considered by the Committee of Public Accounts. With the creation of the Northern Ireland Assembly (which is temporarily in abeyance), the Comptroller and Auditor General for Northern Ireland now reports to the Assembly, which has established a committee to consider his audit reports. A separate committee performs the funding and supervisory functions previously undertaken by the Westminster Public Accounts Commission, which is discussed below.

The Northern Ireland Comptroller and Auditor General is supported by some 100 staff in the Northern Ireland Audit Office, which is totally independent from the National Audit Office. But the two institutions enjoy a close working relationship, and each year the Northern Ireland Audit Office carries out about 25 audits on behalf of the Comptroller and Auditor General in areas such as Social Security for which he remains responsible.

The Auditor General for Scotland and Audit Scotland

The Scotland Act 1998, which established the Scottish Parliament, created the post of Auditor General for Scotland to audit from April 2000 the accounts of bodies funded by the new Scottish Parliament and to conduct value for money studies of those bodies. The Auditor General is appointed by the Queen following a recommendation from the Scottish Parliament. He is supported by a new body, known as Audit Scotland. This consists of the staff previously employed by the National Audit Office in Scotland and the Accounts Commission for Scotland – a total of around 140 staff.

The Auditor General has a wide remit. He is responsible for auditing or appointing the auditors of almost all public bodies in Scotland, other than companies and local authorities. The Scottish Parliament has established an Audit Committee to consider reports from the Auditor General for Scotland, and to make appropriate recommendations to the Scottish Executive.

The Auditor General for Wales

An Auditor General for Wales was created by the Government of Wales Act 1998, which established the National Assembly. The Auditor General audits the accounts of the Assembly, and its sponsored bodies, to check that funds have been spent on the purposes intended. He is also empowered to investigate whether value for money has been achieved. The National Assembly has established an Audit Committee to consider the reports of the Auditor General.

The Auditor General for Wales is appointed by the Queen on the advice of the Secretary of State for Wales. The Government of Wales Act allows the Auditor General for Wales to make arrangements with the Comptroller and Auditor General for audit and other support services. The Auditor General for Wales is currently supported by 30 National Audit Office staff based in Cardiff. There is a proposal before the UK Parliament to transfer all National Audit Office and Audit Commission staff in Wales to the Auditor General for Wales, and make the Auditor General responsible for auditing the functions of both the National Assembly and local and health authorities in Wales.

The Public Audit Forum

The Public Audit Forum was launched formally in 1998 following a recommendation in 1996 of the Committee on Standards in Public Life, an advisory body which reports to the Prime Minister. The Forum provides a focus for developmental thinking in relation to public audit.

The Forum is chaired by the Comptroller and Auditor General (who is currently also the Auditor General for Wales). The other members are the Comptroller and Auditor General for Northern Ireland, the Auditor General for Scotland and the Controller of Audit of the Audit Commission for England and Wales. The Comptroller and Auditor General of the Republic of Ireland attends the Forum as an observer. A Consultative Forum has also been established which consists of key stakeholders in the public audit process, such as government departments, local government representatives, private sector accountancy firms and consumers' representatives. The full Consultative Forum meets around three times a year.

To date the Public Audit Forum has published papers on the principles of public audit, the implications for audit of the government's modernizing agenda, the service public sector bodies can expect from their auditors, and propriety and audit in the public sector. Work in progress includes the development of papers on data matching and the role of public sector auditors, the implications for audit of electronic service delivery, and the relationships between audit, inspection and regulation.

THE GOVERNMENT ACCOUNTING SYSTEM

Each government department, agency or public body is required to produce annual accounts. Most departments produce several, each covering a specific area of activity. The accounts are presented in a format determined by the Treasury and the financial year runs from April to March.

Public accounts in the UK were prepared on a cash basis, but in 2000 the government introduced a new law requiring government departments and other central government public bodies to prepare accruals accounts showing income and expenditure. The same law also introduced a requirement on departments to produce information on objectives and performance alongside their accounts.

Departmental accounts are submitted to the Comptroller and Auditor General for audit. The accounts, along with the Comptroller and Auditor General's certificate and report, are laid before Parliament. The Comptroller and Auditor General is also responsible for presenting to Parliament the accounts of executive agencies. The arrangements for other public bodies vary and are determined either in statute or in the financial memoranda that govern their activities.

THE AUDITING PROCESS OF THE NATIONAL AUDIT OFFICE

Financial Audit

In the UK the main purpose of financial audit is to form an independent opinion on the financial statements. Each audit is planned and performed to obtain sufficient, appropriate evidence on which to base this audit opinion, and the form of the opinion depends on the basis on which the financial statements are produced. Where financial statements are produced on an accruals basis a 'true and fair view' opinion is normally given. All the Comptroller and Auditor General's audit opinions also explicitly state whether the money has been applied for the purposes intended by Parliament and whether the financial transactions conform to the authorities that govern them.

During audit work the National Audit Office performs a variety of procedures, depending on the judgement of the audit staff and the nature of the account. For example, as part of its audit the National Audit Office may examine a sample of transactions, selected using statistical techniques after an assessment of the financial systems in operation. The audit of departments, agencies and other large bodies can occur throughout the year as interim audit work is conducted in many cases during the year of account. This enables the audit to be completed within a few months of the end of the financial year and ensures that the information Parliament receives on public spending is timely. At the completion of the audit a letter is sent to each audited body setting out the audit findings and highlighting aspects of accounting or financial control where improvements might be made. The quality of financial audit is assessed by internal review processes; the National Audit Office has also invited the body that examines private sector auditors in the UK to assess its work as well.

Inspection Rights

The Comptroller and Auditor General has a duty to ascertain that the grants made by Parliament have been used for the purposes Parliament intended. To enable him to carry out this function at those bodies funded by Parliament where he is not the appointed auditor, he has been granted a right of inspection. These inspection rights are either provided by the statute that sets up the body or, more commonly, by agreement with the department that supervises it. Such rights are exercised periodically. In most cases the Comptroller and Auditor General also has rights to examine value for money issues at these bodies.

Value for Money or Performance Audit

Formal powers to examine the economy, efficiency and effectiveness with which central government departments have used their resources were granted to the Comptroller and Auditor General in 1983. This legislation built on established practice whereby the Comptroller and Auditor General traditionally included the results of value for money examinations in reports on the appropriation accounts. Since 1983 he has reported the value for money work of the National Audit Office in some 40–50 reports each year covering a wide range of government activities. The Comptroller and Auditor General can carry out value for money examinations at all departments and bodies audited by statute and most audited by agreement.

The terms 'economy', 'efficiency' and 'effectiveness' are not defined in legislation but the National Audit Office works to the following internationally recognized definitions:

- *economy* – minimizing the cost of resources used for an activity having regard to appropriate quality;
- *efficiency* – the relationship between output, in terms of goods, services or other results, and the resources used to produce them;
- *effectiveness* – the extent to which objectives have been achieved and the relationship between the intended effects and actual effects for an activity.

The Comptroller and Auditor General decides on the subjects to be covered by value for money audits but is not entitled to question the merits of policy objectives. Examinations are therefore focused on the means departments have employed to achieve the policy objectives set by the government and approved by Parliament.

The National Audit Office adopts a structured approach to value for money work. Areas of government are monitored routinely using departmental information, academic work, parliamentary debates and the specialist press. Each year the National Audit Office conducts a strategic planning process whereby staff develop study proposals. Units consider the range of study proposals submitted by their staff and put forward to the Comptroller and Auditor General a plan of value for money work. Studies are selected according to a variety of criteria, including the amount of money involved; prima facie evidence of poor value for money; the level of political, parliamentary and public interest; and the likely added value to be derived from a National Audit Office study.

The National Audit Office is concerned to ensure good relations with government departments and its programme of work is discussed with them. Where possible it takes account of departmental comments, for example on the scope or timing of proposals. These discussions can smooth the progress of studies and lead to more focused reports. From preliminary study to final report the process typically takes about a year but the National Audit Office has also recently started to carry out shorter and more quickly executed studies in response to matters of particular public concern.

There are two stages to producing a report: the preliminary and the full study phases. The preliminary study establishes whether a full study should proceed and outlines the objectives of the study, identifies the tasks, and assesses the likely impact of the work. Where possible the views of the audited body are incorporated at this stage. The full study involves detailed fieldwork and the collection of sufficient, relevant and reliable evidence to support conclusions drawn. National Audit Office study teams are often supplemented by experts in particular fields.

The National Audit Office discusses its findings with departmental staff throughout the progress of its value for money studies. It agrees the factual accuracy of the final report formally with departments and this process, known as clearance, can take some time. Opinions, conclusions and recommendations in reports are the responsibility of the National Audit Office. If there is a dispute about the facts and their presentation that cannot be resolved, the department's views are incorporated in the text. The need to agree the factual accuracy of value for money reports requires close and constructive working relations with audited bodies. The clearance process ensures a balanced and fair report and enables the Committee of Public Accounts to focus on lessons to be learned rather than discuss conflicting accounts of what the facts are.

In order to test the quality of value for money reports the National Audit Office has in recent years developed comprehensive systems of review, including feedback from audited bodies and quality reviews by independent academics. And, as noted, nearly all value for money studies are produced by joint teams of National Audit Office staff and outside experts. The techniques of value for money studies go far beyond the examination of documents and discussions with public officials. Issue analysis, stakeholder panels, interviews with private sector suppliers of public services, focus groups, customer satisfaction and other surveys, and systems modelling are some of the tools and methods used. Some recent studies are listed in Table 2.1.

Table 2.1   Some of the studies in 2002 and 2003

Subject area	Report title and content
Agriculture	Reaping the rewards of agricultural research – the management of agricultural research
	The 2001 outbreak of foot and mouth disease
Cross-cutting studies involving a number of government departments and public authorities	Developing effective services for older people
	Improving service delivery by the Food Standards Agency, which is responsible for monitoring the quality of many foods in the UK
	Using call centres to deliver public services
Defence	Building an air manoeuvre capability through the introduction of the Apache helicopter
	Progress in reducing stocks
	Helicopter logistics
	The construction of nuclear submarine facilities at Devonport
Education	Individual learning accounts – a programme to help people improve their working skills
Environment	Dealing with pollution from ships
	The Environment Agency – protecting the public from dangerous waste
Customs & Excise	Report on Customs and Excise accounts 2001–02
Inland Revenue	Tackling fraud against the Inland Revenue
Law and order	The work of Victim Support, a body established to help the victims of crime
National Health Service	A safer place to work: protecting NHS hospital and ambulance staff from violence and aggression
	Ensuring the effective discharge of older patients from hospital, so that they can receive appropriate care when they leave

Table 2.1   (continued)

Subject area	Report title and content
	The regulation of medicines in the UK to promote safety, quality and efficacy
Overseas	Department for International Development: maximizing the impact of British aid programmes concerned with water, e.g. water purity and irrigation
Parliament and Treasury	Construction of Portcullis House, the new Parliamentary building
	Financial management in the European Union: Annual Report of the European Court of Auditors for the year 2000
Public–private Partnerships and the Private Finance Initiative	PFI: construction performance – the use of private finance in public construction projects
	The PFI contract for the redevelopment of the West Middlesex University Hospital
	The Public–private partnership for National Air Traffic Services Ltd
Regulation	Department of Trade and Industry: regulation of weights and measures
	Office of Fair Trading: progress in protecting consumers' interests
Transport	Highways Agency: maintaining England's motorways and trunk roads
Work and pensions	Tackling benefit fraud
	Tackling pensioner poverty: encouraging the take-up of legal entitlements to social security benefits

Relations with Parliament and the Government

The Comptroller and Auditor General and National Audit Office staff work closely with the Committee of Public Accounts – a senior select committee of Parliament – which consists of 15 Members of Parliament. The Committee meets twice a week when Parliament is sitting, approximately 45 times a year in total. These 'hearings' are normally based on a Comptroller and Auditor General's report, either on the accounts of a department, agency or public body or more commonly on a value for money report. Committee meetings are held in public unless the matters under discussion relate to national security or are commercially sensitive.

The Comptroller and Auditor General provides a briefing for the Committee in advance of its hearing, and he or the Deputy Comptroller and Auditor General is present throughout each hearing to answer further questions that may arise. The main witness before the Committee is the senior official (the Accounting Officer) of the department or body on which the report is based. Representatives from the Treasury attend all hearings to answer any questions about wider issues of financial control.

As an Officer of the House of Commons the Comptroller and Auditor General is independent from government and this is emphasized by his complete discretion in the exercise of his duties. When planning the programme of value for money work the Comptroller and Auditor General is required to take account of the views of the Committee of Public Accounts but the final choice rests solely with him. The Committee can make requests throughout the year for particular examinations and has a formal opportunity to do so each year when it considers the National Audit Office's two-year forward work programme.

Members of Parliament and members of the public also write to the Comptroller and Auditor General raising specific matters of concern about the propriety and value for money of public spending – he receives some 300 such requests each year. The Comptroller and Auditor General determines what action to take in reply and some matters may lead to examinations which he reports to Parliament.

The budget of the National Audit Office is determined by another Parliamentary Committee – the Public Accounts Commission. It receives proposals from the Comptroller and Auditor General, and reports from the private sector audit firm that it appoints to carry out an annual financial and value for money audit of the National Audit Office. When the Commission has reached its conclusion, the Chairman invites the House of Commons to vote the money for the next financial year to the Comptroller and Auditor General. Unlike many countries, the approval of the audit office's budget does not pass through the Ministry of Finance; that is, the UK Treasury.

Reporting

The Comptroller and Auditor General's audit opinion is set out in the audit certificate which is published with the financial statements. The Comptroller and Auditor General may additionally be required by statute to report on that body. If the Comptroller and Auditor General has anything to report he will set this out in a separate report, also published with the financial statements. Otherwise he will add a paragraph to the audit certificate stating that he has no observations to make. In addition, the Comptroller and Auditor General may report to Parliament on any matter he believes should be brought to its attention. He usually does this in his main report published with the appropriation accounts volumes. Most of the Comptroller and Auditor General's audits are conducted under statute with the requirement that the audited financial statements and audit certificate are laid before Parliament.

The Comptroller and Auditor General's value for money reports are also laid before Parliament and published by order of the House of Commons. In addition the National Audit Office publishes an Annual Report of its activities. The results of the work of the Comptroller and Auditor General (and the National Audit Office) are therefore readily available to the public and can attract considerable media attention. Reports are also available on the National Audit Office's Internet website (www.nao.gov.uk).

The Committee of Public Accounts issues its own reports following its hearings. These are based on drafts submitted by the National Audit Office and draw conclusions and make detailed recommendations aimed at ensuring that errors are not repeated. The government publishes a response to the Committee's report, normally within two months, in which it sets out the action taken or planned to meet each of the Committee's recommendations. Where the government does not accept the Committee's recommendation, explanations are offered and the Committee has the option of raising the matter again with Treasury officials in a follow-up session.

In addition to the Committee sessions there is a further annual opportunity for the House of Commons to discuss the work of the Committee of Public Accounts in full session. This debate is normally focused on a selection of the Committee's reports and the government's replies and concludes by passing a motion noting the contents of the reports of the Committee during the year. Furthermore, the National Audit Office's reports are often taken into account in the work of other parliamentary committees, and reference is also made to them during debates in Parliament.

Overseas Work

The National Audit Office and the other public audit institutions in the UK undertake work overseas, such as in contracts from the United Nations to audit particular agencies and in work from the European Commission to assist countries who are joining or are candidates to join the European Union. Other work derives from links with countries in the British Commonwealth, other countries which, like the UK, are members of the International Organization of Supreme Audit Institutions (INTOSAI), and international authorities such as the World Bank.

In 2004, current appointments include the external audits of the International Labour Organization, the International Atomic Energy

Agency and the World Food Programme. The National Audit Office also had twinning contracts with the European audit offices of Latvia, Lithuania, Slovenia and Turkey.

During 2003, over 600 representatives from 70 countries visited the National Audit Office. The Office often includes in its teams performing value for money studies expertise drawn from across the UK and beyond. For example, with help from the World Bank the National Audit Office was able to work with the Office of the Comptroller and Auditor General of India, providing input to their modernization plans.

The UK's audit authorities are pleased to work with and learn from colleagues overseas. International comparisons are often included in reports made to UK authorities, and this is very much welcomed by the auditees and Parliament. All the international work is separately financed by recipients or donors and is not funded by the audit offices themselves.

The Media

The National Audit Office and the other public audit authorities in the UK are concerned to present their reports in an attractive and readable way. Close attention is paid to graphics, pictures and executive summaries. The aim is to help the various readers of the reports to understand the analyses and recommendations quickly, but without sacrificing intellectual rigour or fairness of presentation. The public audit authorities appreciate that most citizens will come to know their work through newspapers, radio and television, and great care is taken when dealing with the media to show that the external auditor can deal with politically contentious subjects – as most programmes of public expenditure are – in an independent and non-political way that accords with the principle that the auditor is not concerned with the merits of particular policies, but with their implementation and management.

Impact

The National Audit Office has a target to save £8 in public spending for every £1 it costs to run the office. It measures the impact of its work each year by calculating the number of significant changes made by audited bodies as a result of National Audit Office recommendations. In 2002 over 1000 significant changes arose following financial audit work and a further 212 significant improvements arose from value for money work. For the same year, the National Audit Office estimates that its work led to identifiable savings or economies of some £19 million from financial audit and over £400 million from value for money audit.

Recommendations of the National Audit Office have also led to a number of recent non-financial improvements. For example:

- Following National Audit Office recommendations on dealing with pollution from ships, the Maritime and Coastguard Agency introduced improved contingency plans for dealing with oil spills at all UK ports and harbours.
- After a National Audit Office report on the level of violence against staff in the National Health Service (NHS), the NHS established a new organization to implement the report's recommendations, including developing a national system to record physical assaults on staff, developing and delivering conflict resolution training, and improving the effectiveness of the partnership between the NHS and the police in order to ensure a nationally consistent approach to investigation and handling of cases.
- National Audit Office recommendations to the government agency responsible for regulating the safety of medicines and healthcare products on monitoring the impact of its safety alerts and warnings, led to the agency's agreeing that it should expand the work it does to measure the effectiveness of its messages to the public.

In short, the National Audit Office is concerned to promote both efficiency and compassion in the delivery of public services.

BIBLIOGRAPHY

Gary, O. and Barry K. Winetrobe (2003), *Parliamentary Audit Scrutiny: Innovative and Effective*, London: The Constitution Unit, School of Public Policy, University College London.
Jones, P.C. and J.G. Bates (1994), *Public Sector Auditing*, 2nd edn, London: Chapman and Hall.
Likierman, A. (1988), *Public Expenditure*, London: Penguin Books.
Ling, T. (2003), 'Ex-ante Evaluation and the Changing Public Audit Function', *Evaluation*, **9** (4), 437–52.
The National Audit Office (2001), *State Audit in the European Union*, London: The National Audit Office.

Official Publications

Audit Commission. A review of the work of the Audit Commission's appointed auditors in 2001.
Audit Commission. *Audit Commission Annual Report*, year ended October 2002.

Audit Scotland. *Audit Scotland Annual Report 2002–03*.
Audit Scotland. *Hospital Cleaning* (2003).
Auditor General for Wales. *Annual Report of the Auditor General for Wales*, for the year ended 31 March 2003.
Auditor General for Wales. *ELWa – The National Council for Education and Training for Wales: Financial Management of Partnership and Innovation and Development Projects* (2003).
National Audit Office. *Hip Replacements: Getting it Right First Time* (HC 417, Parliamentary Session 1999–00).
National Audit Office. *Dealing with Pollution from Ships* (HC 879, Parliamentary Session 2001–02).
National Audit Office. *National Audit Office Annual Report 2003. Hip Replacements: An Update* (HC 956, Parliamentary Session 2002–03).
National Audit Office. *A Safer Place to Work: Protecting NHS Hospital and Ambulance Staff from Violence and Aggression* (HC 527, Parliamentary Session 2002–03).
National Audit Office. *Safety, Quality, Efficacy: Regulating Medicines in the UK* (HC 255, Parliamentary Session 2002–03).
State Audit in the European Union (2001).

Legislation

Audit Commission. Audit Commission Act 1998
Audit Scotland. Scotland Act 1998
Audit Scotland. Public Finance and Accountability (Scotland) Act 2000 (Act of the Scottish Parliament)
Auditor General for Wales. Government of Wales Act 1998
National Audit Office. Exchequer and Audit Departments Act 1866
National Audit Office. Exchequer and Audit Departments Act 1921
National Audit Office. National Audit Act 1983
National Audit Office. Government Resources and Accounts Act 2000
National Audit Office. Government Resources and Accounts Act 2000 (Audit of Public Bodies) Order 2003
National Audit Office. Government Resources and Accounts Act 2000 (Rights of Access of Comptroller and Auditor General) Order 2003
Northern Ireland Audit Office. Audit (Northern Ireland) Order 1987
Northern Ireland Audit Office. Northern Ireland Act 1998
Northern Ireland Audit Office. Government Resources and Accounts Act (Northern Ireland) 2001
Northern Ireland Audit Office. Audit and Accountability (Northern Ireland) Order 2003

3. Public expenditure control in the Netherlands[1]

Saskia J. Stuiveling and Rudi W. Turksema

THE NETHERLANDS – INTRODUCTION

Economic and General Information

With a surface area of less than 42,000 square kilometres and a population of some 16 million, the Netherlands is one of the most densely populated countries in the world. Half of the land requires constant protection against flooding. The country's development has been influenced to a large extent by its situation at the estuary of the rivers Rhine, Maas and Scheldt.

A few facts and figures. Rotterdam is the largest port in the world, a position that it has occupied for over 30 years. Amsterdam's Schiphol Airport is one of the four largest in Europe. Dutch freight companies account for 40 per cent of waterborne freight and a quarter of overland freight in the European Union. The Netherlands is one of the world's major agricultural exporters and the largest producer of natural gas in Western Europe.

Amsterdam is the capital of the Netherlands, but the seat of the head of state and the government is in The Hague. This is why the Netherlands Court of Audit – like many other government bodies – is located in The Hague.

The Dutch economy is heavily oriented towards the services sector, with around 60 per cent of GDP coming from this source. A further 30 per cent comes from the manufacturing sector and agriculture contributes much of the remainder. The Netherlands has been a major trading nation for centuries, with banking, shipping and general commerce contributing to its balance of trade and payments surplus.

The Structure of the Dutch State

The Kingdom of the Netherlands, as the country is officially known, is a constitutional monarchy, with the monarch as the head of state. Even the highest office in the land, however, is explicitly subject to the rules laid down in the Constitution, under which the government is formed jointly by the monarch and the ministers of the current administration. Responsibility for the government's actions is borne entirely by the ministers, however.

The present head of state is Queen Beatrix. If and when her eldest son, Crown Prince Willem Alexander, accedes to the throne, we shall have a king as head of state for the first time since 1890, following four generations of queens.

The hereditary monarchy operates in conjunction with a democratic parliamentary system, under which the members of parliament are elected by the people. Parliament is responsible for overseeing government policy. Variations on this system of government can be found in other countries including the United Kingdom, Denmark and Spain.

Central government: ministries
The Netherlands has 13 ministries:

- Ministry of General Affairs
- Ministry of the Interior and Kingdom Relations
- Ministry of Foreign Affairs and Development Cooperation
- Ministry of Defence
- Ministry of Economic Affairs
- Ministry of Finance
- Ministry of Justice
- Ministry of Agriculture, Nature Management and Food Quality
- Ministry of Education, Culture and Science
- Ministry of Social Affairs and Employment
- Ministry of Transport, Public Works and Water Management
- Ministry of Health, Welfare and Sport
- Ministry of Housing, Spatial Planning and the Environment.

Each of these is headed by a minister, who bears political responsibility for the policy pursued by that ministry. He or she is supported in this task by one or occasionally two state secretaries. The civil servants in each ministry assist the minister and state secretary or secretaries in their work. They maintain an apolitical stance (loyalty principle). After elections, the civil servants continue to work at the same ministry for the newly appointed ministers and state secretaries.

In addition many government tasks are devolved to other bodies. These have regulatory functions in addition to their judicial, administrative and advisory duties. They exercise these functions independently but can be influenced where necessary by ministers, and can be both public and private entities. There is also state involvement in enterprises, including telecommunications, airports and seaports. The level of state participation varies from 1 per cent to 100 per cent ownership of capital. Many of the ministries' tasks are carried out by decentralized governmental services. These employ over half of all civil servants and are within the hierarchy of ministries, but enjoy significant independence.

Decentralized government

As far as local government is concerned, the Netherlands is divided into 12 provinces and 483 municipalities.

The provinces are administered by a Provincial Council, a Provincial Executive and the Queen's Commissioner. The members of the Provincial Councils are elected directly. Each Provincial Council appoints its own Provincial Executive, which is responsible for the administration of the province. The Queen's Commissioner is appointed by the Crown and acts as chairman of both the Provincial Council and the Provincial Executive.

Each of the municipalities is administered by a Municipal Council, a Municipal Executive and a Mayor. The members of the Municipal Councils are elected directly. Each Municipal Council appoints its own Municipal Executive, which is responsible for the administration of the municipality. The Mayor is appointed by the Crown and acts as chairman of both the Municipal Council and the Municipal Executive. The desirability of a new system in which the Mayors will be elected is currently under debate.

The Electoral System

The Dutch Parliament (the States General) has two chambers. The Senate (the upper chamber) has 75 members, who are elected for a term of four years by the members of the 12 Provincial Councils, who in turn are elected directly by the inhabitants of the particular provinces. The 150 members of the House of Representatives (the lower chamber) are elected directly by the people, also for a four-year term. The House of Representatives has much more substantial powers than the Senate, which can only accept or reject a decision by the House of Representatives in its entirety.

Elections in the Netherlands are based on a system of proportional representation, under which each party is allocated a number of seats in Parliament corresponding to the proportion of the overall vote won by that party. Thus the distribution of parliamentary seats reflects the popularity of the various parties among the electorate fairly accurately, and virtually every shade of political opinion has the opportunity to be represented in Parliament. Because of the large number of political parties resulting from this system the country is always governed by coalitions.

The Political Environment

Ministers are not members of the legislature but the Cabinet must have the support of the House of Representatives of the States General. It will thus broadly reflect the political composition of that chamber. The leader of the largest political party in the House of Representatives is usually appointed Prime Minister and will consequently no longer be party leader in the House of Representatives. The Cabinet will be a broad coalition, agreed after consultation with the politicians in the House of Representatives.

Dutch ministers have considerable autonomy in the exercise of their functions, and are subject to little central control. Ministerial responsibility covers both ministers' personal actions and action taken by their ministries. However, in practice ministers are unlikely to resign because of mistakes made within their ministries. Laws are passed when they gain approval in both chambers of the States General, and following signature by the sovereign, the responsible minister and the Minister of Justice who is responsible for the proclamation of the laws.

Each chamber has different powers. The House of Representatives has full-time members and can initiate and amend legislation, although in practice most legislation comes from the government. The Senate has part-time members and can only accept or reject legislation. Both chambers operate a comprehensive committee system, the composition of which broadly reflects the composition of each chamber. The two chambers both have a number of permanent committees and can set up special committees on an ad hoc basis.

The States General has three other ways in which it can hold the government to account. The first is in the setting of the state budget, where it considers the proposals put forward by the executive. The second is the right of interpellation, through which either chamber can question ministers about present or future policies. Finally it has a right of enquiry, whereby it can set up specific investigations.

Institutional watchdogs
In addition to parliament, three independent government bodies play a part in the operation of Dutch democracy, the Council of State (the advisory body which makes recommendations on every Bill), the National Ombudsman (who investigates whether the government has behaved properly towards members of the public), and the Netherlands Court of Audit (which investigates whether public funds are collected and spent legitimately and effectively).

PUBLIC EXPENDITURE AND INTERNAL CONTROL

The Court of Audit's tasks and responsibilities with respect to public expenditure and internal control are laid down in the Government Accounts Act 2001. The 2001 version of this Act came about as a result of two important changes in government accounting in the past two decades, the *Operation Accounting Reform* and *From Policy Budgeting to Policy Accountability*.

Operation Accounting Reform

In the 1980s there were major problems with central government accounts:

- financial statements were five years overdue;
- many items of expenditure were irregular or doubtful;
- financial management at the ministries was poor.

Some of these problems were due to the performance of departmental internal audit divisions. An examination by the Court of Audit in 1985 found significant staff shortages in the audit divisions, lack of qualifications, weak audit programmes and poor accounting procedures in place.

As a result, the mid-1980s saw a radical change in approach, signalled by the Government Accounting Reform Operation. With the support of Parliament, the Minister of Finance introduced this five-year plan to improve financial management in 1986. Its objectives were to:

- improve internal control at the ministries;
- prepare manuals on administrative procedures and control;
- establish internal Ministry Audit Departments (MADs) at all ministries;
- have the Ministry Audit Departments issue unqualified audit opinions on the ministries' financial statements.

These goals were achieved by the mid-1990s. As a result the regularity of expenditure improved from 30 per cent uncertainty about regularity in 1987 to 99.5 per cent regularity in 1999.

From Policy Budgeting to Policy Accountability

In 1999 a new and comparable change process was launched named 'From Policy Budget to Policy Accountability' (Dutch abbreviation: VBTB). One of the main goals of this operation is to focus on the achievements of governmental policy.

The overriding principle of this outcome-based budgeting system is that budgets and accounts should contain related and consistent information on policy objectives and on budget execution and financial resources. This outcome-based system replaces the input-based system. Elsewhere in the world, only Australia and New Zealand have implemented reforms that are as far-reaching as those in the Netherlands. The first official outcome-based budget was presented to parliament in September 2001.

What is outcome-based budgeting?
Budget regimes can be classified by the importance they attach to costs, inputs, instruments, outputs and outcomes. A distinction can thus be made between input-based, output-based and outcome-based budgeting systems. As the name implies, outcome-based budgeting is a government budgeting system that focuses on 'outcomes'. The underlying policy model establishes causal relationships between government resources, such as budgets, timeframe and personnel, to instruments (subsidies, legislation, etc.), and outputs to the final outcomes in society (see Figure 3.1).

Outcome-based budgeting assumes that government actions are ultimately directed at achieving results in society, within a given timeframe. It links the financial resources set out in the budget to outcome objectives. Typically, an outcome system involves defining indicators and setting targets to allow assessment of the government's relative success in attaining its outcome objectives.

Understanding outcome-based budgeting requires a clear distinction between 'outcomes' and 'outputs'. Outputs are defined as 'the goods or services which government agencies provide for citizens (and/or businesses

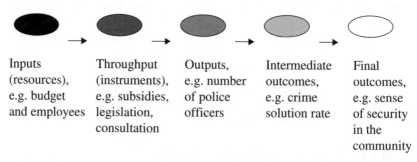

| Inputs (resources), e.g. budget and employees | Throughput (instruments), e.g. subsidies, legislation, consultation | Outputs, e.g. number of police officers | Intermediate outcomes, e.g. crime solution rate | Final outcomes, e.g. sense of security in the community |

Source: The authors.

Figure 3.1   Causal policy model

and other government agencies').[2] Outcomes are defined as the effects on society of outputs from governmental agencies. While 'outputs' are largely controllable by government agencies, 'outcomes' are usually not. A variety of extraneous factors can influence the state of the society that the government is trying to influence. The frequently used term 'performance' does not distinguish between outputs and outcomes. It may refer to both types of result.

Outcome-base budgeting in the Netherlands

How is outcome-based budgeting implemented in the Dutch context and what approach has the Dutch government adopted? Below, the guiding principles of the budget reform, its implementation in regulations and, finally, some subsequent modifications are successively described.

Guiding principles The general objective of the budget reform, as stated in the 1999 policy proposal, is to increase the information value of budget and accountability documents. This objective can be realized, first, through making budget and accountability documents more policy oriented by relating resources to policy and performance, and second, through improving the coherence between budget and accountability documents. The 'three W questions' embody the Dutch government's response to these two challenges, and are three related questions that should be answered by the government's budget:

- What policy goals does the government want to achieve?
- What actions is the government going to undertake to achieve those goals?
- What may those actions cost?

The Annual Report should answer a corresponding set of accountability questions, the 'three H questions':[3]

- Has the government achieved the goals set in the budget?
- Has the government completed the actions planned in the budget?
- Have costs remained within the limits set in the budget?

Structure of the new budget The principles of the three W questions are worked out in the technical details of the new Government Accounts Act. The new Act, which came into effect from the 2002 budget, lays down the requirements that the government's budget and Annual Report must satisfy. Figure 3.2 outlines the new budget structure.

1. Legislative proposal	2.1 Policy agenda
2. Policy paragraph	2.2 Policy articles
3. Management paragraph	– General policy objectives
4. Agency paragraph	– Operationalization of policy objectives
5. In-depth appendix	– Budgetary consequences of policy
	– Budget flexibility
	– Assumptions about effects, efficiency
	and estimates

Source: The authors.

Figure 3.2   The new budget structure

The key focus of the new budget is the policy paragraph. It is divided into a policy agenda and a number of policy articles. The policy agenda, which will be no longer than ten pages, presents a general overview of developments and government priorities in the domain of the ministry. The details are worked out in the policy articles.

The first section of each policy article is the 'general policy objective'. Outcome targets, including timing, are stated and target groups are identified for policies. If the general policy objective cannot be operationalized into SMART-C[4] outcome targets, it should be translated into second-order or intermediate outcome targets in the 'operationalization of policy objectives' section. This section also contains information on the instruments used and the output targets set by the ministry. In the section on the budgetary consequences of policies, the available budget for each policy article is split into the budget available for programme expenditures and that for ministerial operating expenditures. The programme expenditures are further split into the budgets available for each operational objective and within that objective the budget available for each instrument used.

The three W questions are accordingly answered for each operational policy objective and consequently for each general policy objective. Box 3.1 illustrates the structure of the policy articles using an example from the 2002 budget of the Department of the Environment.

Finally, the policy article contains a section on budget flexibility. It indicates the legal restrictions on expenditure (based on international treaties, contracts, laws, obligations) and the percentage of appropriation that can be reallocated if parliament so wishes. Although this modification of the budget structure is not due directly to outcome-based budgeting, its introduction represents international best practice for informing decision-makers on their room for manoeuvre.

BOX 3.1 ILLUSTRATION OF THE THREE W QUESTIONS

What policy goals does government want to achieve?

Final outcome objective: resist climate change

1. Operational outcome objective: reduce emission of greenhouse gases (CO_2). Outcome target: 6 per cent reduction by 2008 to the 1990 level
2. Operational outcome objective: reduce emission of industrial gases. Outcome target: in 2010, the following levels of emission SO_2 46 kton, NO_x 231 kton, etc.
3. Operational outcome: etc.

What action will government take to achieve those goals?

Instruments (operational outcome objective 1): (a) clean development mechanism, output target: reduction certificates of 50–70 Mton CO_2; (b) subsidies, output target: 40 subsidies, 2.5 Mton CO_2

Instruments (Operational outcome objective 2): (a) cost equalization NO_x, output target: not available; (b) other subsidies, output target: not available

Instruments (operational outcome objective 3): etc.

What may those actions cost?

Budget available for operational outcome target 1:

- Instrument a: EUR 83,339,000
- Instrument b: EUR 56,723,000

Budget available for operational outcome target 2:

- Instrument a: EUR 2,723,000
- Instrument b: EUR 1,795,000

Budget available for operational outcome target 3:

- etc.

Source: The authors.

Management statement While the budget system should concentrate politicians' minds on the link between budget and outcomes, it is the responsibility of government managers to transform the available budget into the desired outputs and to monitor outcomes. In recognition of the crucial role of management control, ministers *can* present an 'in control statement' on operational management in their annual reports.

Internal Control

Audit Committee
Since the mid-1990s each of the 13 ministries has had an Audit Committee. The Audit Committee is chaired by the ministry's secretary general, and its obligatory members are the Director of the Financial and Economic Affairs Department and the Director of the Ministry Audit Department. The Audit Committee's task is to advise on the annual audit plan, to take note of the most important audit findings and recommendations for improvement, to advise on and implement measures to overcome short-comings, to advise on internal control and control measures and to advise on audit policy.

Ministry Audit Departments
Under the Government Accounts Act 2001 each minister is responsible for the regularity, orderliness and auditability of his ministry's operational management. The ministers instruct their Ministry Audit Departments (MADs) to audit their operational management, the records kept for that purpose, the financial information in the Annual Reports, the ministerial trial balances and the preparation of information on the policy pursued and operational management. Their audits culminate in a report containing an opinion on the regularity of obligations, expenditure and receipts in compliance with budget acts and other regulations, and on the true and fair view given by each ministry's financial statements. The MADs report primarily to their respective ministers – since the ministers are ultimately responsible to parliament.

MADs were established in the 1980s as a result of Operation Accounting Reform (see p. 59). Twelve of the 13 ministries now have their own audit department. The MADs represent the first audit tier. The second and third tiers are the Ministry of Finance's Audit and Supervision Policy Directorate and the Court of Audit. MADs principally carry out regularity audits, but – as a result of the new outcome-based budgeting system – there is now a trend towards operational and performance audits.

Audit and Supervision Policy Directorate

The Minister of Finance had originally established a second audit tier, the Central Audit Department (CAD), in 1946. Its tasks included the audit and design of the records of the ministries and external departments. The CAD was also authorized to coordinate the MADs and to achieve 'uniformity of concept' with other internal audit departments. Over the years, the policy aspects of the CAD's work became more important than the operational aspects. This specialization was made possible by the establishment of internal audit departments at all ministries, the improvement of the ministries' financial management and the outsourcing of the CAD's audit engagements to external departments. The result was a final farewell to all operational audit work by the CAD and a change of name to the Central Government Accountancy Directorate in 1993. In 2003 it was reorganized and renamed the Audit and Supervision Policy Directorate (ASP).

Pursuant to the Government Accounts Act, the Minister of Finance is responsible for supervising the design of the audit of the execution of state budgets. The ASP performs this supervisory task on behalf of the minister. The ASP's director is the chairman of the Consultative Body of Ministry Audit Departments (CBMAD). The other members are the directors of the MADs. A representative of the Court of Audit attends the CBMAD's meetings. The CBMAD can issue audit directives, recommendations, decisions and advice. Within the CBMAD, Interministerial Consultation Auditing has been established to promote the quality and uniformity of the audit approach in central government. The ASP and the MADs together employ about 700 people.

EXTERNAL CONTROL: NETHERLANDS COURT OF AUDIT

Background Information

'Algemene Rekenkamer' literally means 'General Chamber of Accounts'. The term 'General' refers to the fact that it audits all national government accounts. 'Chamber' reflects the collegiate nature of the Court of Audit's leadership rather than its judicial powers. It does not actually have the powers of a court. The Court of Audit cannot judge or sanction those responsible for public expenditure or act as a court of appeal. The Court of Audit's juridical powers are embedded in the Constitution. Its further authorities and tasks are laid down in the Government Accounts Act. The Court of Audit conducts regularity and performance audits and investigates a variety of bodies that are financed by budgets or grants.

Historical development

State audit in the Netherlands can be traced back to the fourteenth century, when the territories of the current Netherlands came under the influence of the Dukes of Burgundy, who introduced a system of centralized public finance, including Chambers of Audit. In 1447 a Chamber of Audit for the Netherlands was founded in The Hague. In the intervening 550 years, the institute has undergone many changes but its duties have traditionally been carried out by a Board of Auditors on behalf of the sovereign. During the Napoleonic era the state audit system was remodelled on the French structure, which included judicial powers and ex ante audits of proposed expenditure by the Court of Accounts.

The audit institution was given a new legal basis in the 1814 Constitution with the reinstatement of the rule of the House of Orange over the Netherlands. The Court of Accounts became a Court of Audit: a mixture of the French court system, but without judicial powers, and the Anglo-Saxon Auditor General approach.

In 1848, a fundamental revision of the constitution shifted the locus of sovereignty to the States General. From this moment on the Court of Audit reoriented itself towards serving parliamentary requirements more directly, though not to the extent that it became merely an office of the legislature. The Court of Audit is independent, but increasingly supports the work of the States General by responding to requests to carry out specific audits. However, it retains the right either to decline such requests or to postpone the commencement of any audit that does not fit in with its activity programme.

After World War Two the need to control public expenditure and improve government performance resulted in the Court of Audit placing considerable emphasis on developing performance audits to complement its regularity audits, the principal focus of its work. This position is formalized in the Government Accounts Act.

The Court of Audit's profile has increased significantly since the mid-1980s, when the States General began to take account of past audit recommendations in its consideration of new policies. As greater attention was paid to audit reports, their impact increased and the Court of Audit's role in the accountability process was enhanced.

Independence

The Court of Audit is a 'High Council of State', along with the Senate and the House of Representatives of the States General, the Council of State and the National Ombudsman (also see p. 58). High Councils of State are central government bodies created to ensure that the democratic system works properly. Unlike other government bodies they are *independent* of government: their legal status, duties and powers are laid down by law. Like the House of Representatives (the parliament), the Court of Audit is responsible for checking government policy, but the difference is that the Court gives its opinion only *after* a policy has been laid down. Nor does the Court make *political* pronouncements: it will never say, for example, that a particular law is 'not good', although it may say that a law is not working in the intended way.

Relations with parliament and government
The Court of Audit has complete independence in its choice of work although it must approve the State Accounts every year. Both chambers of the States General may request work to be carried out but the Court of Audit determines its final activity programme. The Court of Audit and parliament's State Expenditure Committee meet about three times a year to discuss matters of mutual interest and the latter consults the Court of Audit when it makes recommendations. The State Expenditure Committee is an important parliamentary committee as it has the authority to call ministers to account and seek further evidence from the Court of Audit.

The relationship between parliament and the Court of Audit is often discussed in the States General, for example when politicians request more information on the selection of topics for further examination. However, the Court of Audit resists parliamentary moves to curb its freedom and seeks, without compromising its independence, to maximize the benefits derived from its work.

As an independent body the Court is detached from the day-to-day workings of politics and can thus examine all sorts of topics 'at its leisure'. This does not mean that the Court shuts itself up in an ivory tower: it is always aware that its findings must be capable of practical application. In this light, the Court regards the government and the House of Representatives as its principal 'customers'. Wherever possible, the Court designs its audits to meet the needs and wishes of members of parliament: it sees it as its job to provide concise, relevant information so that parliament can decide quickly whether a minister is on the right track.

The Court of Audit's reports are submitted to the States General and the government and, as official parliamentary documents, are in the public domain. All reports are published on the website of the Court of Audit (www.rekenkamer.nl), which also has an English version. Any parliamentary committee can discuss the reports but they are usually considered by the State Expenditure Committee.

The relationship between the Court of Audit and the States General has evolved gradually. Until the mid-1980s there was little public or political concern about matters of financial accountability and as a result the Court of Audit's work received little attention. The increased importance of financial accountability in the mid-1980s altered this situation. The House of Representatives now frequently uses the Court of Audit's reports to question ministers. The Court of Audit also recognizes that it needs parliamentary interest for its work to be successful, and this interest can be measured, for example, by the number of questions asked of the government by the States General.

Organization

Audit mandate
The Court of Audit has a very broad mandate to audit central government. The Constitution states that it 'is responsible for auditing state receipts and expenditure'. To further define its role, the Court of Audit has formulated the following mission statement:

> The Netherlands Court of Audit aims to audit and improve the regularity, efficiency, effectiveness and integrity with which the State and its associated bodies operate. It also audits compliance with the Netherlands' obligations under international agreements. As part of this process, it passes on the results of its audits, as well as its accumulated experience, to the government, to parliament and to those responsible for the bodies audited. As a rule, this information is also available to the public. It consists of audit findings, opinions and recommendations concerning organisation, management and policy. Another task of the Netherlands Court of Audit is to contribute to sound public administration through cooperation and knowledge exchange at home and abroad. The Netherlands Court of Audit sees quality, reliability and utility as the hallmarks of its work, and independence, efficiency and effectiveness as the hallmarks of its working methods. It strives to be a transparent organisation, continually investing in the quality of its staff and procedures.

The Court of Audit has extensive rights of access to all documentation, even personal notes. Its relations with audited bodies are generally good and they are helped by the physical location of the Court of Audit's staff within ministries.

Strategy
The Court of Audit periodically revises its strategy. It tries to respond as effectively as possible to issues and developments in its environment and to introduce order into its work (or to re-order it). The Court's strategy for 2004–09 is centred on the concept of *Good governance*. This term is defined with reference to the 'good governance' diagram developed by the United Nations, which is based on eight characteristics. In accordance with its statutory task and mission, the Court considers four aspects of good public

administration to be within its domain. They are *transparency, public accountability, effectiveness and efficiency* and *responsiveness*. The Court of Audit has incorporated these aspects into the two pillars of its strategy: *accountability and supervision* and *link between policy and implementation* (see Figure 3.3).

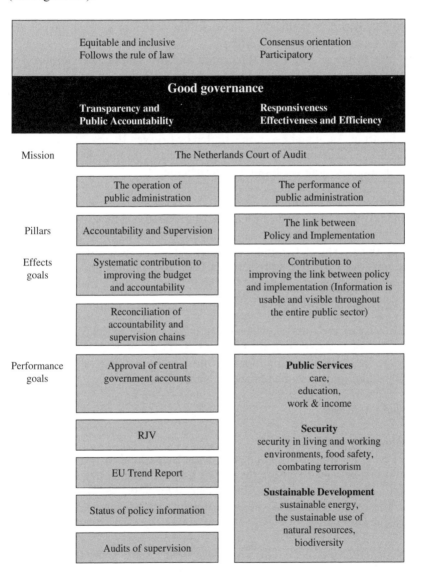

Figure 3.3   The NCA strategy 2004–09

Structure
The Court of Audit has a board with three members, including the president, each of whom is appointed by the government on the recommendation of the House of Representatives. Each member is appointed for life or until the retirement age of 70 (in practice recent presidents and members of the board have retired at the age of 65). The composition of the Court of Audit's board is politically balanced. The secretary general advises the board and heads the organization.

The Court of Audit has three audit and two support directorates. The audit directorates are divided into audit sections, most of which are based in the ministries. This process of situating staff in the audited bodies started in 1930 and, the Court of Audit believes, has the advantage of facilitating communication between itself and the audited department. At the moment a Court of Audit audit section – staffed by between 10 and 20 auditors – is located in each ministry. The support directorates and the government-wide audit sections are located at the headquarters.

Staff and other resources
In 2003 the Court of Audit had about 320 staff. Of these some 220 were involved directly in audit work and the remainder were support staff. Eighty per cent of the auditors are graduates in such disciplines as economics, law, political and social sciences, accountancy and statistics. All employees undergo a one-year internal training course that explains the Court of Audit's audit approach.

The Court of Audit's budget is set following discussions with the Ministry of the Interior, which submits the budget to the States General. In case of disagreement, the Court of Audit may raise the issue with the State Expenditure Committee but must rely on members of the States General to propose amendments to the budget.

Audit Activities

Regularity audits
There is a strong onus on ministers in the Netherlands to have systems and controls in place to ensure the proper use of public money. Ministers are actually accountable to the States General for doing so. They are assisted in this by the Ministry Audit Departments, which form their own opinion on the accounts.

Systematic approach The Court of Audit's audit approach is systems based and relies heavily on the work of the Ministry Audit Departments. This is permitted by section 86 of the Government Accounts Act. MADs share their findings with the Court of Audit, which examines their audit programmes and the conclusions reached, and plans its own audits accordingly. The Court of Audit carries out further regularity audits as necessary.

This systematic approach means that the Court of Audit's opinion on each account is based largely on the results of internal audit work. The Court of Audit must therefore be confident that it can place reliance on internal audit. To this end, it investigates the planning, execution and closing of the MADs' audits to determine whether it can rely on them. It also carries out additional investigations. If it considers the MADs' audits to be reliable, which is usually the case, it adopts the MADs' audit findings. The Court then determines whether errors or uncertainties at budget article level are sufficiently material to warrant reporting to parliament. It also considers which shortcomings in the financial management control systems should be reported.

If the Court of Audit believes the MADs' work is weak or has short-comings, it can carry out further investigation. After reviewing the MADs' audit work and completing its own investigations, the Court issues 24 reports on the annual reports prepared for each budget (ministries, special budgets and budget funds). The reports set out the findings and opinions regarding the operational management and financial statements of the ministries, departments and budget funds. Most of the Court of Audit's reports on annual reports refer to weaknesses in financial control systems. The Court's opinion relates to both the true and fair view given by the financial statements and the regularity of obligations, expenditure and revenue in compliance with budget acts and other regulations. The Court's audit reports are amalgamated to produce an opinion on the State Accounts, which the Court of Audit is required to approve before discharge can be granted by the States General. The annual reports of the ministries and budget funds are not yet consolidated with those of state-owned enter-prises and public bodies.

If the Court of Audit objects to some elements of irregular expenditure and the minister refuses to accept recommendations for changes, the Court can report its objections and thus force a minister to submit a bill to elim-inate the objection. This bill is known as an Indemnity Act and permits the inclusion of 'irregular' expenditure in the State Accounts. Once the Court of Audit has issued its reports on the annual reports and the final budgets acts have been passed, parliament discharges the minister for his or her financial management during the year.

Consequences of VBTB for auditing   Clearly, Dutch budget reform will not leave the Court of Audit (or the MADs) unaffected. Most importantly, the traditional distinction between information included in the budget for information purposes and information included for the legally binding vote has lost its relevance. The alignment of financial information with policy information (information on outputs and outcomes) and targets is increasing the importance of policy information in the appropriation process and extending the Court's traditional duty to audit financial statements. Traditionally, the Court has fulfilled this duty by means of regularity audits. Auditing policy information used to be the domain of performance audits. With the adoption of outcome-based budgeting, policy information has entered the field of regularity auditing. Since the emphasis in the annual reports has shifted from financial information towards non-financial information on government performance, audits (both internal and external) of the annual reports should be adapted accordingly. To this end, MADs are being reorganized into audit departments that can also audit non-financial information.

Integrity

The Court has no competence or powers to investigate individual cases of corruption as defined in criminal law. If the Court discovers potential cases in the course of its work, its policy is to hand the case over to the responsible authorities and urge them to notify the public prosecutor. Owing to the Court's role and position, it is very rare for the Court to consider notifying the police or the public prosecutor.

The Court is currently conducting a study to update its own audit approach in relation to the integrity of the public sector. It is concentrating on how integrity can be systematically embedded in the various types of audit it conducts. The new approach will also include specific audit activities in relation to integrity.

Performance audits

Performance audits form an important part of the Court of Audit's work. The statutory basis for this work is section 85 of the Government Accounts Act 2001, which requires the Court of Audit to 'examine the effectiveness and efficiency of the policy pursued, and the efficiency of financial and tangible asset management, of the records kept for this purpose and of the organisation of central government' (Government Accounts Act 2001). The legislation also enables the States General to ask the Court of Audit to carry out a particular audit. They cannot order it to do so since it is free in its choice of audit, but in practice the Court tries to incorporate such requests into its activity programme. The importance attached to performance audits has increased since the mid-1980s, largely as a result of the increased parliamentary attention paid to it.

The Court of Audit can examine the efficiency and effectiveness of government policy but not the policy itself. The audit process is well established, starting with the policy decision and then adopting the criteria to evaluate the policy. The specific criteria vary with each audit. However, criteria on policy goals and policy information are used in almost all performance audits.

The Court of Audit aims to secure future change rather than apportion blame. It believes early intervention will highlight cases in which ministers should clarify or further define their objectives. It interprets its *a posteriori* audit mandate as a means to examine a subject as soon as a minister takes a decision that has financial consequences.

There are two elements to the Court's performance audits: (1) audits of the government's obligation to evaluate policy, and (2) audits of outputs and outcomes.

Audits of the government's obligation to evaluate policy   In 2002, the Court of Audit examined how well the ministries were meeting their obligation to set up practicable policy evaluation systems. This was the first in a series of audits to be conducted over several years regarding the structure and operation of the ministries' evaluation systems.

A properly working system of evaluation instruments is important for two reasons. First, periodic evaluations and monitoring are essential to provide sound information on policy results and operational management. This is an important requirement of the From Policy Budgets to Policy Accountability process. Second, periodic policy evaluations and monitoring provide information on the effectiveness and efficiency of policy; such information is indispensable for the further development of policy.

Audits of outputs and outcomes   Performance audits investigate whether public funds are spent *to good effect*. The best possible result has to be achieved with the least amount of money. After all, the financial resources at the government's disposal are all 'public funds'. Ministers are responsible for the correct expenditure of funds and for their policies having the desired effects. For a variety of reasons, this is not always the case in practice. Sometimes it emerges that the goal of a particular policy was not formulated clearly, in which case it is impossible to determine whether the policy has been effective. Sometimes, policies include rules that turn out to be too complicated or too restrictive. Sometimes a policy does not have the desired effect because the minister did not provide enough money for it or did not oversee its implementation properly. Alternatively, unexpected developments in society may result in a policy having effects other than those intended. Often there are multiple reasons.

Audits of outputs and outcomes are divided into four types, ranging from relatively easy to difficult. All commence by establishing whether the policy objectives are clear (is it formulated SMART-C?) and by examining whether ministers themselves have information to track the implementation of policy.

The first type is the audit of *goal realization*, which examines whether policy goals have been achieved. Did the minister produce the promised outputs and/or have the desired societal outcomes been realized? In this type of audit no causal relationship between outputs and outcomes is investigated, and it is therefore relatively easy. Most of the Court's audits are of this type.

A second audit type is the *target group* audit. Some policies are aimed at specific target groups. For policy to be effective it must reach the target group. If the audit shows that this is not the case, one can wonder whether policy was effective.

The third and fourth audit types (efficiency and effectiveness respectively) are complicated because they examine causal relationships. An *efficiency audit* examines how an organization's performance relates to the resources deployed; that is, the causal relationship between inputs and outputs (or outcomes). *Effectiveness audits* examine the causal relationship between outputs and outcomes. Did the intended social effects actually occur, and were they a result of government policy? This is difficult to establish. Even if the social situation has moved in the desired direction, this might not necessarily be a result of policy.

Selection of performance audits   In its selection of performance audits, the Court of Audit has given priority in recent years to policies relating to basic public needs: safety, income, healthcare, education, housing and the environment. These six priority areas were defined in the strategy for 1999–2003.

An important topic in the strategy for 2004–09 is the gap between policy and implementation. Anyone reading the 2003 Dutch budget will be impressed by the government's ambitious policies in such fields as security, care, integration and education. But what becomes of all these policy plans? In March 2003, the Court of Audit published a study comparing the findings of 29 audits it had carried out in recent years with the situation at the end of 2002. The comparison reveals a government that announces policy after policy and invests a great deal of energy in drawing them up, but puts far less effort and professionalism into carrying them out and has even less interest in their results.

The consequences are dire. Although there are no hard statistics, it can be concluded from the many examples in the Court's audits that a substantial amount of policy is not implemented as agreed, if at all. In consequence, there is a divergence between policy and its implementation. And since there is generally insufficient information on policy implementation and results, it is most unlikely that the House of Representatives is even aware. The answer is yet more policies to make up for the perceived inadequacies of current policy. The Court considers this divergence – if not gap – between policy ambition and implementation to be a serious threat to the government's credibility and the public's confidence in government.

Legal entities with statutory duties (quangos)
The Court of Audit's mandate was extended in 1989 as a result of a public debate on subsidies to Dutch shipyards that resulted in a parliamentary inquiry. The inquiry concluded that there was a need for greater audit of loans and guarantees. Additional pressure was brought to bear by the growth in the volume and cost of social security in the 1980s and the States General's realization that it had no information on this important area of public spending. In short, the law was changed because the States General wanted an independent opinion on key spending decisions. This is extremely important in a country in which a large part of public administration – for example, the social security payment system – is already undertaken by non-government bodies. Section 91 of the Government Accounts Act 2001 enables the Court of Audit to examine (not certify) both the regularity and the performance aspects of:

- public limited liability companies and private companies whose issued share capital is completely or partially held by the state (minimum 5 per cent share and a financial interest greater than EUR 500,000);
- corporate entities and partnerships to which the state has directly or indirectly given a grant, loan or guarantee;
- corporate entities performing a function regulated by statute and funded wholly or partially by receipts from levies instituted by statute – for example, social security, education, employment intermediaries and broadcasting bodies.

Such audits are carried out initially by inspecting audit reports and files held by the relevant ministry but the Court of Audit can call for further information from the organizations themselves. If it is still not satisfied, it can inspect the organization's books after giving notice to the appropriate minister. The Court of Audit views its power of access to state aided bodies as 'an excellent tool to obtain information from agencies and public bodies at a distance from their former ministries'.

Europe
The Netherlands contributes approximately EUR 4.5 billion to the European Union each year and receives about EUR 1.5 billion back from it (year 2002). Much of this is in the form of agricultural subsidies, grants from the structural funds for social projects at provincial and local government level and grants for technology policy to support the development of new technology. This money is paid not only to ministries, provinces and local authorities but in many cases also directly to Dutch companies and individuals. The same applies in the other EU Member States.

Audits of local government are outside the Court of Audit's mandate. An exception is made for European funds. Since the extension of the Court of Audit's mandate pursuant to the eighth amendment of the Government Accounts Act (1 May 2002), the Court of Audit may also audit beneficiaries of these funds that are not part of central government in so far as the State is accountable under or pursuant to the treaties establishing the European Communities for the obligations arising from the grants.

The Netherlands Court of Audit believes it is important that European funds are spent properly. In the current situation the European Court of Auditors' (ECA) remit does not include the Member States. It can only audit European expenditure for the European Union as a whole; that is, through the EU budget. Consequently the focus of the ECA audit is on the European Commission, not on the Member States. The Netherlands Court of Audit is therefore in favour of a more transparent auditing structure within Europe. In its opinion the European Court of Auditors should function as the external auditor of the European Commission, whereas the Member States' supreme audit institutions should audit the European grants spent within the Member States.

Procedures

The clearance process
The Court of Audit submits its reports to the auditee for comment although it is not required to do so. The audit findings will normally be discussed with the responsible civil servants of the ministry audited and their responses will be considered in the final draft. The relevant minister is also invited to comment on the audit findings and is given six weeks to respond. Depending on the findings and the ministry's responses the Court of Audit may choose to treat the audit as complete and 'close the file', but in most cases the audit results and conclusions will be submitted to the States General. The final report includes the response of the auditee (usually the minister) to the Court's findings and the Court's final comments.

Reporting

The Court of Audit reports to the States General at various times during the year. Before 1 April each year it is required to produce an Annual Report on its activities. Its statutory reports on the annual reports of the ministries are published on the third Wednesday of May.

The results of performance audits are published throughout the year. Any report that the Court of Audit publishes through the States General automatically passes into the public domain as parliamentary documents and is thus available for public scrutiny.

The impact of a performance audit is difficult to assess. The Court of Audit estimates that the government accepts a large majority of its recommendations but the extent to which remedial action follows is less clear. Since the mid-1980s the Court of Audit has followed up audits to ensure that the promised action is delivered.

The Court of Audit assesses the impact of its work by carrying out follow-up audits on a regular basis. These normally take place between one and three years after the initial report is published and the results of the follow-up are published in the Annual Report. In its follow-up work the Court of Audit indicates which of its recommendations have been implemented.

Other Activities

Local audits

Both the provinces and the municipalities in the Netherlands have responsibility for different aspects of administering and managing local and regional services and programmes. Each tier of government is financed by a combination of central government grants and local taxes. Financial audit of the organizations and bodies associated with these services and programmes is a responsibility of the regional and local authority audit institutions and is outside the Court of Audit's mandate.

Pursuant to the Local Authorities (Separation of Powers) Act 2002, all local authorities must have an audit office or function by January 2006. Something similar is laid down for the provinces in the Provinces (Separation of Powers) Act 2003. Financial statements are audited not by the local audit office but by external auditors.

The Court of Audit regards it as its task to support local and provincial authorities with its knowledge. With this in mind, it organizes on-site workshops entitled 'Build Your Own Audit Office' in various municipalities and provinces and participates in the Board of Governors of the Association of Local Audit Offices, for which it also hosts the secretariat.

The Court of Audit and other countries

The Court of Audit also looks beyond its own national borders. As an institution it tests its theories, gains new insights and shares know-how in other countries. It is of the opinion that a properly functioning audit office is a necessary component of sound financial management in government. In the field of development cooperation, the Court of Audit endorses the concept of good governance by supporting other audit offices. It concentrates its activities on a number of regions in the belief that this will increase their effectiveness. In doing so, it bases its work on the policy of the relevant minister and international organization.

NOTES

1. In writing this article, the authors drew on texts that the Netherlands Court of Audit published earlier on its website (www.rekenkamer.nl), in its 2003 Brochure and in the NAO publication *State Audit in the European Union* (2001). The authors wish to thank Ina de Haan, Robert Tjon Tsoe Jin and Ferrie Pot for their contributions.
2. Definitions are adopted from OECD, PUMA, 2002.
3. To indicate that the scope of accountability has increased, the term 'Annual Report' is used rather than the term 'Financial Statement'.
4. Specific, Measurable, Agreed, Realistic, Time-bound and Consistent.

4. Public financial control in Europe: the example of the Federal Republic of Germany

Hedda von Wedel

INTRODUCTION

Article 20(1) of the Constitution states that the Federal Republic of Germany is a Federal State. The main characteristic of federal states is the division of governmental functions between the central government (Federation) and the regional governments (the Länder). In the Federal Republic of Germany, Articles 30 and 70 of the Constitution lay down the division of functions between the Federal Government and the Länder. Financial responsibilities are also allocated in accordance with this division (Article 104(a) of the Constitution), as are tax revenues (Article 106 ff of the Constitution). The separation of responsibilities, expenditure and revenue between the Federal Government and the Länder also affects the budget system. Article 109(1) of the Constitution states that the Federal Government and the Länder are autonomous and independent in terms of their budgets. The establishment of the budgetary autonomy of the Federal Government and Länder also sets a limit as regards content. It aims to prevent the Federal Government or the Länder claiming financial powers to which the Constitution does not entitle them. Nevertheless the principle of budgetary autonomy does not apply without reservation. Articles 91(a), 91(b) and 104(a)(4) of the Constitution are in contrast with this basic principle.[1]

Despite the budgetary autonomy of both Federal Government and Länder, their budget legislation must at least agree in terms of its basic principles. The twentieth Amendment of 1969 extended Article 109(3) of the Constitution so that common principles could be introduced for budgetary law. The Federal Government then promulgated the Law on the Principles of the Budgetary Laws of the Federal Government and Länder (Law on Budgetary Principles) of 19 August 1969. The Law on Budgetary Principles consists of two parts. Part I contains the principles to be respected by the

Federal Government and Länder to ensure legal uniformity and Part II contains regulations that apply uniformly and directly to both the Federal Government and the Länder.

Article 1 of the Law on Budgetary Principles required the Federal Government and the Länder to introduce legislation that would bring their legislation into line with Part I of the Law on Budgetary Principles by 1 January 1972. The Federal Government fulfilled this requirement by promulgating the Federal Budget Code and the Länder followed with their own Regional Budget Codes.

The Regional Budget Codes largely follow the Federal Budget Code both in substance and formally in terms of paragraph order. Some Regional Budget Codes differ in some respects from the Federal Budget Code, above all where the Law on Budgetary Principles allows alternative solutions.

In accordance with Article 42(1) of the Law on Budgetary Principles, the entire budgetary and financial management of the Federal Government and the Länder, including their separate assets and companies, must be audited by public audit institutions. For the Federal Government, this task is allocated to the Bundesrechnungshof. In the Länder, it is carried out by Landesrechnungshöfe.

The Rechnunungshöfe differ from internal audit bodies in that they are not organizationally embedded in the administration, but, as supreme federal/regional authorities, are independent financial control bodies that are subject only to law, the Rechnunungshöfe are generally held to be 'sui generis' institutions (Stern, 1989, p. 41; see also note 126, with further evidence).

EXTERNAL FINANCIAL CONTROL IN GERMANY AT THE FEDERAL LEVEL

Legal Bases

Independent auditing has been carried out in Germany for 290 years. In Prussia, an independent audit body the 'General-Rechen-Kammer' was set up as early as 1714. It was organized collegiately and answered only to the King. Today, federal external financial control is carried out by the Bundesrechnungshof, which is based in Bonn and has a branch office in Potsdam.[2] The status of the Bundesrechnungshof and its essential functions are guaranteed by the Constitution. The institutional financial control guarantee contained in Article 114 of the Constitution not only guarantees the existence of the Bundesrechnungshof, but also ensures the fulfilment of its tasks. In accordance with this provision, the

Bundesrechnungshof audits the efficiency and regularity of the budget and the financial management of the Federation. The judicial independence of its Members is also laid down in this article. Under this provision, the Members of the Bundesrechnungshof may only be dismissed before the expiry of their term of office, lastingly or temporarily relieved of their office or transferred or retired by a court decision, and only for reasons and in ways that are established by law. In technical matters, they are not subject to any instructions. Article 114 of the Constitution is supplemented, on the one hand, by the Bundesrechnungshof Act (which contains regulations for the setting up and organization of the institution and for the appointment of its Members) and, on the other hand, the Law on Budgetary Principles and the Federal Budget Code, which specify its tasks still further.

Organization of the Bundesrechnungshof

The Bundesrechnungshof currently has 61 Members. In addition to the President and the Vice-president, who are both elected by the Bundestag and the Bundesrat on a proposal from the Federal Government, there are a further 59 members, who are appointed by the Federal President on a proposal from the President of the Bundesrechnungshof. In addition to its Members, the Bundesrechnungshof has approximately 700 employees.

In accordance with Article 2(2) of the Bundesrechnungshof Act, the Bundesrechnungshof is divided into Audit Divisions, which are, in turn, divided into Audit Units.[3] Currently, there are 50 Audit Units, which are distributed among nine Divisions, which are each led by a Senior Audit Director (a Member of the Bundesrechnungshof). The Audit Units are each led by an Audit Director (Member of the Bundesrechnungshof) whose work is supported by auditors.[4] The organization of the Audit Units depends partly on the government department that they audit, partly on horizontal aspects and partly on their basic responsibilities. The arrangement by Division means that each Audit Unit corresponds to a federal department. In the case of horizontal competencies, areas such as personnel expenditure, organization or IT are combined into fields under one Audit Unit. In this way, comparable findings are evaluated by means of uniform standards and principles. In addition to this, there are fundamental activities that concern basic questions such as budgetary law, principles of financial control or EU affairs.

The Bundesrechnungshof is organized according to the collegiate principle; this means the individual members do not have a final right of decision. Usually, the Head of Unit and the Head of Division responsible decide together in what is known as a 'two-man College'. The three-man

College – Head of Unit, Head of Division and President or Vice-president – comes into play where the President or Vice-president or a Member of the Bundesrechnungshof feels that a three-man College is required. Where these Colleges fail to obtain unanimity, and in matters of special importance, the (Divisional) Senate decides.[5]

The competence of the General Senate is laid down in Article 14 of the Bundesrechnungshof Act. The Senate deals with important decisions, such as the inclusion of contributions in the Annual Report or the Special Reports to the Bundestag and the Bundesrat (Article 99 of the Federal Budget Code). It issues the Audit Standards.

The General Senate consists of the President, the Vice-president, the Senior Audit Directors and at least three Audit Directors.[6]

Since 1998, the Bundesrechnungshof has had nine Regional Audit Offices. The Regional Audit Offices have around 900 employees and assist the Bundesrechnungshof in its audit of the Federal Government's budget and financial management. They are supervised by the Bundesrechnungshof. They carry out their audit tasks under the regulations applicable to the Bundesrechnungshof and in accordance with its instructions. The Regional Audit Offices are subdivided into sectors and each sector supports one or more Colleges of the Bundesrechnungshof. The creation of the Regional Audit Offices has, of course, considerably increased the audit coverage of the Bundesrechnungshof and its offices. Coordination is carried out via an integrated annual planning system, for example the audits that are carried out by the Regional Audit Offices alone, in teams or together with the Bundesrechnungshof are contained in an annex to the annual programmes of the Bundesrechnungshof's Audit Units and are adopted via an agreed procedure. This prevents any overlapping.

Auditees

Supplementary regulations concerning audit tasks, audit subjects and audit standards are laid down in the Federal Budget Code, the Law on Budgetary Principles and some special laws. Under Article 88(1) of the Federal Budget Code, all bodies belonging to the Federal Government are subject to the Bundesrechnungshof's audit. The constitutional bodies of the Federation are therefore also subject to the audit in respect of their budgets and financial management. The federal administration includes all federal institutions, the special estates of the Federal Government, federal undertakings and Federal Government activities in private companies in which the Federal Government participates either directly or indirectly. Further audit fields include public law legal entities, like, for example, the Federal Institute for Labour and Social Security Institutions that receive subsidies from the Federal budget, and the Federal Insurance Office for Employees. Bodies outside the Federal administration are audited where they implement parts of the Federal budget or receive compensation for expenditure from the Federal Government, manage Federal funds or assets or receive financial contributions from the Federal Government.[7]

Audit Criteria

The Bundesrechnungshof's audit criteria are the efficiency and regularity of administrative activity. Both audit criteria are enshrined in the Constitution (Article 114(1)(1)). The Bundesrechnungshof's audits are based on them, as are those of the Regional Audit Offices under it.

Audit of regularity

Financial control from the point of view of regularity is an audit of legality and the observance of the laws, the budget and the administrative regulations, including the audit of documents. The audit of regularity even goes as far as to examine whether the Federal Government actually has competence over the expenditure in question according to the Financial Constitution (Zavelberg, 1993).

The efficiency criterion

The efficiency audit examines whether there is an optimal relationship between cost and benefit in the administrative activity concerned. Here, we must distinguish between the maximum principle (for example to achieve the best possible result with a given outlay) and the minimum principle (to obtain a given result with as low an outlay as possible). The aspect of economy, as it is specified in Article 90(3) of the Federal Budget Code, is a sub-category of efficiency. Unlike the audit of regularity, there is no rigid, mathematically precise audit standard for this. Therefore, the financial audit of efficiency always involves a judgement on appropriateness (Zavelberg, 1993).

Political decisions

The Bundesrechnungshof must respect political decisions in the form of laws. They are the standard by which its audits are carried out and are not the subject of its audit activity.[8] The Bundesrechnungshof can only examine whether a political decision has been implemented in the most efficient way possible, it cannot examine whether the political decision itself was correct. It must take into account that, in the last analysis, political objectives are set by the Parliament.

Powers

The Bundesrechnungshof has far-reaching powers to enable it to fulfil its functions. It has access to all bodies that are subject to its audit. It may look at all files. The audited bodies are obliged to provide the Bundesrechnungshof with the required documents and information. Thus, for example, Article 95 of the Federal Budget Code specifically states that any such supporting documents must be made available to the Bundesrechnungshof as it should deem necessary.

The Bundesrechnungshof's audit procedure is only partly laid down in the Federal Budget Code. Fundamental powers are however addressed. Thus, the Bundesrechnungshof is entitled, at its own judgement, to restrict the audit and leave accounts unchecked. It determines the time and type of the audit, decides whether on-the-spot checks should be carried out and whether experts should be consulted if the need should arise.

The contradictory procedure is provided for in Article 96(1) of the Federal Budget Code. In accordance with this provision, audit findings must be communicated to the auditee for comment. In November 1997, the Senate of the Bundesrechnungshof issued supplementary regulations together with its adoption of its Audit Standards. These lay down the principles and procedure for the fulfilment of the tasks of the Bundesrechnungshof and its Regional Audit Offices. They are intended to guarantee uniform standards and rules of procedure.

Advisory Function

In addition to its audit task, the Federal Budget Code gives the Bundesrechnungshof an independent advisory function on the basis of its audit experience. This advice can be addressed to Parliament,[9] the Federal Government or an individual Ministry.[10] In this respect, the Bundesrechnungshof may take action either at the express request of these institutions or on its own initiative. The Bundesrechnungshof may also give advice in the context of the annual drafting of the Federal budget. The Bundesrechnungshof may give expert advice on the draft budget so as already to enforce the efficiency requirement at the preliminary stage of the drafting of the budget.

The Bundesrechnungshof must inform the Bundestag and the committees created for this purpose (Budget Committee and Audit Committee) with regard to significant audit and advisory results agreed in the contradictory procedure with auditees.[11]

How the Audits and Advice are Put into Effect

The Bundesrechnungshof has no power to give its auditees instructions or impose penalties. Nevertheless it is not ineffective. The observations that it submits annually to the Bundestag are discussed by the Audit Committee (a sub-committee of the Bundestag's Budget Committee established specifically for this purpose). If the Audit Committee agrees with the Bundesrechnungshof's observations, it asks the Ministries responsible to make concrete changes.[12] The Audit Committee usually requires the Ministries to report back so as to ensure that these measures have been carried out. Where applicable, it suggests legislative changes. Parliamentary control can therefore be used to make the public administration alter its procedures.

EXTERNAL FINANCIAL CONTROL IN GERMANY AT THE REGIONAL LEVEL

Legislation

The Regional Constitutions, Regional Rechnungshof Acts and Regional Budget Codes contain an individual Länder's regulations for external financial control. The regulations largely correspond to those of the Federation. The Landesrechnungshöfe are also institutionally guaranteed and their Members also enjoy judicial independence. The Landesrechnungshöfe are Supreme Regional Authorities that are independent of the administration. They are only subject to law and cannot be given instructions either by the executive or by the legislative body.

Competence of the Landesrechnungshöfe

The principle is that, for the audit of the budgetary and financial management of Federal Budget of Germany, the Bundesrechnungshof is responsible for auditing the budgetary and financial management of the Federal Government, and the 16 Landesrechnungshöfe (Regional SAIs) are responsible for the audit of the budgetary and financial management of their respective Regions. All the SAIs perform their tasks autonomously and independently of each other. This is due to the federal structure of the Federal Republic of Germany, and the constitutional principle of budgetary autonomy and independence of the Federation and the Länder.[13] No Rechnungshof can give instructions to another. In the same way as the Bundesrechnungshof has no competence over the audit of the budgetary and financial management of the Länder, the Landesrechnungshöfe can not audit the budgetary and financial management of the Federation (Zavelberg, 1993).

Organization of the Landesrechnungshöfe

The Regional SAI Acts lay down the internal structure and the organizational and decision-making procedures for their respective areas. Like the Bundesrechnungshof, their Members have judicial independence. The collegiate principle applies in all 16 Regional SAIs. In terms of organization most Landesrechnungshöfe are broken down into divisions. However, as at the Bundesrechnungshof, this divisional principle is supplemented with horizontal competence and/or, where applicable, basic competence. Where this is not the case, it must be taken into account that the varying size of the SAIs is one of the causes. In Baden-Württemberg, Bavaria, Brandenburg, Hessen, Lower Saxony, North Rhine Westphalia, the Rhineland-Palatinate, Saxony, Saxony-Anhalt and Thüringen the Landesrechnungshöfe have audit bodies under them, which are generally called 'Audit Offices'.

Audit Procedures of the Landesrechnungshöfe

As already mentioned, the Law on Budgetary Principles lays down the tasks of the Regional SAIs uniformly for the whole Federation in framework regulations. These are converted individually for each Region in its respective Regional Budget Code. The Federal Budget Code and the Regional Budget Codes are largely similar. We will therefore forgo describing the individual regulations for the Landesrechnungshöfe with regard to audit standards, audit powers and the like, since this would be repetitive.

INTERNAL FINANCIAL CONTROL IN GERMANY

Pre-audit Units

Up to the reorganization in 1998 and the introduction of the Regional Audit Offices, the Bundesrechnungshof's work was supported by pre-audit units. The legal basis for this cooperation consisted of provisions of the Federal Budget Code, and further details were contained in a Pre-audit Code for the federal administration. The purpose of the pre-audit was to prepare for and supplement the audit of the Bundesrechnungshof. Supplementing the Bundesrechnungshof's activity was possible, in particular, where it restricted its audit scope (Article 89(2) of the Federal Budget Code).

In the Federal Government's field of administration, there were about 100 pre-audit units with approximately 2400 auditors. The creation of the pre-audit units and their areas of competence were decided on by the competent Federal Ministers in agreement with the Bundesrechnungshof. The pre-audit units were organizationally integrated in the administrations to be audited. However, they were bound by the Bundesrechnungshof's technical instructions in their audit activities. In the field of indirect federal administration (for example the Federal Institute for Labour and the Federal Social Security Institutions), the pre-audit tasks are still carried out by the units provided for by law or in the statutes. Otherwise this type of control has been abolished in favour of external audit.

Internal Control Offices

The financial control of the Bundesrechnungshof is referred to as external control, because it is carried out by bodies outside the body being audited. Institutionalized internal control, as is normally carried out via an internal or administrative audit is traditionally unknown in the public administration of the Federal Republic and the Länder. Instead, there is 'internal supervision', and the appointment of Budget Officers who are allocated certain 'supervisory' functions.

A Budget Officer must be appointed at each public body that manages revenue or expenditure where the head of the body does not fulfil this function. He or she answers directly to the head of the body in accordance with Article 9 of the Federal Budget Code. The budget officer is responsible for the drafting of the financial planning documents and the implementation of the budget, and must be kept informed in respect of all measures of financial importance.

DISTRIBUTION OF GOVERNMENTAL TASKS BETWEEN THE FEDERAL GOVERNMENT AND THE LÄNDER

The fundamental separation of activities, expenditure and revenue between the Federal Government and the Länder leads on to the basic rule, laid down in Article 109(1) of the Constitution, that the Federal Government and the Länder are autonomous and independent from each other in terms of their budgets. Accordingly, the audit of the budgetary and financial management of the Federal Government and Länder is conferred on the Bundesrechnungshof and the Landesrechnungshöfe respectively. Nevertheless, the financial systems are closely intertwined; activities and expenditure responsibilities overlap considerably (Schäfer, 1977). In order to be able to find out which body (Federation/Land) is responsible under the federal system for an activity and its financing, reference must be made to the rules for legislative and administrative competence laid down in the Constitution.

Legislative Competence According to the Constitution

Article 30 of the Constitution establishes the principle that the Länder bear fundamental responsibility for govermental functions. Only when the Constitution expressly or tacitly authorizes the Federal Government to exercise a function is the Federal Government able to do so. The legislative competences of the Federal Government are substantially laid down in Articles 70 ff of the Constitution and its fiscal competences are given in Article 105(1).[14]

In practice, however, legislative powers have shifted towards the Federation. In the case of concurrent legislative powers in particular, the Federation has taken control of important regulatory fields involving the protection of legal and economic unity in order to ensure uniform living conditions. So the Länder have been left mainly with regulatory powers in the fields of culture, education and local and police law.

Administrative Powers

The fundamental principle
The implementation of laws largely falls under the competence of the Länder. This ensues from Articles 30 and 83 of the Constitution, which state that the Länder are basically responsible for the exercise of governmental powers and the discharge of governmental functions. This also applies to the execution of Federal Laws, which is carried out by the Länder as their own business or, in certain cases, on the Federation's behalf.

The Federal Government, on the other hand, is necessarily responsible for certain fields laid down in the Constitution, such as, for example, the Foreign Office or the Federal Finance Department (Article 87(1) of the Constitution) as matters of federal administration. Even in fiscal matters, the Federation is only responsible for customs, financial monopolies and indirect taxes laid down by Federal Law. Otherwise, the Länder are responsible.

Administrative activities not laid down by law
The administrative activity of the Federal Government and the Länder is, however, not limited to the implementation of laws. The Federal Government and Länder perform numerous tasks where there is no legal framework (extra-legal administration). The allocation of responsibilities in this field is also based, first of all, on the principle laid down in Articles 30 and 83 of the Constitution, according to which, in the field of extra-legal administration, the Länder may perform all tasks for which the Constitution does not grant a special competence to the Federal Government.[15]

Financial Competence

Under the Constitution, each level of government must finance its own activities. The burden of expenditure follows the administrative responsibilities laid down in the Constitution. On the basis of the link between administrative and financial competence, it is possible to arrive at an (albeit contestable) assumption concerning the financial competence of the Länder. The Federal Government may only finance activities for which it has written or unwritten competence under the Constitution.

Co-financing

There are, however, exceptions to the principle of strict separation of financial responsibilities between the Federal Government and Länder. Because of its overall national and economic responsibilities, the Constitution grants the Federal Government competence for the co-financing of the activities of the Länder.

Co-financing fields

Joint activities For certain of the Länder's fields of activity, which are of substantial importance for the future development of the country as a whole, the Constitution provides for the Federal Government's participation in the implementation and financing of any activities where this is necessary for the improvement of living conditions.[16] These are known as 'joint activities'. Article 91(a) of the Constitution provides for the extension and construction of institutions of higher education, including university clinics, the improvement of regional economic structures and the improvement of the agrarian structure and coastal preservation as joint activities.

The Federal Government exercises influence via joint Federal Government/regional government framework planning over the way the Länder implement their activities. As the Constitution states, joint implementation is mandatory for joint activities. In addition, Article 91(b) of the Constitution allows for the possibility of the cooperation between the Federal Government and the Länder in educational planning and the promotion of research.

Financial assistance   With financial assistance, the Constitution gives the Federal Government the possibility of making funds available to the Länder for particularly important investments (Article 104(a)(4) of the Constitution). The granting of financial assistance is tied to the following conditions – it must serve to:

- prevent disruption in the overall economic equilibrium; or
- compensate for varying economic strength over the territory of the Federation; or
- promote economic growth.

Examples of this are public housing, the development of roads in towns, or urban development/redevelopment.

Federal statutes granting payments   A further exception to the principle of the separation of expenditure occurs in the case of statutes granting payments within the meaning of Article 104(a)(3) of the Constitution. Where the Federal Government grants payments to citizens within the framework of its legislative competence, for example under the Federal Educational Grant Act, the Rent Subsidy Act or the Federal Family Allowance Act, the Constitution provides that the Federal Government should be responsible for all or part of these payments.

Other Exceptions to the Rule on the Separation of Expenditure

Administration by the Länder on the Federation's behalf

In addition to this, another exception to the principle that each level of government must finance its own activities is when the Länder implement Federal Laws on behalf of the Federal Government. In this case the Federal Government bears the cost of the expenditure that is directly related to implementation of the given task ('Zweckausgaben'). In these cases, the Länder bear the administrative costs, such as personnel expenditure (Article 104a(2) of the Constitution). The reason why the Federal Government bears the cost is because of the stronger influence that it can bring to bear on the Länder when they act on its behalf. Examples of this type of administration are the federal motorway administration, the administration of other long-distance federal highways or joint taxation (Art. 108(3) of the Constitution).

Overlapping on the revenue side
As well as in activities and expenditure, overlaps also exist on the revenue side. Revenue from certain types of taxes (joint taxes), goes to the Federal Government, the Länder and the municipalities. This is done partly on the basis of fixed shares and partly on the basis of shares that must be laid down by law. Article 106(2) of the Constitution establishes which tax revenues accrue to the Länder. Examples of these are the taxes on donations *inter vivos* and inheritance, motor vehicle tax and the tax on real estate transactions. The financial endowment of the Federal Government and the Länder, however, depends substantially on the distribution of joint taxes, which make up the bulk of tax revenue (approximately 80 per cent). The ratio of apportionment for income tax, including wage and corporation tax, is specified in the Constitution. For VAT, on the other hand, Article 106(3) of the Constitution states that the ratio of apportionment must be established by simple law, which requires the agreement of the Länder.

DISTRIBUTION OF TASKS AND COORDINATION AMONG THE SAIs

The Bundesrechnungshof and Landesrechnungshöfe

The aforementioned exceptions to the rule on the separation of expenditure brought about by co-financing and other special arrangements have consequences for the distribution of tasks among the SAIs. There are a number of legal provisions to avoid conflicts over the implementation of audit tasks.[17] In addition to this, there is the Conference of the Heads of the German SAIs, with its various working groups. This body which was established decades ago, contributes, among other things, towards resolving any conflicts via the conclusion of agreements.

The Conference of the Heads of the German SAIs
After the re-establishment of the German SAIs at the time of the construction of the Federal Republic of Germany, the federal structure of external financial control quickly led to the creation of a Joint Conference of the Heads of the Bundesrechnungshof and Landesrechnungshöfe (Zavelberg, 1993).[18] Comparable Ministerial Conferences exist for all Departments.

The Conference of the Heads of the German SAIs still exists as the highest coordination body today. It meets twice a year and its chair rotates on a yearly basis. The Heads of the SAIs of Austria and Switzerland and the German Member of the European Court of Auditors participate as observers. To date, there has been no written agenda.

The rules are unwritten, but they must be adhered to and are carefully handed down. The decisions of the Conference can only be passed unanimously; at the same time they are not binding for the SAIs. Each SAI is entitled to a vote. At the Conference, the SAI Heads must participate personally or may be represented by their vice-presidents. Other representatives are not permitted. The Conference does not normally deal with specific questions, but with matters of principle from the audit field or questions of procedure.

The technically more intensive consultation takes place in the Conference's working groups, among which the working group for Budget Law and Basic Issues is of particular importance.[19] The individual SAIs decide whom they will send to which working groups. The chairmanship of the working groups is determined as required. The Heads of the Landesrechnungshöfe are also represented in the Budget Law and Basic Issues Working Group at their own request. The Bundesrechnungshof is traditionally represented by the Head of the Basic Issues Division.

From time to time, the Conference also sets up ad hoc working groups. However, it tries not to increase the number of permanent working groups. For example, no working group for European issues has so far been set up, although funds from the European Union actually give rise to overlaps in competence between the Federal Government and the Länder in respect of activities and expenditure.

Legal provisions
In all the cases of co-financing and the other exceptions to the rule on the separation of expenditure, the SAIs (the Bundesrechnungshof and the Landesrechnungshöfe) come into contact with each other in the fulfilment of their tasks. Problems regarding their respective audit rights and the organization of audit rights and where applicable, joint audits, can only be solved via cooperation (Zavelberg, 1987).

The budgetary regulations of the Federation and the Länder (Article 45 of the Law on Budgetary Principles, Article 93 of the Federal Budget Code and the relevant Regional Budget Codes) provide that, in cases where both the Bundesrechnungshof and a Regional SAI have competence, the audit should be carried out jointly. Furthermore the SAIs can, by agreement, transfer audit documents to or from other SAIs. The purpose of these regulations is to avoid the duplication of audits, use the SAIs' limited audit capacities effectively, spread the benefits of special audit experiences and, lastly, reduce the load placed on the auditees (Zavelberg, 1993).

Because of the overlapping of responsibilities, Article 56(3) of the Law on Budgetary Principles requires that the SAIs should keep each other informed about their work plans and audits. The aim of this rule is, on the one hand, to avoid areas being left unaudited and, on the other, to avoid multiple audits. This requirement can be met ad hoc depending on the particular circumstances. However, it must also partly be fulfilled on the basis of agreements between the SAIs.

Today, the objective of the aforementioned Conferences of the Heads of the SAIs is to reach a uniform view in general matters of financial control, conclude audit agreements and guarantee the mutual exchange of information and specific audit experiences and audit approaches (Zavelberg, 1993).

Joint or parallel audits by several SAIs take place, however, independently of the Conference's working group meetings. They can nevertheless be discussed at the Conferences.

The technical cooperation of the SAIs is facilitated by the fact that, so far, they have all worked in the governmental field on the basis of almost identical legal backgrounds and very similar budget structures and accounting methods. Only in the area of local audits have responsibilities and other audit principles varied from one Region to another.

This will change with the introduction of budgetary and administrative reforms in some Länder.[20] The consequences of this for the coordination between the Federation and Länder remain to be seen.

Despite these common bases, there are naturally conflicts of interest between the Federal and Regional SAIs. Examples of this are the numerous observations by the Bundesrechnungshof concerning accounting errors by the Regional administrations at the expense of the Federal Government. Comparable observations by the Landesrechnungshöfe are rare. The Landesrechnungshöfe naturally attach more importance in their random sampling procedures to fields in which the Regions' own expenditure/revenue are more strongly affected.

Cooperation agreements

A description of all the agreements between the SAIs would go beyond the framework of this chapter. However, some particularly important agreements are presented below.

Agreement in connection with the overlaps on the revenue side   Under Article 93(1)(1) of the Federal Budget Code, in cases of dual competence, audits should be carried out jointly wherever possible. In practice, this rarely happens. However there are agreements, like, for example, the Trierer

Empfehlungen, which establish how to proceed in cases of dual competence. This agreement is an important example of the coordination of individual audits in the area of joint taxation. It was developed by the 'Taxation' Working Group and was put into an agreement between the Federal and Regional SAIs by the Conference of the Heads of the SAIs.[21] The purpose of these recommendations is also to keep the Bundesrechnungshof out of the audit of the organization of the Regional Tax Administration. This agreement states that the Bundesrechnungshof and the Landesrechnungshöfe should inform each other as early as possible at the beginning of each financial year about their schedules for their audits of the tax offices. The planned audits should take place at the same time so as to relieve the burden on the tax offices. The SAIs should carry out their on-the-spot checks simultaneously, but independently. The drafting of the audit letters and their implementation are the responsibility of the SAI involved. In the Trierer Empfehlungen, it was also agreed that the SAIs should inform each other of audit findings of general interest. In addition to these recommendations, the Bundesrechnungshof has irrevocably declared itself to be ready to inform the Regional SAIs in good time before the beginning of each calendar year of its planned focus and horizontal audits in the field of taxation (Zavelberg, 1993). In this context, it should be noted that, in the tax field, there are no doubts as to the Bundesrechnungshof's audit rights. An exception, however, is Bavaria's refusal to allow the Bundesrechnungshof to carry out checks on bodies under the Bavarian Ministry of Finance. This was, however, a refusal by the Ministry itself and not by the Bavarian SAI. In this matter, the Federal Administrative Court decided in favour of the audit powers of the Bundesrechnungshof.[22]

Agreement on joint activities   Unlike the overlaps on the revenue side, the Federal Government is involved directly in the implementation of regional activities in the context of joint activities under Article 91(a) of the Constitution. Given that the Bundesrechnungshof and the Landesrechnungshöfe have differing legal opinions as regards the scope of their audit rights, they have agreed to approach these joint tasks in accordance with the 'Reichenhaller Erklärung'.[23]

The Reichenhaller Erklärung states that the Bundesrechnungshof is entitled to carry out checks at the relevant Regional Ministries. However, it has not been possible to obtain a uniform opinion regarding further audit powers for the Bundesrechnungshof in the Länder. With regard to the procedure to be implemented, it has been agreed that the Landesrechnungshöfe and the Bundesrechnungshof should inform each other in good time when audits related to these joint tasks are planned.[24] In addition to this, significant findings concerning audits are to be communicated.

Legal situation with regard to financial aid   In the field of financial aid under Article 104(a)(4) of the Constitution, Federal Funds are entered as revenue in the budgets of the Länder. On the basis of an administrative agreement, the Länder are required, after conclusion of the audit, to inform the competent Federal Ministry of the use of the funds and communicate the relevant audit findings of their supreme audit institutions within the meaning of Article 93 of the Federal Budget Code.[25]

In this field, the Federal Constitutional Court has also decided, in the context of its constitutionality control procedure, that, in the case of financial aid, Regional authorities that use Federal Government Funds are subject to the control of the Regional Parliaments and the Landesrechnungshöfe.[26]

The Federal and Regional SAIs also agreed in February 1980 to inform each other of relevant audit findings.

In the meantime, there has been an increase in the number of people that have spoken out against the system of co-financing practised so far.[27] In 2002, the Federal Commissioner for Efficiency in the Administration went as far as to recommend that the system of co-financing should be abolished (Bundesbeauftragter für Wirtschaftlichkeit in der Verwaltung, 2002).[28]

Relations between the European Court of Auditors and the German SAIs

In this relationship, we must differentiate between general cooperation and cooperation on specific audits.

General cooperation with the European Court of Auditors essentially takes place within the framework of the Contact Committee and the regular meetings of the liaison officers. Only the Bundesrechnungshof is represented at the Contact Committee and liaison officers' meetings. It deals with all questions regarding external financial control independently of whether or not it has the audit rights in the particular case under consideration. This has so far not been called into question by the Landesrechnungshöfe, although there is no definitive consensus on the Bundesrechnungshof's rights of representation (Isensee, 2001).

As for the actual audits, the European Court of Auditors cooperates with the SAI responsible for the individual case and it sends both the letter announcing its audit and its sector letters. The SAIs concerned decide themselves whether or not to participate in the audits. In most cases, they only accompany the audits. Joint audits are rather the exception.

In addition, all the SAIs concerned exchange their audit programmes. This exchange of audit programmes has, however, a basically informative character, because although the audit programmes all contain the topics of the audit, they do not name the actual auditees. These are only given, both on the European and German sides, in the audit notification letters that are addressed to the auditees and copied to the SAIs and the Federal Finance Ministry. As these letters are sent out four weeks before the actual visit, there is not really enough time to prepare a joint audit.

For this sort of audit, longer preparation and coordination work is needed to satisfy the necessary requirements, involving, in particular, the drafting of joint or, at least coordinated, audit plans. This coordination effort is greater than in the domestic field because of the language barriers and the difference in audit cultures between the European Court of Auditors and the various SAIs. In Germany, the coordination requirement may be still greater, because, in the case of the Structural Funds and agriculture, an ECA audit usually takes place in several places in Germany, and this usually involves several Landesrechnungshöfe and in some cases the Bundesrechnungshof too.[29] Despite these problems, both the European Court of Auditors and the Bundesrechnungshof have repeatedly expressed their desire for cooperation.

There is an enormous gap between wishes and reality in this area, as a 2001 inquiry on actual audit cooperation by the Swedish SAI shows.[30] As far as we know, little has changed since in relation to the results of this inquiry.

NOTES

1. Articles 91(a) and 91(b) of the Constitution regarding the so-called joint tasks, Art. 104(a) of the Constitution on the distribution of expenditure.
2. The German Bundestag adopted the law on the establishment and tasks of the Bundesrechnungshof on 27 November 1950. It came into effect retroactively on 1 April 1950.
3. There is also the Presidential Division, which falls under the President and carries out administrative functions.
4. The auditors may be senior or executive officials of the civil service. Exceptionally, they may also be employees who do not have civil service status.
5. The Divisional Senate consists of the Head of Division of the Division concerned, all Audit Unit heads in the Division, another Audit Unit Head and the President or Vice-president. In practice this regulation is almost never applied.
6. These rotate.
7. Subsidies are granted to bodies outside the federal administration for certain purposes, in whose fulfilment the Federal Government has a substantial interest and which could not be fulfilled without subsidies or could not be fulfilled to the necessary extent.
8. Constitutional Court 56, p. 96 ff.
9. Where this advice is addressed to Parliament, it is discussed in the Audit Committee.
10. Article 99 and Article 88(2) of the Federal Budget Code.
11. The Bundesrechnungshof may only exceptionally report audit findings that have not yet been discussed with the auditees in the contradictory procedure. Article 96 of the Federal Budget Code grants this possibility for the Budget Committee, where it deems this necessary for a particular reason.
12. The rate of agreement over the years is above 90 per cent.
13. Article 20 of the Constitution and Article 109(1) of the Constitution.

14. Articles 71, 73 and 105 (1) of the Constitution contain the exclusive legislative powers of the Federation, while Articles 72, 74, 75 and 105 (2) of the Constitution lay down the concurrent legislative powers of the Federation. In the case of the concurrent legislative powers, the Länder have the legislative authority, as long as, and to the extent that the Federation does not use its legislative power.

15. Beyond this, there is a constitutionally unwritten administrative responsibility of the Federation. The Federal Constitutional Court has expressly recognized the competence of the Federal Government, where certain tasks, by their very nature, are outside the field of competence of the Länder. The Constitutional Court felt that these cases must concern tasks with a clearly supra-regional character, which, by their very nature, cannot be carried out effectively by the Land on its own.

    On the basis of this judgement, the Federal Government and the Länder produced a draft 'administrative agreement on the financing of the public tasks of the Federal Government and Länder', which, in practice, is known as the 'Flurbereinigung-sabkommen' (the reparcelling agreement). In this 'reparcelling agreement', the Federal Government and the governments of the Länder have laid down a catalogue of tasks that the Federal Government may finance even though the Constitution does not specifically say so. Although this reparcelling agreement is still a draft, it represents an important guide for governmental practice. Within narrow limits, it enables the Federal Government to provide funding for activities in the fields of national representation, foreign affairs, large-scale research, etc.

16. The provisions on co-financing laid down in the Constitution were created within the framework of the 1969/1970 financial reform. This involved the creation of a constitutional system of mixed financing that had hitherto been practised outside the constitution.

17. Article 45 of the Law on Budgetary Principles; Article 93 of the Federal Budget Code.

18. The creation of the joint conference originally goes back to a meeting in Klingenberg am Main, which took place on 8/9 September 1947 between the Head of the SAI of the British zone of occupation and the Heads of the SAIs of the Länder of the American zone of occupation.

19. At present, there are ten working groups, for example, Budget Law and Basic Issues, Universities and Research Establishments, Tax, The Economy and Participation, Broadcasting, Construction, Organization and Information Technology, Social Matters, Personnel and Schools.

20. The Bundesland Hessen, in the context of a comprehensive administrative reform to be carried out by 2008, wants, inter alia, to introduce a new accountancy system with double-entry bookkeeping and cost–benefit analysis. The intention of this is to reduce to a minimum the government accounting that is currently prevalent in the public administration.

21. January 1971, revised by a Decision of the Conference of the Heads of the SAIs of 6–8 May 1996.

22. Federal Administrative Court, NVwZ 2002, p. 988 ff.

23. Reichenhaller Erklärung of 18/19 October 1976.

24. Further audit agreements dating back to 1 January 1979 exist with all Regional SAIs in this connection, with regard to the use of subsidies given to the Max Planck Society for the Promotion of Research as well as numerous single agreements with individual Landesrechnungshöfe.

25. MinBlFin 1986, p. 238 ff.

26. Constitutional Court 1.299 (315).

27. Financial policy guidelines of the Federal Ministry of Finance of November 2000, p. 24.

28. The role of the Federal Commissioner for Efficiency in the Administration is traditionally conferred on the Head of the Bundesrechnungshof.

29. The way German domestic competence is broken down is extraordinarily complicated because of the federal structure and is not yet unequivocally legally clear.

30. Minutes of the meeting of the liaison officers of the SAIs of the Member States of the European Union of 13/14 March 2002.

REFERENCES

Bundesbeauftragter für die Wirtschaftlichkeit in der Verwaltung (ed.) (2002), *Bericht zu den Finanzbeziehungen zwischen Bund und Ländern*, vol. 9, Stuttgart.

Isensee, Josef (ed.) (2001), *Aussenvertretung der deutschen Rechnungshöfe in der Europäischen Union*, Heidelberg.

Schäfer, Hans (1977), 'Finanzkontrolle im Bundesstaat', in Dieter Wilke and Harald Weber (eds), *Gedächtnisschrift Friedrich Klein*, Munich, 451ff.

Stern, Klaus (1989), 'Die staatsrechtliche Stellung des Bundesrechnungshof', in Heinz Günter Zavelberg (ed.), *Die Kontrolle der Staatsfinanzen – Geschichte und Gegenwart – 1714–1989 Festschrift zur 275. Wiederkehr der Einrichtung der Preussischen General-Rechenkammer*, Frankfurt am Main.

Zavelberg, Heinz Günter (ed.) (1987), 'Gelebter Föderalismus, Die Zusammenarbeit der Rechnungshöfe des Bundes und der Länder', in *Dem Staat in die Kasse geschaut, Festschrift zum 175-jährigen Bestehen des Bayerischen Obersten Rechnungshofes*, Munich, 115ff.

Zavelberg, Heinz Günter (ed.) (1993), *Mut zur Veränderung, Festschrift für Heinz Günter Zavelberg*, Frankfurt am Main.

5. The system of public control in Spain

Milagros García Crespo

INTRODUCTION

For nearly 40 years, and up to 1975, when General Franco died, Spain was ruled by a dictatorship. As has been said many times before, the transition towards a democratic system was exemplary and allowed in a short time the adoption by consensus of a Constitution, approved in 1978, which after four decades signalled the beginning of modernization.

The State model established by the new democratic Constitution is a parliamentary monarchy. There is strict separation of duties between the legislature, the executive and the judiciary. Legislative power is vested in the Cortes Generales, which consist of the Congress of Deputies (the lower house) and the Senate (the upper house). The Congress is the more powerful of the two chambers and can revoke decisions made by the Senate.

The international isolation of Spain during the dictatorship period resulted in a set of political, social and economic organizations which were highly centralized. The new Constitution had to tackle the question of decentralization, giving way to the creation of autonomous regions, the Comunidades Autónomas, enjoying a considerable degree of self-government. Since 1978, the process of decentralization has gone a long way, although not without tensions, and the Spanish territory has finally been divided into 17 autonomous communities, varying greatly in size, population, economic capacity and desire for self-rule.

The territorial arrangement set up by the Constitution incorporates also the province and the borough as autonomous bodies for the management of their own particular interests. Side by side with provinces and boroughs, there are other entities contained under the umbrella denomination of 'local entities' (Entidades Locales). These constitute an ensemble of more than 15,600 entities, ranging from basic territorial organizations enjoying important financial resources (such as provincial councils or big town halls), to small institutions that are financially irrelevant.

In accordance with the European Chart of Local Autonomy, ratified by Spain, the running of local entities will also be affected by a second decentralization, not as yet implemented. This decentralization adopts the two principles of subsidiarity and proximity in the running of public affairs, principles which had also been adopted at the time of the creation of the autonomous communities. The development and financing of local autonomy will, in its greater part, depend on the autonomous communities, but we cannot forget that the State has its own competence in the regulation of the autonomic and local financing models and in the decentralization of the running of certain services and functions. The final decentralization will have to be implemented by the autonomous communities and the town councils through cooperation agreements and procedures.

Since the nineteenth century, public control in Spain has been entrusted to two different institutions: the Intervención General del Estado (IGAE), in charge of internal control, and the Tribunal de Cuentas, in charge of external control. The Tribunal de Cuentas followed the French model, and, consequently, acted from its inception as a real court, holding judicial proceedings over the accounts given by the accounting entities. Now, in the sphere of public sector control, the constitutional mandate meant in practice the passage to a radically new situation, leaving behind the old model characterized by an internal control whose main role was the pre-auditing of expenditure and an external control without democratic legitimacy, given that the members of the Tribunal were not independent.

The reform of the IGAE was initiated after the approval of the Budget Act (Ley General Presupuestaria) of 1977. Apart from improving the norms for the control of legality, two new types of internal control were established: financial control and efficiency control. This Act, in its original form, was short-lived due to the fact that it was passed before the adoption of a new Constitution, and therefore before the new State arrangement. The law underwent important modifications during the following years, particularly in matters of public accounting. The classic administrative accounting method was substituted by a new one based on computer advantages and double-entry accounting, which made it possible to put in order and classify all financial transactions performed by the State. Finally, the Budget Act of December 2003 introduced all the standards necessary further to improve the financial and economic management of the public sector (Blasco, 2003). Updating the law, it sets up the following guiding principles:

- budget stability
- multiannuality
- transparency of information
- efficiency in the allocation and use of public resources.

An objective-based budget together with greater flexibility will facilitate the task of assessing public policies.

The Spanish Constitution invests the task of external control of public expenditure in the Tribunal de Cuentas declaring that 'the Tribunal de Cuentas is the superior audit organ of the accounts and financial transactions of the State and of the public sector'. It also sets out some of its basic features, such as:

- the recognition of its own jurisdiction,
- its dependence on the legislative power,
- the recognition that the members of the Tribunal de Cuentas enjoy the same independence as ordinary judges and cannot be removed.

The Constitution no longer confers on the Head of State the power of electing the members of the Tribunal de Cuentas, and as it is directly dependent on the legislature, the Cortes Generales, it is also independent from the executive. Another important innovation consists in the fact that the Tribunal de Cuentas is assigned not only the control of the State and public sector accounts, but also the analysis of their financial management; thus assuming a task that other democratic countries had undertaken after World War II. In this respect, the Constitution declares that the assignment of public resources, together with their programming and implementation will follow the criteria of efficiency and economy.

The coexistence of integration processes and decentralization processes has been observed internationally in many instances, and Spain is no exception. The process of decentralization has meant a reproduction, on a smaller scale, of the State model, the autonomous communities having set up institutions similar to those of the State.

As the political and administrative organization defined by the Constitution of 1978 recognizes the existence of a regional and local public sector side by side with the State public sector, it follows that there is a possibility of creating public control bodies (for both internal and external control) at those same three layers of government. Thus in every autonomous community there is a General Intervention in charge of internal control, and dependent on the executive body; at the same time, there has been a gradual creation of regional bodies taking charge of external control.

The relations between the IGAE (the State General Intervention) and the Tribunal de Cuentas involve the State public sector alone. It is evident to the observer that the activities of both institutions overlap in cases where the same objectives are shared, for instance verification that public accounting duly reflects the reality that is being controlled; verification that the law is being respected; and control of public management. But there are, of course, many other features that are not shared between both types of control. Thus the ultimate goal of the Tribunal de Cuentas is to oversee the actions of the government in application of the budget, whereas the IGAE works along the principle of self-control, according to which the administration establishes its own control structures.

On the other hand, Spain has been a Member State of the European Union since 1986 and, as such, is the beneficiary of transfer payments from the European budget. These transfers are often co-financed by the central administration or by the regional administration, and must therefore be controlled by the IGAE or by the corresponding regional intervention body as far as internal control is concerned. The Tribunal de Cuentas, or its regional equivalent, deals with external control of the part co-financed by the State or by the region, and ultimately also by the European Court of Auditors, as this is the only body controlling the funds of the European Union budget.

The aim of the present chapter is to point out the duplications and overlapping that occur in such a complex system, many of them stemming from the lack of normative decisions in this matter. The present contribution begins by showing the character of those institutions, both national and regional, in charge of internal and external control, and then proceeds to analyse the problems of coordination resulting from the process of decentralization undergone by the Spanish State in parallel with the process of European integration.

INTERNAL CONTROL: GENERAL INTERVENTION OF THE STATE ADMINISTRATION

History and Functions

Internal control is the control performed by an organ which is itself part of the structure of the controlled body; it can also be the case that the controller and controlled bodies both belong to a larger organization (Pedroche Rojo, 2003). In Spain, the organ in charge of internal control is the IGAE.

Following the steps of the continental model, the Administration and Accounting Act of 1850 established a system of jurisdictional or competence-based budgeting that extended accounting to the accrual phase, including all rights and duties. This system was more advanced than the cash-based budgeting that reduced accounting to the recording of receipts and payments accounts by the Treasury (Gutiérrez Robles, 1993). In the same year of 1850, the first budget was approved and the first State Accounts (Cuenta General del Estado) were drawn up.

The IGAE was established in 1870 by the Administration and Accounting of the Treasury Act, that dedicated one section to the function of intervention in which it is stated: 'The General Director of Public Accounting is invested with the duties of General Interventor of the State Administration.'

For a short span of time (between 1924 and 1930, coinciding with Primo de Rivera's dictatorship) the Spanish control model, characterized by the existence of one institution in charge of internal control and another in charge of external control, was modified as a result of the creation of the Treasury Supreme Court that took charge of both the pre-audit and the post-audit of financial transactions by the administration, and whose president acted also as General Interventor. After 1930, only the regulation of the intervention function remained in place until 1995.

We must now make some reflections on the running of control institutions during General Franco's regime. First of all, we ascertain the co-existence of an economy subjected to an infinity of controls, interventions and regulations, and a Treasury whose control organisms did not function or were simply suspended. Up to 1952, that is for some 13 years, the regulation of contracts for public works and services was suspended, and the Tribunal de Cuentas was not re-established until ten years after the end of the Spanish Civil War. Despite the difficulties, the IGAE managed to complete the historical series of public accounts and to produce the State Accounts for each and every year. On the other hand, in 1963 the Budget Directorate-General was created, and this entailed the separation of the IGAE from the services drawing up the budget, a task it had performed since 1870.

Turning now to the present, we must point out that the Budget Act of 1977 reformed in depth the responsibilities of the IGAE. Up to that time, internal control had had a rather 'a priori' character, but since then it has taken on a post-audit character as well, with the two being complementary with each other, as the law of 1977 added financial control to the intervention functions, as one component of internal control, while at the same time entrusting the IGAE with the management and running of public accounts. Thus the present responsibilities of the IGAE are:

1. internal control, which includes the intervention function and financial control,
2. the management and running of public accounts,
3. the drawing up of the public sector accounts.

Intervention and Financial Control

The function of intervention is to control all transactions involving economic rights and duties that are performed by the State administration and the State's autonomous agencies; it also controls receipts and payments derived from these transactions, as well as the collection, investment and general allocation of public resources (IGAE, 2002). Up to 1977, internal control was a task entrusted exclusively to the IGAE. Its scope was rather limited, as the function of intervention had a pre-audit character, centred on legal aspects and performed on a case-by-case basis. The idea underlying the activity of intervention is the lack of trust in the public manager. Therefore, the intervention procedure – the most basic form of control – follows a simple principle: decisions regarding expenditure and orders of payment are never dependent on the free choice of a single person (Pascual García, 2002).

In accordance with its a priori nature, the action of intervention is preventive, and its aim is to ensure that all transactions are made according to law. When discrepancies arise between the auditing and the audited entities, a contradictory procedure is applied, in which the Council of Ministers has the ultimate power of decision. The procedure of intervention is applied to services, agencies and entities with a limited budget.

After the law of 1977, the scope of internal control was widened with the introduction of financial audit. As we know, financial audit evaluates the legality, effectiveness, efficiency and economy of all transactions made by the public sector (IGAE, 2002). The process of internal control is performed after the actions that are being controlled have taken place (post-audit), and it provides a global assesment of these actions, and contributes, through recommendations, to better management of public funds.

Financial control, as under the remit of the IGAE, has two modalities:

1. *Permanent control.* This is performed permanently and shortly after the actions to be controlled have taken place. It is done within the auditee entity by interventors delegated by the General Interventor. In cases where this control is carried out within the general administration and autonomous entities for which permanent control has not been envisaged as the exclusive type of control, it has a complementary character. In the remainder of cases, permanent financial control is a substitute for the intervention function. Nevertheless, given the lack of detailed regulation on this type of control, it has gradually assumed the function of merely verifying that all transactions are done in compliance with existing norms, rather than assuming a pre-audit character.

2. *Ordinary control.* This is part of the annual audit plan approved by the IGAE, which includes the entities to be controlled, the type of control and the organ that will perform it. This control is compatible with other types of internal control. As a general rule, ordinary financial control is performed in those public sector organisms and entities that are not subject to permanent control.

It is evident that in the area of financial control there is overlap between the actions of the IGAE and the competences that the law invests in the Tribunal de Cuentas. This generates, or may generate, overlapping and duplications that demonstrate the need to coordinate the tasks of both institutions.

Public Accounting

The IGAE is the entity responsible for public accounting management, and must therefore introduce into its operations improvements that have been internationally adopted. During the last 25 years a considerable effort has been made in order to modernize the public accounting system in Spain.

We can distinguish four phases in the normative development of public accounting in Spain (Montesinos, 2002):

- The phase of administrative accounting, up to 1977, during which single-entry accounting was generally used and there was no articulation between the different accounting records.
- The Budget Act of 1977 marked the beginning of a new phase in which the double-entry accounting system was introduced and developed. This radical reform of accounting was not brought into the 'State' subsector until 1986. We must mention two important aspects in this phase: the adoption of a general plan of public accounting and the instauration of a system of accounting information disclosure.
- The third phase brought about the adoption in public accounting of internationally accepted advanced accounting principles. A set of accounting principles and a new conceptual framework were put in place, and a new general plan of public accounting was adopted.
- The fourth and last phase can be conceived in terms of international compatibility and pre-eminence of national accounting (Contabilidad Nacional). The accrual basis of accounting is adopted as the main criterion for public accounting; financial disclosure is required for all entities constituting a unity of decision and control; there is macroeconomic aggregation of all information; and the

development of management indicators in some sectors of public activity. Where control is directly concerned, one factor to be noted is the regulation of consolidation in the way the State Accounts are presented.

From the point of view of coordination, we observe a lack of homogeneity in public accounting between the state sector and the autonomous communities enjoying a normative capacity in this field. Besides this, there is a significant delay in the process of adaptation of the local bodies' accounting systems to the general public accounting plan of 1994, given that the law of 1988 regulating the local treasuries has not been adapted to the innovations in the area of internal control procedures. This delay in coordination cannot be justified, as the power of decision at the local level rests in the Treasury and not in the autonomous communities, even if local bodies are part of the autonomic public sector.

It seems necessary to take pertinent measures towards the homogenization of the degree of control of public resources and, therefore, within the sector of local bodies, a proper structuration of financial control as a part of internal control is needed. This is the aim of the coming reform. At present, and given the diversity in size and economic importance among the local bodies, a simplified model is used apart from the general model, but the creation of a new basic model is envisaged for the smaller bodies, reducing the amount of records and information they are obliged to provide. This simplification aims at a better fulfilment on the part of these smaller bodies of their duty of accountability, which in many cases has been neglected.

The internal coordination promoted by the IGAE is different according to the sector involved: State, autonomous (or regional) and local. In the case of the State sector, there is a commission in place charged with the formulation of principles and guidelines, whereas in the autonomous sector its role is limited to the presentation of proposals that must be discussed by the Fiscal and Financial Policy Council. In the case of the local sector, the power of decision lies in the hands of the Ministerio de Hacienda, and therefore the IGAE has drawn up the blueprint for the new accounting standards for local bodies.

Finally, it has to be pointed out that despite the advances introduced, international accounting harmonization is at present far from sufficient.

State Accounts

As the body responsible for public accounting management, the IGAE is in charge of drawing up the State Accounts. The budgetary cycle in Spain begins when the State budget is drawn up, then approved and put into practice, and it ends when the Parliament approves the State Accounts. Since the reform of 1999, the State Accounts include not only the State administration and the autonomous agencies, but also social security entities, public enterprises and state-owned trade companies, as well as state foundations. The document has been renamed the State Sector General Accounts (Cuenta General del Sector Estatal). It is composed of three different accounts:

1. Accounts of the Public Administrations of the State,
2. Accounts of the State Enterprises,
3. Accounts of the Foundations of the State Public Sector.

The content of the new State Accounts is not homogeneous: whereas the Accounts of the Public Administrations of the State (which includes the central administration, autonomous agencies and social security sector) follows the Public Accounting Plan, the other two accounts follow enterprise accounting procedures – in the case of public foundations, the model for non-profit enterprises is followed.

The IGAE draws up directly the general administration account; for the rest of the accounts, it requests the preceptive audit reports for the autonomous agencies and social security institutions to be sent to the Tribunal de Cuentas. The accountable entities have a three-month deadline to send their accounts, together with the management and audit reports, to the general intervention.

It is an internationally accepted principle that governments present consolidated annual accounts so that a global picture can be drawn from them, quite apart from the degree of government decentralization in the country. In Spain, a law promulgated in December 2000 and regulating the State Accounts, aims at initiating the process of account consolidation for the public administrations sector, while postponing the consolidation of other accounts until the IGAE takes a decision in this respect. It is not easy to fulfil the consolidation requirements, mainly because the standards applicable to the private sector are not extensible to the public sector. Other difficulties lie in the excessive number of state public sector entities in Spain (around 460), and in the co-existence of two different systems of accounting. Another, more serious difficulty, would arise if the autonomous communities accounts were to be added to the State Sector Accounts. The IGAE has begun timidly to consolidate the accounts of the State administration, to which the standards for public accounting apply, but up to the present the three documents that make the State Sector Accounts are presented in aggregated fashion.

Once the State Accounts have been drawn up by the IGAE, they are delivered to the government and from there to the Tribunal de Cuentas before 31 October of the year following that to which the accounts refer. The Tribunal de Cuentas must state an opinion about the content within six months, and send its report to Parliament.

EXTERNAL CONTROL: THE TRIBUNAL DE CUENTAS

Evolution and Present Structure

The study of the historical precedents of the Tribunal de Cuentas must begin at the time when an external control independent from the executive made its appearance in the context of the establishment of a constitutional State. It is thus agreed that, in what concerns the Tribunal de Cuentas, the first organic set of rules of procedure dates from 1820. A few years later, in 1828, a royal decree incorporated the denomination of Tribunal Mayor de Cuentas and invested it with governing and judicial powers.

The ups and downs of the Tribunal de Cuentas as a democratic institution during the nineteenth century corresponded with the political upheavals in Spain at that time. The present normative developments of external control in Spain began in 1982 with the promulgation of the Ley Orgánica del Tribunal de Cuentas, followed in 1988 by the law of procedure (Ley de Funcionamiento), in accordance with the guidelines set by the Constitution of 1978.

The Tribunal is made up of 12 Counsellors, six appointed by each of the lower and upper houses of the Cortes Generales by a qualified majority of three-fifths. They are elected for a nine-year period, but can serve for a second term. The composition of the Tribunal usually reflects the political balance within the Cortes Generales. The law specifies that in order to qualify for election as a Counsellor an individual must have at least 15 years professional experience. The President of the Tribunal is appointed by the monarch for a three-year period, on the recommendation of the Counsellors.

In line with its collegiate nature, the supreme decision-making body of the Tribunal is the Full Session, which comprises all 12 Counsellors and the Attorney General. Among its competences, the following are of major importance:

- to approve the annual audit programme that the Tribunal presents to Parliament,

- to agree the inception of government audit and to approve the technical guidelines for its implementation,
- to approve the reports, memoranda, motions and written statements derived from the audit procedures, as well as those measures to be suggested in order to improve the financial management of the public sector.

One of the main innovations introduced by the law of 1982 was clearly to differentiate between the two most important tasks entrusted to the Tribunal de Cuentas:

1. Audit of the economical and financial activities of the public sector. The law defines the public sector as the State administration; the autonomous communities; local corporations; social security management bodies; autonomous public agencies, state corporations and other public enterprise. The Tribunal also has responsibility for auditing subsidies, credits and other public sector assistance to companies or individuals.
2. Jurisdiction. The characterization of this supreme audit institution as a court ('tribunal') is a clear indication of its judicial activity in the hearings for accounting responsibility of those in charge of handling public funds.

In keeping with the presence of these two functions, the Tribunal is divided into two sections: the Sección de Enjuiciamiento (jurisdiction) and the Sección de Fiscalización (audit). Each Counsellor, with the exception of the President, is ascribed to one of these sections. These organizational arrangements are specified in law. Each Counsellor has responsibility for the work of his own division, but the Tribunal adopts a collegiate approach to decision-making on matters such as draft reports. The jurisdiction section is composed of the President of the section and six other Counsellors. It is organized into five sectoral divisions corresponding to the main areas of economic and financial activity of the public sector, and two territorial divisions dealing with the autonomous communities and local entitites. The jurisdictional section is composed of its President and three other Counsellors, and it exercises the jurisdictional powers that the Constitution invests in the Tribunal de Cuentas.

Up to 1982 the jurisdictional and audit functions were conflated. Audit was derived from the jurisdictional function as an appendix, necessary in order to examine the public accounts and to arrive at a verdict. It was therefore a subordinate function. The law of 1982, following the principles set up in the Constitution, separated these two main functions.

In addition to the Counsellors the Tribunal has a staff of some 480, of whom approximately 180 are professional staff and 300 assistants. Around 50 per cent of staff work on audit and 25 per cent in the field of jurisdiction, while 25 per cent are administrative staff. The professional staff are normally lawyers or auditors. In addition there are other functional specialists. The staff are regarded as civil servants. The Tribunal has the power to recruit its own staff and to propose its own budget, which it submits to the Parliament for approval, as part of the general state budget.

The Audit Function

Present legislation states that the control function is external, permanent and consultative, and that its aim is the compliance of all economic and financial activities of the public sector with the principles of legality, efficiency and economy in the running of public revenue and expenditure programmes. This characterization goes much further than the previous one, which limited itself to the control of legality.

Audit is a technical public function carried out by an institution that also enjoys a technical nature. It is a technical activity, not only because it must be carried out according to a set of knowledge parameters, but also because it places in the public domain the findings of a public sector audit (Navas, 2002). The audit tools are reports, memoranda, motions and written statements.

The Tribunal can also make use of auxiliary elements, such as:

● audit findings from internal controls,
● audit findings from the external control institutions of the autonomous communities,
● the use of audit procedures in the control of single entities belonging to the public sector,
● the requirement of the duty to collaborate.

The reports are subject to contradictory procedure, and the Tribunal informs those responsible in the audited entities of the proceedings, allowing them to put forward whatever documents and evidence they deem appropiate prior to the final drawing up of the report.

The law sets out the controls to be performed, apart from those included in the annual audit programme adopted by the Tribunal. Those controls are the Annual Report and the Final Declaration on the State Accounts. Besides scrutiny of the activity of the public sector, the Tribunal is also in charge of the audit of electoral accounting and the ordinary accounting of political parties. These competences are attributed to the Tribunal by the law regulating the electoral system and the financing of political parties.

The report on the State Accounts represents the peak of the audit activity, synthesizing the annual economic and financial activity and closing the budgetary cycle. As it has already been pointed out, from 1999 onwards this account includes the whole of the state public sector.

Twenty years after the coming into force of the law, and with the benefit of hindsight, we think that a simplification of the State Accounts audit procedure should be considered, given that it constitutes in many instances a duplication of effort, as it may overlap with audits by the IGAE, and the external control institutions and general interventors of the autonomous communities. In fact, the Tribunal de Cuentas inspects the way the IGAE performs the control of legality (Martínez Noval, 2003). The Final Declaration on the State Accounts should consist only of a formal evaluation of the accounts submitted by the IGAE, the social security intervention and the audits from other autonomous entities, with the Tribunal limiting itself to pointing out the eventual shortcomings in the reports. A non-negligible result would be to shorten the delay for the drawing up of the final Declaration.

The audit procedure comes to completion when recommendations in view of improving financial management, which are included in the report, are taken to Parliament. More precisely, motions on particular matters, such as control of subsidies or the structure of the State Accounts, are presented to the Cortes, thus giving way to changes in legislation. Apart from being discussed in Parliament, the reports are published in the Boletín Oficial del Estado (the official Spanish gazette) and by the Tribunal itself.

The Jurisdictional Function

Since 1982, the jurisdictional function invested in the Tribunal has complied with the strict concept of jurisdiction required in a constitutional state, being limited to matters of accounting responsibility. Thus, while in the field of control the Tribunal de Cuentas is 'the supreme audit institution', in the jurisdictional field, a High Court appeal can be lodged in order to annul or revise the verdict of the Tribunal (Sala Sánchez, 2002).

Accountability trials are judicial proceedings in which the objective, subjective and formal elements of every judicial hearing concur. The objective element is the accountability of those in charge of handling public resources, in cases where those resources are misused, either with premeditation, guilt or negligence. The subjective element is composed of the

Accounts Counsellors and the Courts of Appeal, together with the persons subjected to control. Those entities legitimated to intervene in a trial for accounting responsibility are the Office of the Attorney General and the Public Administration, as well as, passively, those allegedly responsible, either directly or subsidiarily.

Public action is also possible, as the requirement of accountability can be claimed by 'any citizen regardless of the fact that he holds a subjective right or has any direct interest in a particular matter' (1982 Organic Act).

There are two different kinds of judicial proceedings, one for account- ing trial (juicio de cuentas) and another one for debt repayment (reinte- gro por alcance). There is no doubt that the existence of two separate types of proceedings following different paths of action is in itself prob- lematic. The creation of a single judicial procedure for accounting respon- sibility is therefore envisaged. This single procedure would be simpler and faster, and would involve only the essential references to existing legislation.

Relations to Parliament

The relationship between State Audit and Parliament is a usual feature in almost every democratic system. In some instances, the supreme audit insti- tution helps the government in the implementation of expenditure, but even then it is obliged to inform Parliament.

In Spain, the Tribunal de Cuentas is an institution enjoying consti- tutional rank that assists Parliament in the exercice of its financial powers. The legislative chambers encounter a great deal of difficulty in carrying out direct audit given the complexity and variety of legal and economic formulae of the public sector, the volume of public expenditure, and so on. The Tribunal represents the appropriate response to this challenge.

Parliamentary consideration of the reports of the Tribunal, excepting the Annual Report, is delegated to the Joint Committee for the Relations with the Tribunal de Cuentas. This committee consists of 14 members of both the Congress and the Senate. Where the report on the State Accounts is concerned, it is the Cortes Generales that considers and resolves to accept the accounts. Parliament can require further information but in practice the report is accepted without question. The President of the Tribunal de Cuentas presents the reports to the Committee.

We may ask ourselves if there is a degree of contradiction in the fact that the Tribunal de Cuentas is the 'superior audit organ' while being directly dependent on Parliament, and indeed when the Organic Act of 1982 asserts that the Tribunal de Cuentas is fully independent in the performance of its functions and subject to the law (García Crespo, 1998).

Direct dependence on the Cortes Generales is needed in order to ensure that the audit institution is independent from the government. This does not mean that the Tribunal is influenced by Parliament, as can be inferred from the principle of independence and irremovability of its members, and from the fact that it enjoys exclusively a functional sphere of its own. The principle of hierarchy is not applicable to the relationship between the different State organs, thus the concept of direct dependence on Parliament articulates the status of the Tribunal de Cuentas from the constitutional perspective, and it does not determine the audit activity, the permanence in office of the Counsellors or their enjoyment of jurisdictional powers.

We have a clear example of this in the task of analysis and verification of the State Accounts, a task the Cortes Generales delegates to the Tribunal. The Constitution declares that the legislative chambers have the power to control the government's actions and that they have the duty to consider the proposals presented by the Tribunal in relation to the State Accounts. The Tribunal presents a declaration or technical report on the financial and accounting regularity of public expenditure. The Cortes then, on the basis of this report, makes an appraisal of the government's actions and gives, when needed, its approval. It would be erroneous to interpret that Parliament makes an assessment not of the government's actions but of the actions of the Tribunal de Cuentas, approving or rejecting the audit report and not the Accounts themselves.

In short, the Tribunal suggests and Parliament decides on the approval of the State Accounts. Parliament does not call into question the audit findings, but it may ask for a wider or deeper scrutiny on certain issues, or for the auditing of areas that are unexplored. Parliament, on the basis of the report presented by the Tribunal, exercises political control over the administration's activities, gives its approval to motions based on the report's recommendations and urges the government to comply by them.

On the other hand, Parliament enjoys the power of audit initiative; that is, it can ask for a particular audit to be carried out. Nevertheless, the growing use of this power at both the State and regional levels can also be a source of concern, as the parliamentary audit initiative may become excessive and frequently bows to political opportunism. We are allowed thus to speak of a deficit of objectivity. In the face of this development, the Tribunal de Cuentas and the rest of audit entities must continue to feel free in the exercise of their functions. They do not need immediately to introduce the requests made by Parliament into the audit programmes they have already approved, as these could suffer severe distortions.

AUDIT INSTITUTIONS OF THE AUTONOMOUS COMMUNITIES

The Autonomous Communities

The Spanish Constitution of 1978, in its section VIII entitled 'Territorial organization of the State', did not close the constituent process. The nationalities and regions which at present comprise the Spanish territorial framework did not know, at the time when their creation was approved, how many or which ones there would be. It could not be predicted that there would be 17 of them nor the concrete powers they would enjoy. The end result, after 25 years, has been also the consequence of jurisprudence emanating from the Constitutional Court, negotiations between political parties, and so on, following a path that was not foreseen in the Constitution.

The immediate historical precedent of regional autonomy dates from 1931, the advent of the Spanish Second Republic. The Constitution of 1931 tried to satisfy the movement of Catalonia towards autonomy, establishing at the same time the right for any region to follow a similar trend, as the Basque Country and Galicia did. We could say that the accommodation of nationalist feeling required the generalization of the regional autonomy principle. This process was interrupted during the Civil War of 1936 and the subsequent dictatorship of General Franco.

The process was restarted in 1978 and has reached at present a level of regional self-government unthinkable at the time when the Constitution came into force. Although Spain is not a federal state – nor was it envisaged to became one – the system has evolved towards a quasi-federal arrangement. In fact, the present territorial arrangement was conceived as an alternative to federalism, in which those nationalisms aspiring to full independence could feel comfortable.

There has been a continuing process of power devolution, and the concept of regional autonomy, originally meant to be purely administrative, has become political autonomy and is gradually becoming also financial autonomy. As the number of devolved competences grew, it was necessary to modify the financing system, gradually substituting state money transfers for the surrendering of tax powers, together with the cession of fiscal normative powers and an increase in fiscal co-responsibility.

The creation of institutions with an economic character has, as a rule, followed the same pace as power devolution, and throughout the process there has been a phenomenom of emulation of the State by the autonomous communities, as these have adopted the same political and administrative arrangement as the State. Despite the fact that the Constitution foresees two different models of autonomy enjoying different levels of self-government, the same phenomenon of emulation has taken place along horizontal lines as the 17 autonomous communities tend to place themselves at the same level of devolved powers and self-financing arrangements.

This process of vertical devolution of competences from the State to the autonomous communities, and the subsequent creation of institutions analogous to those of the State, has produced the partial voidance of State institutions such as the Consejo de Estado, the Ombudsman and, indeed, the Tribunal de Cuentas.

The decentralizing process has not been completely without tensions, as the new institutions tried to maximize their sphere of power while the old institutions tried not to lose all of theirs (Nieto de Alba, 2002). At present, the issue of the relationship between the State, taken in a strict sense, and the autonomous communities is yet undecided. The problem is that the criteria for the distribution of competences did not allocate clear-cut powers among them, but rather attributed to the State an exclusive power over a series of matters, thus allowing the autonomous communities to take on all matters that were not explicitly attributed to the State. The result is that in many instances, both powers overlap.

Internal Control

Each one of the 17 autonomous communities enjoys normative powers in the field of public accounting, invested in its General Intervention, the entity that carries out internal control of the autonomous administration and draws up the Accounts of the region's public sector.

The normative capacity for the design of public accounting has resulted in marked differences among the accounting systems adopted by the different autonomous communities. In 1988 the situation was as follows:

- the area of public budget was compulsory for every autonomous community,
- financial accounting was being carried out in 11 communities, and setting this up was foreseen in the rest,
- only two communities were carrying out management accounting, and in most communities this possibility was not even contemplated.

In the following years, however, this situation changed considerably. The autonomous communities have adapted themselves to the General Public Accounts Plan of 1994, with slight variations. This makes possible the comparison of accounting and financial information, facilitating the task of analysis and the aggregation and consolidation of microeconomic data between different autonomous communities. We may conclude that the adoption of the General Plan as the general normative framework has been decisive in this process of convergence (Montesinos, 2002).

External Control

Following the general institutional pattern, the audit institutions of the autonomous communities have adopted the State model, that is, the model of the Tribunal de Cuentas. As it has already been said, the Constitution and the Organic Act of the Tribunal define it as the 'supreme audit organ'. Although the Constitution does not explicitly foresee the possibility of creating external control organs at the autonomous community level, it does not declare either that the Tribunal de Cuentas must be the only such institution. This has allowed for the succesive creation of devolved audit institutions, by virtue of the conferred general powers of self-government institutional arrangement and, this time explicitly, by virtue of the Estatuto de Autonomía (Devolution Act) or other specific legislation.

This set of norms constitutes precisely the foundations of the constitutional edifice where the external control of public accounts is concerned, as it has been recognized by the Constitutional Court. This enlargement of the constitutional framework is coherent with the progressive development of competences and institutions within the 'devolved State' ('Estado de las Autonomías').

The autonomous communities are ruled by their own Estatuto de Autonomía. In eight of these Estatutos, the creation of autonomous audit institutions is explicitly envisaged. In three cases (Catalonia, Galicia and Asturias), the Estatutos were approved before the Organic Act of the Tribunal de Cuentas of 1982, which does not make any significant reference to this fact. Article 1 of the Organic Act states that the jurisdiction of the Tribunal de Cuentas covers the whole national territory, despite the eventual establishment of autonomous audit organs as foreseen in various Estatutos de Autonomía. Article 4 specifies that the public sector also comprises the 'autonomous communities' and, according to article 13 and in harmony with the procedures established for the state central administration, the Tribunal will draw up an annual report comprising an assessment of the General Accounts of each autonomous community.

In another section dealing with judicial procedures, the law states that in the autonomous communities that have established their own public audit bodies, the Tribunal may delegate to these bodies the conducting of judicial proceedings in cases of accounting responsibility.

As a consequence, there are in this area two superimposed layers; the Organic Act gives the Tribunal supremacy over public control issues, while acknowledging at the same time a sphere proper to the autonomous audit bodies in accordance with the Estatutos. The same concurrence is reproduced in the Rules of Procedure Act of 1988, when there were several autonomous audit bodies already in place.

The external control bodies are created by a law approved at the regional Parliament. There are at present 11 autonomous communities that have created their own audit body. For the other six communities, inspection of the public accounts is still in the hands of the Tribunal de Cuentas. It would be desirable that all communities should have such an audit institution, so that the whole system were more homogeneous and consistent.

The audit bodies of the autonomous communities reproduce, in the legislation that shapes them, the audit function of the Tribunal de Cuentas. This should mean, in principle, that the procedures are also homogeneous. In their organizational structure they follow the model of the Tribunal de Cuentas: we find in all of them a Full Session, a President and a Secretary General. The structure of membership is nevertheless different: the organ is embodied by a simple person in Navarre, Castile-La Mancha and Aragon, and in the remainder of cases it is composed of three, five or seven members, which in every case elect a President and work as a collegiate organ. All members serve for a six-year term and can be re-elected by a qualified majority of the regional chambers. They are also the regional Parliament's advisors in economic and financial matters and, according to the principle of functional independence, they recruit their own staff following the legal norms regulating the recruitment of public servants.

The relation between the autonomous control bodies and their respective parliaments usually takes place in parliamentary committee, which in some cases is a specific committee for public expenditure and in others is the treasury and budget committee.

The audit function includes the control of legality, the control of financial regularity and the control of effectiveness, efficiency and economy. The autonomous public sector is composed of the autonomous administration and the local entities, although in the case of local entities the control powers of the audit bodies are not homogeneous, due to the fact that in some autonomous communities there are legal restrictions.

None of these regional audit bodies has a judicial capacity. When in the course of the audit proceedings there are signs of irregularities on the side of the accountable entities, the Tribunal de Cuentas must immediately take over, as the judicial capacity is exclusively its own. But the regional audit bodies can initiate judicial proceedings in view of a possible accounting trial (juicio de cuentas), as it is these bodies who, in the audit process, have detected the responsibilities in the first place.

THE NEED FOR COORDINATION BETWEEN DIFFERENT CONTROL INSTITUTIONS

Coordination of Internal Control

While the intervention function is carried out exclusively by the IGAE, whether directly or through delegated interventors, in the case of financial control, some organisms and public entities have a specific control arrangement with their own internal control organ, although they are subject to General Intervention. It is thus necessary to coordinate financial control at this level.

The specific control organs are integrated within the structure of the controlled body, always in organic dependence to the person in charge; that is, the General Interventor. In such cases, internal control works at two different levels:

- The first level is constituted by an effectiveness control conceived as a tool for management, and which is carried out within those administration bodies.
- The second level corresponds to the IGAE as it is by nature an internal but independent organ, autonomous in relation to the controlled organs.

It is clear that this plurality of internal control organs calls for the establishment of coordination procedures in order to improve their effectiveness.

Coordination between Internal and External Control

Internal and external controls coincide in their objectives only in the area of financial control. The Organic Act attributed to the Tribunal de Cuentas the control of efficiency and economy, whereas the Budget Law ascribed the control of efficiency and effectiveness to the IGAE. Taking the law as a starting point, both control models have evolved from a mere inspection of legality to an assessment of public management effectiveness, as well as moving towards a methodological adaptation and the use of control tools suitable for the new objectives.

According to the IGAE (Díaz Zurro, 2002), this institution follows the criteria set up by the Tribunal de Cuentas. We can affirm that these criteria, as far as financial control is concerned, are similar in both institutions. The IGAE takes the Audit Programme as the basis of its activity, whereas the Tribunal follows the Financial Control Action Plan. It is clear that in this area there can be duplication of efforts. In order to prevent this from happening, or at least in order to benefit optimally from the work carried out by both institutions, collaboration practices could be established on three different levels:

- mutual exchange of information on their respective control programmes,
- common use of the reports drawn up by both institutions,
- normative and methodological development.

In cases where time coincidences arise, the rule applies that the IGAE does not interfere with the activity of the Tribunal. Application of this rule can cause delays, for instance in the audit of annual accounts. Clearly, clashes of this sort must be minimized by means of the prior coordination of plans and programmes.

With regard to the use by the external control body of the reports drawn up by the IGAE, it is already envisaged that the findings of the annual accounts audit will be sent to the Tribunal de Cuentas. Since 1999, by virtue of a legal mandate, the accounts have been sent from the IGAE to the Tribunal in order to have a professionally assessed document on the representativity of the accounts. When trading enterprises or some public foundations are involved, the accounts are delivered together with a report made by a registered auditor; otherwise the document is acompanied by a report by the IGAE, drawn up either by the National Audit Office or by the Delegated Interventions.

The delivering of other control reports to the Tribunal de Cuentas at the initiative of the IGAE is not yet forecast. Nevertheless, there is a legal obligation to collaborate with the Tribunal de Cuentas, and the Tribunal has the power to require and make use of the findings of any internal control performed in a public sector entity. The IGAE has already pointed out the desirability of setting up a procedure in order to speed up access and use of audit findings on the part of the Tribunal de Cuentas.

Common procedures are being set up in the form of audit rules, and a committee – on which a representative from the Tribunal sits – has been created in order to establish the necessary technical standards.

Coordination between the Tribunal de Cuentas and the Devolved Audit Bodies

As we analyse the co-existence of the Tribunal de Cuentas and the devolved audit bodies of the autonomous communities in the context of a decentralization process, we come to the conclusion that it is necessary to define the different spheres of activity and to make a clear distinction between exclusive and shared competences. We could conceive an ideal, rational system in which all competences were perfectly distributed and all areas of overlapping or concurrence were absent; but in the real world – and public control is no exception – discrepancies and difficulties arise as part of the organization itself.

In Spain, overlap of competence in the area of external control arises from a twofold coincidence:

- From the perspective of territorial organization, the activity of control bodies in their respective territories does not prevent the Tribunal de Cuentas from performing its activity in the whole public sector.
- The economic activity of regional governments is sometimes interlaced with that of central government, particularly when it comes to the management of the European Union budget funds; thus obliging the Tribunal de Cuentas and the devolved audit bodies to coordinate their activity in order to unify their criteria.

The Rules of Procedure Act, which was approved at a time when the first devolved audit bodies were already running, does consider the issue of institutional coordination; as does, implicitly, the safeguard clause included in the laws regulating the regional control institutions. In the Rules of Procedure Act, coordination is derived from the principles of effectiveness and hierarchy, rather than from the principles of cooperation and effectiveness.

If we examine the doctrine expressed by the Constitutional Court as supreme interpreter of the Constitution, we find a sentence from 1988 in which the Court establishes that the Tribunal de Cuentas is the supreme audit body but not the only one, and claims that in its relations to the different regional control bodies it holds a position of supremacy, adding that 'the competence that may be attributed to these audit organs does not exclude nor is it incompatible with that of the Tribunal de Cuentas over those same public administrations'. In another sentence, from 1991, the Constitutional Court insists on the idea of supremacy but declares that there is no exclusive reservation or proviso in favour of the Tribunal de Cuentas as far as the auditing of the public sector is concerned. We are dealing, thus, with an absence of constitutional proviso – an absence of 'audit monopoly'.

We may ask ourselves what is the content of this relation of supremacy. Article 153 of the Constitution enumerates the types of control that affect the autonomous communities, including among them economic and budgetary control by the Tribunal de Cuentas. This is also recognized in

Section VIII of the Constitution, which defines the State's territorial arrangement and whose Chapter III deals with the autonomous communities. If we were to take the principle of the supremacy of the Tribunal de Cuentas in a strict sense, it would render the whole of Section VIII meaningless. It would also be in contradiction with the constitutional provisions giving way to the creation of self-government institutions and the financial independence of the autonomous communities, albeit in harmony with the principle of coordination with the State Treasury.

Another, in our view more decisive, argument is that if the constitutional structure of the State does not allow us to postulate the subordination of the devolved parliaments to the Cortes Generales, neither should we postulate the hierarchical subordination of the devolved audit bodies to the Tribunal de Cuentas (Fariña Busto, 2002).

If the Tribunal de Cuentas is in charge of economic and budgetary control, it is because the only control body mentioned by Constitution is the Tribunal, as at that time nobody knew if those legitimated to exercise the right to autonomy were going to make use of this right, or even if after the creation of autonomous communities and parliaments they were going to create their own control bodies. In fact six autonomous communities have never set up an audit body of their own.

In short, the Constitution attributes a control function to the Tribunal de Cuentas, and at the same time the Estatutos attribute a control function to the devolved audit bodies. Their respective spheres of action are as follows: the Tribunal is responsible for the audit of the economic and financial performance of the whole public sector, which comprises also the autonomous communities and the local entities, while the devolved audit bodies are in charge of controlling the economic and financial performance of their respective regional public sector, which by virtue of a sentence from the Constitutional Court comprises also the local entities.

The concept of supremacy does not entail an ideology, but a functional necessity that manifests itself in the principles of prevalence and supplementarity. The principle of prevalence means that in cases of conflicting norms, those of the State prevail over those of the autonomous community in matters that are not the exclusive competence of the latter. The principle of supplementarity means that State law is suplementary to the laws originated in the autonomous communities (García Crespo, 2002).

That said, supremacy must be compatible with autonomy, thus making it necessary to articulate collaboration and cooperation procedures. The only legal disposition on the matter of coordination is to be found in Article 29 of the Rules of Procedure Act; Article 29 does not specify what coordination tools are to be used, but it urges the Tribunal de Cuentas and the regional audit bodies to establish common audit criteria and procedures in order to avoid malfunctions and duplications that work against the principles of efficiency and economy.

The law allows for a degree of freedom to choose how to achieve this coordination. The important thing is to develop a pattern of action common to all control institutions, aiming at effectiveness of performance. This common pattern of action may consist in audit plans programmed and allocated between the Tribunal de Cuentas and the regional audit bodies, in accordance with their respective spheres of competence and the principle of proximity or subsidiarity (as understood in EU law) and with the aid of common procedures and criteria that would facilitate the achievement of more homogeneous results.

Coordination based on a principle of supremacy postulates the existence of a directive power in the search for harmonized action. As an alternative to coordination, the devolved audit bodies advocate the concept of cooperation, which implies equality between autonomous institutions that agree to bind themselves in specific actions. It is an active principle, indispensable in decentralized organizations whose members share a number of competences; a principle based on mutual loyalty that works not by imposition but through agreement.

It is clear that legislation concerning the Tribunal de Cuentas does not sufficiently develop these areas, partly because of the complexity of the system that needs to be tackled in practice.

The Constitution explicitly points out that coordination is the faculty enjoyed by the State in order to create a formal relationship framework between the coordinated entities. Nevertheless, the principle of cooperation is not mentioned in the Constitution although, as the Constitutional Court has declared, the State and the autonomous communities are all under a general obligation to cooperate – an obligation that does not need to be justified in specific legal terms because it is part of the essence of the State's territorial organization introduced by the Constitution.

Cooperation goes a step further than coordination as it implies the participation of all the institutions concerned in a single decision-making process. In addition to that, the procedures of cooperative federalism tend to predominate in politically decentralized states. In this respect, there is a legal precedent in the Legal Regime and Common Administrative Procedures of the Public Administrations Act of 1992. This law declares that public administrations are governed by the principle of cooperation, and establishes the method of sectoral conferences. In 1999 the law underwent a modification that introduced a clear distinction between coordination, cooperation and other formulae found in positive law, as alternatives to collaboration.

After the creation of the first devolved control bodies in the mid-1980s, it became clear that it was necessary to harmonize the principles of supremacy with those of autonomy and coordination. In order to do so, a Coordination Committee was established in 1989. This committee has done some valuable work in specific areas such as staff training, the establishment of audit rules and information exchange, but the main issue, that is, the supremacy of the Tribunal de Cuentas in cases of material concurrence, remains to be tackled.

It would be advisable to observe the following rules:

- When the autonomous community, by its nature as a public entity and in accordance with the Constitution and the Estatuto de Autonomía, takes on exclusive competence in a given matter, the exercise of this competence will correspond to the devolved institutions, along the classical lines of separation of powers, so that the activity of the executive power will be controlled through the intervention of a technically qualified control organ.
- Only in the case that no regional control organ has been created, will the Tribunal de Cuentas, in its capacity as supreme audit organ, exercise control in order to avoid the existence of unaccountable areas of power.

That said, we must insist on the need to apply further the principle of cooperation so that present situations of mistrust can be avoided. It is also possible to draw up a catalogue of matters in which a cooperation procedure is applicable, such as:

- *The planning of audit activity.* Through planning, objectives are defined and procedures established, and coordinated planning, without interfering with the functional autonomy of the devolved audit bodies, serves to potentiate the perception of the public sector as a single reality that manifests itself at State, regional and local levels. A positive consequence of coordinated planning is synchronicity and proximity to the audited activity, thus facilitating the adaptation of the public management system when detected deficiencies are corrected.
- *Horizontal audit, aimed simultaneously at a set of entities performing similar activities.* The objective of this kind of audit is to analyse the organizational systems and internal control procedures, in order to assess possible common deficiencies and take corrective action.
- *The use of common criteria and procedures.* This is the logical consequence of coordinated planning involving a common methodology. In the carrying out of coordinated audit in which the efficacy of control cannot be assessed individually but globally, it is important

to set up technical guidelines accepted by all audit bodies involved. In any case, these guidelines would constitute a set of complementary standards, separate from those standards followed in each control body.

- *Method of reporting audit results and parliamentary procedure.* In the same way as every audit institution has its own norms on the procedure for delivering the audit results, and its own formal and timing patterns for its presentation in the regional parliaments, it is necessary to establish the standards that must be followed in coordinated audit. These standards affect not only the internal running of an audit, but also the external relations associated with the activity, culminating in the integration of the partial audit findings into a general report and its processing in Parliament.

- *A coordinated liability procedure in cases of mismanagement of public resources.* In such cases, the logical consequence of the audit activity is the inception of judicial proceedings. The exclusive competence of the Tribunal de Cuentas in jurisdictional matters cannot result in different standards of injunction for liability, depending on the fact that the audit is performed by the Tribunal or by a regional audit body. The aim of coordination at this point is to avoid inequalitites in the way the law treats public managers. Such inequalities do happen when the devolved audit bodies do not refer to the judicial section of the Tribunal de Cuentas the cases of accounting liability they may have detected.

In addition to encouraging cooperation in the areas already mentioned, it is necessary to expand the culture of cooperation, delimiting the spheres of competence and sharing the same objectives and procedures in order to optimize the control function by taking advantage of the synergy created within it by the different audit entities.

Coordination with the European Court of Auditors

Spain joined the European Union in 1986, and must therefore comply with its basic legislation. Integration also affects public control. EU actions in Member States are controlled by the European Court of Auditors, and taking into account that many projects are co-financed, the need for coordination is clear if duplication of controls on the same object is to be avoided.

The EU treaty declares that the European Court of Auditors must carry out its control activity in contact with the State Audits of Member States. That said, the reality of the relations between these institutions is not always satisfactory, given the difficulties of implementing joint audits or of using in the European Court of Auditors the reports drawn up by State institutions.

In the Spanish case, as in the case of other countries where there are regional external control bodies, the situation is even more complex, as many EU spending programmes are managed and co-financed by the regional governments. According to the EU treaties, the European Court of Auditors always deals with the State audit institutions. It would be more coherent, and indeed advisable, if, in the case of Member States with a decentralized political system and regional audit bodies, the European Court of Auditors dealt with these regional bodies when the controls affected only the regional governments (Castells, 2002). But it is the Member State who must take the decision, and since there are some problems of coordination between the Tribunal de Cuentas and the regional audit bodies, it is not easy to arrive at a solution. The supreme audit organ, which is considered by the EU treaties as the sole representative entity at the European level, must relinquish some of its rights in favour of the regional audit bodies.

On the other hand, the relation with the audited entity takes place between the European Court of Auditors and the IGAE. There are norms set up to perform national controls, namely:

- regularly to verify that the actions financed by the European Commission are duly implemented;
- to prevent, detect and punish irregularities;
- to recover public funds lost by mismanagement, embezzlement or negligence, and for which the State is subsidiarily accountable.

In addition, the IGAE is the organ that centralizes information about irregularities and, according to the Budget Act, it must coordinate with the different administrations the control of EU funds. Consequently, the IGAE has signed a number of agreements with the Treasury departments of the autonomous communities and has created a committe for every EU fund in order to coordinate controls at State level. Despite these remarkable coordination efforts, the IGAE cannot be certain as to the existence of a homogeneous and satisfactory degree of control in every autonomous community (Lázaro Cuenca, 2002).

REFERENCES

Blasco Lang, J.J. (2003), 'La nueva Ley General Presupuestaria', *Cuenta con IGAE*, **8**, October.

Castells, Antoni (2002), 'El Tribunal de Cuentas Europeo y sus relaciones con el Tribunal', *Revista Española de control Externo* **12**, September.

Díaz Zurro, Alicia (2002), 'El control externo visto desde el control interno', *Revista Española de Control Externo* **12**, September.

Fariña Busto, Luciano (2002), 'El Tribunal de Cuentas y los OCEX', *Revista Española de Control Externo* **12**, September.

IGAE (2002), 'Diccionario terminológico', *Publicaciones y documentación del Ministerio de Hacienda*, Madrid.

García Crespo, Milagros (1998), 'Las relaciones entre el Tribunal de Cuentas y el Parlamento en el Estado español', Lisbon EURORAI Seminar, Lisbon.

García Crespo, Milagros (2002), 'La coordinación entre los distintos niveles de control externo', *La contabilidad y el control de la gestión pública*, Civitas, Seville.

Gutiérrez Robles, Augusto (1993), 'Historia de la Intervención General de la Administración del Estado', *Ministerio de Economía y Hacienda*, Madrid.

Lázaro Cuenca, Jesús (2002), 'La auditoria de los fondos estructurales europeos', *La contabilidad y el control de la gestión pública*, Seville.

Martínez Noval, L. (2002), 'La fiscalización en los albores del siglo XXI', *Revista Española de Control Externo* **12**, September.

Montesinos Julve, Vicente (2002), 'Situación y reforma de la Contabilidad Pública en España', *La contabilidad y el control de la gestión pública*, Civitas, Seville.

Navas Vázquez, Rafael (2002), 'El Tribunal de Cuentas y los OCEX', *Revista Española de Control Externo* **12**, September.

Nieto de Alba, Ubaldo (2002), 'Una reconstrucción doctrinal de la descentralización: aplicación al control externo', *Revista Española de Control Externo* **12**, September.

Pascual García, José (2002), 'Régimen jurídico del gasto público; presupuestación, ejecución y control', BOE, Madrid.

Pedroche Rojo, Luis (2003), 'Control de la actividad economico-financiera del sector público estatal', *Cuenta con IGAE* **7**, June.

Sala Sánchez, Pascual (2002), 'Poder Judicial y Tribunal de Cuentas', *Revista Española de Control Externo* **12**, September.

6. External audit institutions: the European Court of Auditors and its relationship with the national audit institutions of the Member States

Antoni Castells

INTRODUCTION

The purpose of this contribution[1] is to examine some current issues related to the public sector's external audit institutions. In the first section, we examine three phenomena which deeply affect the current framework of action of these institutions. First, the impact of current processes of supranational political integration and decentralization which are currently being experienced in Europe, often simultaneously. Second, the growing demand for transparency and accountability of activities carried out in both the public and private sectors. And third, the problems that arise from the blurring of the line that separates the public and private spheres.

In the second section, we describe the characteristics, principal activities and specificity of the European Court of Auditors (ECA). One of the European Union's five institutions, the ECA is responsible for providing support to the European Parliament for controlling the budget management of the European Commission. This body, though perhaps not very well known, plays a relevant role as an institution involved in the external audit of the EU executive.

In the third section, we consider the issues arising from the coordination of the tasks of the European Court of Auditors and the tasks of the external audit institutions of each Member State. This coordination is complex and perhaps insufficiently regulated, and its difficulty will only be increased by the incorporation of ten new members into the European Union, with the consequent impact on the European Court of Auditors itself.

With these reflections, we intend to highlight the importance of the tasks undertaken by external audit institutions in democratic societies, and to discuss some of the most important aspects of the issues currently affecting these institutions.

THE CHANGING FRAMEWORK OF ACTION OF EXTERNAL AUDIT INSTITUTIONS

External audit institutions play an indispensable role in democratic systems. They help the legislative branch to control the executive branch in such a key area as budget, and thus make an essential contribution to the balance of powers and citizens' control over their government.

These institutions are currently subject to three phenomena that, although different, do share one common element: the fact that they have a relevant impact on the mission that these institutions must carry out. First, the territorial area of action of public authorities is being restructured and readjusted by processes of supranational integration and decentralization. Second, we are seeing a growing importance of mechanisms to ensure transparency and accountability in financial administration, for private companies or political authorities. Third, the blurring of the line separating the private sphere from the public sphere is bringing a new level of complexity to the tasks of external audit.

Supranational Political Integration and Decentralization

The first phenomenon that we will discuss is the processes of supranational political integration and decentralization, which often occur simultaneously. Europe is undergoing a process of supranational political integration while, at the same time, many countries (including Spain) are experiencing intense processes of political decentralization. This means that, in a specific territory, several different political authorities act simultaneously: the European Union, the State, the regional (or intermediate) government, and local governments, which in turn are usually subdivided into two tiers.

Each of these governments has its territory, its responsibilities and its revenues. Certainly there is also a hierarchy as regards sovereignty. However, all of these governments have democratic legitimacy and are held accountable to the citizenry for their actions, the use of the resources entrusted to them, and the efficacy of their administration. Thus – at all levels, in one form or another, and with one name or another – external audit mechanisms are in place. These are public institutions normally linked to the legislative assembly, whose essential function is to assist the assembly in its task of controlling the executive branch and, more specifically, to allow it to truly audit the budget execution.

This means that these external audit institutions are not alone. When the European Union's external audit body audits the execution of the EU budget, it must bear in mind that the citizens who are the final recipients of its action must also benefit from the action exerted by the external audit institutions of the national and regional levels of government and, possibly, those who are responsible for auditing the accounts of local entities. The same goes for all of them, because none works alone.

The actions of the several external audit institutions overlap in different areas. On the one hand, the social issues on which the different levels of government work are often quite similar or have points in common. Generally speaking, there are not very many exclusive areas of responsibility which shut off one level of government from another. More and more, public authorities must address global problems with local implications. This is the case for issues such as security, organized crime, environmental preservation, and immigration. Thus it is easy to see that, in this or that area, the different public administrations act simultaneously. This could be because they hold different vertical responsibilities over the same material functions: EU directives, basic national laws, regional legislation, and municipal administration. Or this could also be because there are financing mechanisms which involve different levels of government in one way or another. Therefore, despite constitutional or statutory divisions of responsibilities between different levels of government, in fact reality shows an extensive confluence of these different governmental levels in similar spheres of responsibilities. And this must inevitably be reflected in the audit tasks entrusted to external audit institutions.

On the other hand, there are also legal, political and institutional relationships that link the external audit institutions of the different levels of government. These relationships are partly the regulatory translation of the confluence of the same aforementioned material areas, with a view to effectiveness. They are also partly the result of the distribution of political power – and, ultimately, of sovereignty – between the different levels of government. Thus the European Court of Auditors and the National Audit Institutions of the Member States are independent in their respective areas of audit, as are the Courts of the *Länder* in the Federal Republic of Germany. The Courts of the Autonomous Communities of Spain also enjoy independence. This means that no external authority or body may interfere with the exercise of their functions, nor influence the reports that these bodies submit to their respective parliaments. However, on the other hand, they do not enjoy exclusivity as auditors of the accounts of the Autonomous Community governments, since, in certain circumstances, these accounts could also be audited by the Spanish Court of Auditors. Furthermore, the accounts of local governments must be audited by State or Autonomous Community external audit bodies according to the level of government holding responsibility over local administration. But this must not be detrimental to the powers of control held by the local legislative assembly, which in all cases must be the preferential recipient of the results of this audit.

All this creates a situation with one prominent fact: the different external audit institutions cannot act in isolation from one another, because such a situation would be detrimental to the effectiveness of their actions, their services to citizens, and, often, the coherence required of a decentralized political system. Therefore, when speaking of relationships between different external audit institutions, the key question is how we can maintain the balance between, on the one hand, the independence and autonomy of these entities and, on the other hand, coordination and cooperation between these entities on issues where they have common interests.

Greater Demand for Transparency and Accountability

The second phenomenon we will discuss is the growing concern about control over the management of private corporations as well as public administrations. There is an ever-increasing awareness of the issue of transparency of corporations listed on the stock market, which has come from the realization of the extent to which their owners – the shareholders – can be deceived through accounting practices which hide the real management results. Recent events that have occurred on the securities markets of several countries (especially the USA) have illustrated the importance of the sound functioning of audit mechanisms in the private sector. As a result of this concern, the need for rules of good corporate governance has become widespread. And if this concern for transparency is so vivid in the private sector, then it should be even more so in the public sector. And it is thus: we are now seeing growing demand by society for public authorities to exhibit transparency and accountability.

Naturally, although this concern for transparency is shared by the public and private sectors, we should not forget that they are two different circumstances. The private sector aims to guarantee that shareholders are able to exert control over agents and be informed of the true profitability of the company. Here, we have a clear definition of who the owners are, which allows the audit pressure to be more intense. Furthermore, the market forces themselves sanction the behaviour of agents, automatically suppressing corporations that are inefficiently run. But, if one thing has been taught by the recent episodes of corruption, it is that, even when private interests are concerned, the market (in this case the securities market) is unable to perform correctly without public regulations and audit systems with clear, strict criteria, which in all likelihood can only be established by public powers. This is to the extent that a publication like *The Economist* – which could hardly be accused of supporting interventionism – has asked whether it might be necessary for public authorities themselves to undertake the auditing of private companies, as a public service.

In the case of the public sector, it is the legislative branch which must be in a position to control the financial performance of the executive branch and properly bring to reality the balance of powers on which all democratic systems are based. Transparency and, above all, appropriate mechanisms of accountability, are essential for this balance to work. The legislative branch must be able to audit and control the actions of the executive branch. Public agents must be held accountable to elected representatives for the results of their administration. More specifically, they must be accountable for ensuring that their administration is in line with the mandate they have been given by the assembly, and for their efficacy and efficiency in fulfilling this mandate. In order to carry out this mission, the legislative branch must have the appropriate technical and institutional instruments at its disposal. It must have mechanisms for evaluating the administration of governments and for holding these public agents accountable before the corresponding institutional bodies. This requires the existence of good external and internal control and audit systems, the design of appropriate systems of indicators, and the submission of the agents to the institutions and entities that politically represent the citizenry. Without these mechanisms, the executive branch has overwhelming means to act on its own and avoid the control to which it should be subjected. And uncontrollable power always ultimately exceeds its functions, and this results in abuse and corruption. The executive cannot be its own political judge.

No government is pleased to be subject to this control. Governments do not appreciate critiques of their administration, and even less so at a time when the power of public opinion is one of the few counterweights to the behaviour of the executive branch. But the best way of avoiding criticism is not to give it motives, rather than to silence it. It is best for the citizenry when there are institutions and procedures whose mission is to make this critique, and when there are governments that, fearing this critique, make pertinent efforts to improve their administration. Evidently, the simplification of messages and the business of media sensationalism carry obvious risks and create a situation in which sometimes what is communicated to the public is not a balanced reflection of the reports prepared by the institutions responsible for auditing public agents, but instead a self-interested caricature of them. And this can have obvious repercussions on the work of these institutions and even on the work of the agents themselves, who may fear that risky decisions may later be turned against them, and thus become inhibited and end up detaching themselves from their responsibilities.

It is true that the demand for transparency and accountability in a context where the media have great power poses a new and very complex problem, making it necessary to revise some postulates which seem very well-entrenched in our consciousness and behaviour. However, what should prevail above all else is the value of the proper operation of the balance of powers, which is the foundation of democracy. An essential corollary to this is the value of criticizing the government's administration, as well as all that which contributes to the existence of appropriate institutional mechanisms for this critique to be used as a judgement tool by those who must control – in other words, approve or sanction – this administration. The sound operation of these mechanisms of critique and control may be inconvenient for government, but it is extraordinarily positive for institutions.

Today there is clearly a strong, pressing demand by the citizenry to ensure transparency and accountability. And the nature of the problem is essentially the same for private companies and the public sector, although, as we have seen, they exist in contexts with very different characteristics. In both cases, it is fundamental for those who are responsible for controlling administration (of private or public agents) to be able to carry out their mission effectively. From this standpoint, the essence of the problem is the same. Only the protagonists vary: in the public sector, the government is subject to the control exerted by Parliament, while in the private sector, the company's executive team is subject to the control exerted by the shareholders.

All of this places external audit institutions in the focus of public attention with particular intensity. In some respects this situation strengthens their role, but in others it makes their weaknesses manifest. Indeed, if even for the control and auditing of private accounts, it has become clear that the market does not function adequately and strict public regulations must exist regulating the exercise of this function, then is it not more than fundamental that this occurs in the public sector? That is, the function of the external audit institutions seems more highly legitimated and any demands that may arise justified, in the sense that these institutions warrant preferential attention, probably to a greater extent than the attention they have been receiving to date. But on the other hand, as mentioned previously, the limitations are also revealed. If private agents, who are in the end subject to the effective control of results and of the market, can escape this control and even fool their own shareholders, would it not be that much easier for public agents to conceal their poor management, inefficiency or, in extreme cases, irregular conduct to protect their status quo or their different kinds of interests?

For this reason, the centrality acquired lately by matters referring to transparency and accountability, while reinforcing the importance of the role of the external audit institutions, also demonstrates the difficulty of their task and the necessity for these institutions to have a constant spirit of excellence in order to improve their audit procedures and be able to respond to the mission that society has placed in their hands.

Changing the Boundary between Public and Private Spheres

These reflections emphasize the parallels existing between the need for external audit of private and public entities. Nevertheless, we must introduce a consideration that lends greater complexity to this matter: the line separating the public and private spheres has become more blurred, and currently, public–private collaboration is the norm and not the exception. Today, we see numerous forms of partnership between the public sector and private interests, in both provision of services and investment projects. This collaboration is the consequence of the fact that, in numerous activities, three circumstances converge: the existence of public interest, the availability of individuals to assume part of the costs of the activity provided by the public sector (through fees, prices or tolls), and the existence of a profit opportunity field for private investors. And all of this without contraindications in terms of equity among individuals.

This convergence has substantially modified the terms by which public–private relations were approached some decades ago. In contrast to the situation then, specific infrastructures can be open to management by private capital, naturally with the supervision of and regulation by the public authorities. The same is true of numerous public services. Society demands public kindergartens, public transport and many other services from the public authorities, although they may have to pay part of the costs via price. And the public sector must attempt to meet this demand, as long as all citizens have equal access to the service (if necessary, establishing due systems of scholarships or subsidies for those with lower incomes). And the same could be said of various types of cultural and sports facilities, in which the initial thrust is very difficult without the involvement of the public sector, but whose operation and management can follow substantially private criteria.

All of this also essentially modifies the traditional framework in which the activity of the public sector was set up. This situation opens up new horizons. Public–private partnership will be the norm in the future and not the exception. But precisely because the areas of convergence between the public and the private sector will increase – indeed, they are already increasing quite significantly – it is more important than ever to avoid confusing the two sectors, to differentiate their respective roles and prevent possible forms of collusion. Partnership and collaboration are positive. Confusion between the activities corresponding to the public sector and those corresponding to the private sector is not only negative but can end up seriously harming joint initiatives and, above all, causing irreparable damage to the credibility of the public authorities. This is because nothing could harm them more than the impression that power leads to money and money provides power. For this reason, public–private collaboration must be multiplied and supported without reserve in all fields where such collaboration is positive, but at the same time, the rules of the game and the respective responsibilities of the public authorities and private interests must be clearly defined.

Therefore, these considerations must be incorporated into reflections on external audit, and the types of formulae of coordination between the mechanisms of external audit of the private sector and those of the public sector must be considered in the future.

THE EUROPEAN COURT OF AUDITORS

Main Features and Activities

The European Court of Auditors (ECA) is the external audit body for the budget of the European Union (EU). Its fundamental mission is to assist the EU legislative branch (the Council and the Parliament) in its tasks of controlling the management and execution of the budget. An especially important point is the discharge (*la décharge*) of the budget, where the Parliament decides whether to approve the liquidation of the budget provided by the Commission.

The ECA was created by the Treaty of Brussels on 22 July 1975 and began operating in October 1977. On 1 November 1993, with the entry into force of the Maastricht Treaty, the Court acquired the status of institution of the European Communities, along with the Parliament, the Council, the Commission and the Court of Justice. And on 1 May 1999, with the Treaty of Amsterdam, it obtained recognition as an institution of the European Union, which extended its sphere of action from the strictly Community field to the three pillars of the EU, and granted it the possibility of appealing before the Court of Justice in defence of its prerogatives.

The ECA currently (until April 2004) consists of 15 members, one for every country in the EU. The members of the ECA are appointed by unanimous vote of the Council, on the proposal of each of the Member States. This appointment must be validated by a non-binding opinion of the European Parliament, effected after a hearing of the candidates before the Committee on Budgetary Control, in which the former are subject to questioning by the members of Parliament integrating the above-mentioned Committee. The President of the Court is elected by its members and holds office for three years.

The ECA is a collegial body, so that it is the Court, acting as such, which approves in the last instance the reports and opinions resulting from its task, and which adopts the decisions of an internal nature regarding its organization and functioning. In order to carry out its audit functions, the ECA is currently organized according to audit sectors, each of which is headed by a Member of the Court. This presents a problem typical of collegial bodies, as its members must be able to properly balance their collegial responsibilities, which oblige them to study and form an opinion on all the matters that must be decided by the plenary of the Court, and their sectoral responsibilities, by virtue of which they must concretely direct the audit of a specific sector.

The ECA organizes its activity, as indicated, according to audit sectors, which are themselves organized in Audit Groups. These Groups can be of a vertical or a horizontal nature. The former define the sphere of action according to one of the material fields of the EU budget: the Common Agricultural Policy, Structural Actions and Internal Policies (regional and social policies, research, etc.), External Actions, Own Resources and Administration. The horizontal Group carries out tasks that commonly affect the different fields: coordination of the Statement of Assurance (DAS), or the audit procedures and working methods.

The mission of the Court, as established by the Treaties, is to carry out audit of accounts, and to examine the legality and regularity of transactions, as well as the sound financial management (performance audit). Thus, on the one hand, the Court must check the legality and regularity of transactions, verifying the compliance of budgetary operations with the treaties and regulations and with generally applicable accounting norms. On the other, it must audit budget management, examining to what extent the budgetary interventions meet established objectives and analysing the costs incurred in order to meet them. The two dimensions are fundamental for the Court to properly carry out the mission with which it has been entrusted.

In order to carry out its functions, the Court must execute an audit task, which is partially carried out directly at the Commission itself or at the main offices of the institutions, agencies or entities being audited, and which must often be carried out in the Member States themselves; then the ECA carries out missions that are prepared in cooperation with the national audit institutions. It must be emphasized that the Treaties grant the ECA the possibility of carrying out its audit tasks, if necessary, at the premises of the final beneficiaries of EU programmes. The Court thus has the power to request documents supporting the operations financed by the EU budget of all entities or private bodies that participate in its execution or are its beneficiaries.

The Court's audit tasks are technically carried out according to the usual stages of any audit task: planning, auditing and reporting. First, the audit plan is methodically and systematically drawn up; then the audit on the spot is materially carried out, examining the necessary documents, which often entails carrying out audit missions in the Member States, as indicated; and finally, drawing up the Reports. For the latter stage, the contradictory procedure with the Commission is very important. In this procedure, the Commission receives the first draft with the observations of the ECA and has the opportunity of formulating its allegations. This process is indispensable for respecting the rights of the entity being audited and normally allows the content of the Reports to be enriched.

The ECA's audit activity is materialized in the drafting of reports and opinions. Of particular importance is the Annual Report, which contains the observations on the execution of the whole of the EU budget. Normally, the Report corresponding to a given financial year is presented before the European Parliament during the first days of the month of November of the following year. Then, towards the month of January, the members of the Court appear before the Committee on Budgetary Control, as well as before the pertinent sectoral Committees of the European Parliament in order to present the different chapters of the Annual Report and reply to any questions and observations that the members of the European Parliament may put forth.

The Annual Report, as well as the Special Reports drawn up by the ECA are an essential element in the procedure of discharge of the budget by the Parliament (called *décharge* in EU jargon). By virtue of this procedure, the Parliament approves the execution of the budget being submitted for its consideration by the Commission, which is the institution responsible for EU budget management. This is a particularly important moment in the political life of the EU, perhaps because it is not a strictly parliamentary system and there is a large degree of independence between the Parliament and the Commission, and the former attempts to particularly demonstrate its control over the Commission during the course of this procedure. The Parliament normally formulates a resolution containing a series of recommendations, some of them particularly critical, which are drafted with the fundamental support of the observations contained in the Court Reports. The resolution of discharge of the budget usually has great political repercussion. In 1999 it was this resolution that definitively originated the resignation of the Santer Commission.

The Singularity of the European Court of Auditors

The European Court of Auditors is, as indicated, the external audit body of the EU budget. From this point of view, its nature and functions are no different from those of the majority of external audit bodies in the majority of Member States: the European Court of Auditors, as with all of these institutions, carries out an ex post audit, in other words, after the budget has already been implemented; and its fundamental aim is to assist the legislative branch in the political control of the executive.

Stated in parenthesis, this confers on the external audit institutions a necessarily instrumental role, which at times is not easy to accept. It is sometimes difficult to understand that certain observations, which the Court considers important, are not taken into consideration, or at least not with the emphasis that the Court would like, by those institutions that should do it: the Parliament, the Council and the Commission. Moreover, this could lead to an attempt to gain recognition or an executive character for these recommendations, which would clearly go beyond the nature that external audit institution activities should have and disrupt the proper balance of power: the legislative branch has to control the executive, and the Court must assist it in this task. The corrective measures proposed by the Court do not have, neither could they have, a directly executive character. It is, in any case, the legislative that should adopt the appropriate rules, in its sphere of action, in order to implement the measures that the European Court of Auditors could recommend.

However, despite these similarities to the other external audit institutions, the European Court of Auditors has some unique characteristics, derived from the originality of the EU framework, which endows it with a certain singularity. We will now discuss these.

- First, *the singularity of the institutional architecture of the European Union*. We have indicated that the fundamental mission of the European Court of Auditors, as with other external audit institutions, is to assist the legislature in its task of controlling the executive. However, the EU institutional building is relatively singular, and neither the legislative branch nor the executive branch can be easily assimilated into those of the Member States. Legislative responsibility is shared between the Council and the Parliament, although the latter has an especially relevant role in the budgetary area. The Commission is an atypical executive, because it has to share this function with the Council, which is the institution in which the power of EU political decision ultimately resides. In this context, the role of the European Court of Auditors in the whole EU budget process acquires, among these three institutions, quite a singular character.

  Contributing to this, without doubt, is the particular nature of the process of European construction. Unlike what occurs in the Member States, this is an ongoing process (much more, in any case, than there could be in any of these Member States) which contains projects of a different nature. Consequently, on many occasions, the critical observations regarding management of the budget that the Court may make, receive a special attention in particular media and are used not only to criticize the management, but to bring the entire process of European integration into question.

- Second, *the confluence of diverse audit traditions*. It has been indicated that, in its essential nature, the European Court of Auditors is similar to the external audit bodies existing in other countries. This is truly the case, but it does not mean that there only exists a single model. The external audit institutions of Member States of the European Union present characteristics responding to extremely diverse traditions. Some of them, those of French and Continental roots, have a collegial character, while those of Anglo Saxon and Nordic origin tend to be single-person bodies (in the tradition of the General Auditor). Some only have the audit function, while others combine this with a judiciary function. In most cases there is a connection with the Parliament, for both the nomination of members and in assisting it in its function; but in other countries members of external audit institutions have a civil servant character. In certain countries there are external audit bodies of a regional nature, which creates the problem, not equally resolved everywhere, of the development of a possible hierarchy among these bodies and that of the central power. Finally, in many traditions, the audit of legality and regularity continues to weigh heavily, while in others (the Anglo Saxon and Nordic) great importance is given to management audit (performance audit).

  This diversity of traditions in aspects so relevant to the activities of the external audit institutions, must necessarily have an influence on the European Court of Auditors, as, although this institution was created *ex novo* based on Treaties, it is clear that it cannot ignore the reality of which it is a part or the inheritance to which it is recipient. On the other hand, this diversity constitutes a great richness, although it also introduces a clear complexity, both in the organization itself and in the functioning of the Court, which to a great extent responds to a synthesis and balance between these diverse traditions, as in the moment of establishing criteria for coordination with the external audit institutions of the various Member States.

- Third, *the specific characteristics of the EU budget*. On the one hand, the two main shares of expenditure in this budget are the Common Agricultural Policy and Structural Actions. Their audit and evaluation imply a great complexity, because these policies respond fundamentally to macroeconomic-type motivations; consequently the techniques traditionally used to evaluate 'typical' public services such as the health or educational systems are not, in these cases, the most appropriate.

On the other hand, a large part of EU spending conforms to a dual characteristic: it is materialized in the form of transfers, not in the direct provision of services; and 80 per cent of it is managed by Member States, that on occasion meet the condition of being co-financers of the same transfers.

Thus, in this way, despite having, as is natural, similar characteristics to the other external audit institutions in essential respects, the European Court of Auditors also possesses somewhat singular features. All of this contributes to the condition where its institutional role, its technical characteristics and the audit procedures employed in the execution of its activities respond to these specifics. One of the most relevant manifestations of this singularity, which is manifest at both the institutional and the strictly technical level, relates precisely to the relations between the European Court of Auditors and the external audit institutions of the EU Member States.

THE EUROPEAN COURT OF AUDITORS AND THE EXTERNAL AUDIT INSTITUTIONS OF MEMBER STATES

As we have seen, powerful reasons exist that advise cooperation between the European Court of Auditors and the National External Audit Institutions (sometimes referred to as Supreme Audit Institutions). On the one hand, a high percentage of EU spending is managed by Member States, thus an effective monitoring of the same cannot be implemented without verification that must take place in the states themselves and with the cooperation of the corresponding administrative services. On the other hand, some of this spending (especially with respect to structural actions) is co-financed with resources coming from the budgets of national administrations (central, regional or local accordingly). This means that while this spending should be subject to the audit of the European Court of Auditors for the part that is the object of EU financing, it should also be subject to the audit of the National External Audit Institutions for the part funded by the budgets of national administrations. However, the object of the audit is the same (the same spending, the same project or the same programme), thus an elementary principle of cost minimization advises the coordination of action of institutions of audit which, ultimately, pursue similar ends.

It is for this reason that the Union Treaty establishes that the European Court of Auditors should carry out its audit tasks jointly with the national audit institutions. In practice, this relationship has been expressed in different forms. Thus the so-called Contact Committee brings together the presidents of the European Court of Auditors and the 15 External Audit Institutions of the current Member States. This Committee normally meets once a year, alternating between Luxembourg, where the European Court of Auditors headquarters are located, and another Member State, and examines various points of common interest related to the activities of the External Audit Institutions. Committee meetings are prepared by the Liaison Officers (*Agents de liaison*), who are the civil servants appointed by each National External Audit Institution to ensure the institutional relationship with the European Court of Auditors. Among other responsibilities, these officers act as interlocutors for the European Court of Auditors for the preparation of the numerous missions that the ECA must carry out in the Member States.

There are numerous relationships between the European Court of Auditors and the National Audit Institutions. These relationships take place on three levels: institutional, operational and technical. The first is based on the various agreements established between the institutions (EU and Member State) responsible for external audit, partly mentioned in the previous section. The second has a more visible expression in the diverse initiatives jointly adopted in order to carry out the activity of audit. The third is expressed in the common development of audit guidelines and control procedures.

These relationships embody a certain complexity, which in part explains why in many areas they have probably not progressed as much as would be reasonable. Without intending to examine all the points on which the relationship between the European Court of Auditors and the National Audit Institutions is based, it would be prudent to refer to three particular aspects which, because of different circumstances, share a central interest: first, some problems related to the carrying out of joint missions, and more generally, to joint audit; second, the basic philosophy that should guide the institutional relations between the European Court of Auditors and National External Audit Institutions; and third, the problem created by the existence of external audit bodies of a regional nature in decentralized countries.

- *The implementation of joint audits.* As indicated, the European Court of Auditors and National Audit Institutions have, on many occasions, coinciding objects of audit. It is clearly this way in the projects or programmes of spending that are co-financed by both the EU and one of the national administrations. But apart from these, several other cases exist when audit occurs in areas in which both institutions should act, and where the sharing of audit activities can only be to the benefit of all.

However, the exercise of joint audit creates difficulties that should not be ignored and which explain, in part, the little use that has been made of this possibility until now. The fundamental reason is the intrinsic difficulty in making compatible the existence of joint audits and reports with the independence of the different institutions of audit. The creation of joint reports supposes unity of action in the different phases of the audit: the preparation of the audit (the set-up of the audit plan), its implementation on the spot, and the approval of the draft report. Up to this point, although with difficulties, nothing would impede a joint team formed of auditors from the European Court of Auditors and one or several External Audit Institutions of the Member States to effectively carry out this task.

This would not be without difficulties, as mentioned before, because the training of the agents is not the same, neither are the audit methods, and because there is some misalignment between the audit timetables of the different External Audit Institutions, and also because previously these audits should have been included in the different work programmes, which are approved in a completely independent fashion by each National Audit Institution. However, if carefully considered, all these difficulties, despite being important, could be resolved. Progress has been made, but not enough, and it would be desirable for each of these problems to be studied with the object of finding practical solutions, and the aim of clearing the way for the realization of joint audits.

Nevertheless, the approval of joint reports is more difficult, and we must be aware of this, because the approval of reports is a prerogative of the bodies that exercise the highest responsibility of the External Audit Institutions, whether these bodies have a collegial or unipersonal nature. Moreover, it is not a question of a minor prerogative, but of a power that is closely connected to the independence and autonomy of the institution. Consequently, it would not be acceptable that at the time the plenary of the institution proceeded with the approval of a report, the judgement of this body were tied to the existence of agreements or report projects previously carried out jointly, on a technical level, with other institutions, as this would impose a reduction of the independence that should characterize external audit institutions.

In other words: to approve a joint report means that two collegial bodies, in principle independent and with full sovereignty, decide to approve the same report. But this is extremely difficult, since two

scenarios can arise. One is that one of the bodies, or both, may wish
to amend the report when discussing its approval. The other is that
those bodies are not allowed to introduce changes on the draft report
set up by the joint audit team, which implies a severe limitation in the
independence of the institution. Anyway, this does not mean that no
solution can be found to that issue. I believe it is possible to set up
institutional mechanisms allowing negotiations (for instance, joint
sessions of the boards of both institutions, mixed commissions
designed to set up agreements on certain aspects, etc.). But we cannot
ignore the fact that all solutions imply to one degree or another a
certain renouncement of the sovereignty of the institutions involved.

Consequently, the problem exists and we should take notice. This
does not mean there is no room to advance in plans that allow, also
in the field of report approval, joint action between the European
Court of Auditors and the External Audit Institutions of the
Member States. Although, certainly, at this political-institutional
level, the difficulties are greater than those that exist on a technical
level in preparing and exerting audits.

However, the levels cannot be totally unconnected, as it would be
entirely incomprehensible to European citizens that the reports
approved by two audit institutions (the EU one and the national one)
on the grounds of the joint audits and the audit reports set up by a
joint team of both institutions, could have diametrically opposed
contents and conclusions. This would be counterproductive to the
credibility of these audit institutions, especially if the differences
were related to the emphasis placed by one or the other on the critique of the management carried out by the Member States, and
would ultimately only have negative repercussions for the work that
these institutions must carry out. It is for this reason that joint audits
should be accompanied by a growing collaboration in the approval
of joint reports, which should be done by always preserving,
naturally, the independence of the various institutions of audit.

- *Collaboration and institutional relationships.* As indicated, respect for
their independence should not serve as a pretext for the appropriate
cooperation between the various institutions of audit to not exist. In
the previous section we referred to a crucial aspect, because it com-
bines technical, operational and institutional elements. However, this
is a question that is brought up often in different contexts and in
general, when it is a question of the utilization of reports already
made by other institutions for the elaboration of one's own reports.

It is clear, as also mentioned, that there are particular technical
difficulties regarding this point, because of, among other reasons,

misalignment of timetables in the production of reports among the different External Audit Institutions, which in part has its origin in the dates on which the national administrations make the documentation corresponding to the liquidation of the budget available to them. However, leaving aside these difficulties, the key question is whether or not greater cooperation should exist in the tasks carried out by the various External Audit Institutions; for example, in the approval of the Annual Report. Some say that the European Court of Auditors could perhaps use the annual reports approved by the respective External Audit Institutions as a starting out point for its own Annual Report. In recent years this question has been very clearly taken into consideration because of the Statement of Assurance (DAS in French). This Statement has been made based on a sample, and on many occasions it has brought up the question as to whether the consequent audits should not be carried out in a decentralized way through Member States.

This type of collaboration, however, is more complex than it seems at a first glance. For example, the use of reports previously set up by National External Audit Institutions by the European Court of Auditors for the elaboration of its own reports could put the EU institution in a dilemma. Or if it were to accept these reports as being good in the form in which they arrive from the National External Audit Institutions, this could clearly be in detriment to their homogeneity, both in terms of the methodology employed and in terms of the level of quality of the content. And, in any case, it would oblige the European Court of Auditors to become responsible for tasks with respect to which it could have well-grounded reservations. Or, it would oblige the European Court of Auditors to establish common rules regarding External Audit Institutions' procedures, and in the final instance, to supervise and, where appropriate, amend the work carried out by these institutions, which could be considered as showing little respect for their independence.

This dilemma conceals a fundamental difficulty that involves the sphere of institutional relations, and here it is vital to find the necessary balance. The relations, between the European Court of Auditors and the National External Audit Institutions do not operate as a confederate-type relationship, in which the European Court of Auditors would be integrated, in reality, by National External Audit Institution delegates. Neither could it operate as a relationship of hierarchical dependency, in which the European Court of Auditors would be located at the summit of external audit on an EU level, and where the National External Audit Institutions would be considered, on occasions, as its mere appendices. While not being explicit, these two models are what have been beneath positions that have sometimes become manifest in the face of certain problems.

The institutional relations between the European Court of Auditors and the National External Audit Institutions should be based on the mutual recognition of their independence and on collaboration on those objectives in which a common interest exists. The absence of collaboration is negative and could lead to a reduction in requirement levels, quality and the scope of the work carried out by the various External Audit Institutions, as each one of these, acting individually, may tend to attenuate the critical content of their observations (due to the indirect effect that these could have for their territory), and supposing that the other External Audit Institutions will behave in a similar way. In other words, one must be aware that the absence of cooperation could lead to a form of downgrading competition in terms of audit requirements.

It is for this reason that we should understand that sharing efforts is positive, and that it can mean seeking systems that also include, in certain cases, joint decision-making. Sharing responsibilities can imply, without doubt, voluntary self-limitation in certain fields, but also implies a greater capacity for involvement in areas in which the decisions are made in a shared way. It is the only way to adequately carry out the work that the citizens have given to the external institutions of audit.

• *Relations with Regional External Audit Institutions.* In certain countries there are external audit institutions in a regional context (disregarding the denominations regions have in each country: Autonomous Communities, *Länder*, etc.). What basically characterizes these institutions is their connection to a territorial political power of a democratic nature. In other words, they are not bodies of a technical nature created by the National External Audit Institution to carry out its functions more efficiently, but external audit institutions attached to the regional legislative assembly, in order to make it able to carry out its task of controlling the executive.

The framework of action of these Regional External Audit Institutions is different in each country. In some they are directly recognized in the Constitution, something which does not happen in others. Some have exclusivity in the external audit of regional governments, while in others this mission is shared with the National Audit Institution. However, whatever their institutional standing, the existence of these institutions introduces a factor that must be taken into account when designing the audit activity of the European

Court of Auditors in the Member States, above all in view of the fact that part of the EU spending programmes is managed and, on occasion, co-financed by regional governments.

Added to this is the fact that the Regional External Audit Institutions of some Member States have addressed themselves, in certain cases, to the European Court of Auditors, invoking the fact that, according to the constitutional laws of their country, it is the regional institutions and not the national that are solely responsible for the external audit of regional governments. The European Court of Auditors can be, without doubt, sensitive to these arguments. But it should be clearly understood that the European Court of Auditors is not responsible for settling constitutional interpretation with respect to the areas of responsibility of the different external audit institutions in a given country. The European Court of Auditors should base its guidelines for action on EU treaties. These are very clear when they establish that the European Court of Auditors' interlocutor in each European Union Member State is the National External Audit Institution.

Consequently, the action of the European Court of Auditors in this area is presided over by a double principle. First, the European Court of Auditors' interlocutor in a Member State (normally for carrying out missions there) is always the National Audit Institution. Second, it would be perfectly logical, and even advisable, that in the Member States with decentralized political systems, in which Regional External Audit Institutions exist, it could be decided that it is these institutions which to all effects would act as European Court of Auditors' interlocutors when the audits carried out in this country concern the regional governments. However, this decision should be adopted in the Member State itself and communicated to the European Court of Auditors which in no case would settle any possible disputes between the National and Regional External Audit Institutions with respect to their respective sphere of influence, as these are disputes that should be resolved by the Constitutional Court of the country in question.

In short, relations between the European Court of Auditors and the External Audit Institutions contain aspects of an unquestionable complexity. This complexity is the expression of the importance of the tasks that both institutions carry out and of the singularity of the political and institutional context in which they are carried out. Without doubt, facing complexity requires effort, dedication and imagination. The challenges to be faced deserve as much.

In the case of the European Union, this complexity will be increased from June 2004 as a result of an additional factor: the incorporation into the Union of ten new Member States, basically from Eastern Europe. The challenge that this provides is placed at least on two levels, one being legislative homogeneity and the other institutional coordination.

On a legislative level, it will be necessary to guarantee the existence of true institutions for external audit of state budget management, promoting the relevant legislative modifications where still pending. The considerations that we have set out concerning their role in the democratic functioning of the states are sufficient in order to understand the vital nature of the existence of external audit mechanisms with similar characteristics to those of the other European Union states.

On an institutional level, the entry of the new Member States will mean their incorporation into the European Court of Auditors. Changing from 15 to 25 members will, in part, mean a significant growth in its activity and consequently in its structure, not always easy to carry out in a short period of time (one should not forget that previous expansions have involved fewer states). However, it also inevitably implies a modification to its internal mechanisms of operation. It is already difficult to adapt to 15 members' procedures designed for fewer representatives. Both the distribution of the operational tasks of the European Court of Auditors and the procedures of internal operation of the Court as a collegial body (type of meetings, prior preparation of the same, etc.) will be profoundly affected. The need to modify these mechanisms will be unavoidable and new viable systems of operation will have to be found.

Moreover, this will have to be done taking into account that the process of expansion of the EU is not closed. More or less gradually and within differing periods, the other countries of Eastern Europe will be incorporated, including those of the former Yugoslavia. It would be appropriate for the new procedures introduced into the European Court of Auditors as a result of the incorporation of the next ten Member States to be of such a nature that they do not require great modifications to permit the incorporation of future members of the European Union.

Mechanisms of operation by chambers, or rotational presence in certain bodies, are just some of the many possibilities that will have to be explored in order to efficiently tackle this 'increase in complexity' resulting from expansion. Believing that the ECA can work with 25 members using the same mechanisms that were already quite inadequate for 15 could have important dysfunctional consequences. It is understood that political considerations should have priority over technical considerations, but not if this leads to a significant reduction in efficiency in the fulfilling of the institutional function itself, which would be to the detriment of the same political action. The European Court of Auditors, but also the Parliament, the Commission and the Council, should make an effort to create a new operating mechanism that would allow the incorporation of the legitimate interests of all the states (including the symbolic ones) without impairing the operating efficiency of the Court.

NOTE

1. This chapter is broadly based on the article 'El tribunal de Cuentas Europeo y sus relaciones con el Tribunal de Cuentas de España', *Revista Española de Control Externo*, **12**, September 2002, pp. 113–30.

PART II

Towards Coordination Strategies

7. A policy to fight financial fraud in the European Union

Alfredo José de Sousa

THE ORIGINS AND FOUNDATIONS OF ANTI-FRAUD POLICY

The Resolution of the European Parliament (2002/2211-INI) on the Commission's report on the protection of the Communities' financial interests and the fight against fraud,[1] stated that in 2001 there was a total of €1275 million in cases of fraud and financial irregularities, broken down as follows:

- Revenues:
  - Own resources: €532.5 million (in 2000: 1143);
- Expenditure:
  - EAGGF-Guarantee: €429 million (in 2000: 576);
  - Structural actions: €249 million (in 2000: 139);
  - Direct expenditure: €64.2 million (in 2000: 170).

This is a substantial reduction in comparison with 2000, where the total amount was calculated to be €2028 million.

The downward trend in terms of fraud was also highlighted in the fourth report on the activities of the European Anti-Fraud Office (OLAF) published in June 2003, which stated that 'the estimated financial impact calculated after the conclusion of surveys in all sectors was €850 million'.[2] By contrast, the European Parliament, in its Resolution on the Commission's report on the assessment of OLAF's activities (COM, 2003, 154) of 4 December 2003, estimated a total amount of €2 billion in financial irregularities and fraud in 2002.

These statistics give a clear idea of the importance of the fight that needs to be waged against the violation of financial interests in the European Union. This is particularly significant when we consider that fraud and the associated corruption often have a cross-frontier nature and are promoted by criminal organizations.

Classic examples of fraud and irregularities with a clearly defined typology in terms of structural funds and direct expenses include ineligible expenses, lack of co-financing, over-billing of unit prices, false billing of supplies, sub-division of expenditure in order to circumvent public tenders, favouritism, conflict of interest of public officials, embezzlement and corruption.

In terms of own resources the main categories of fraud are found in customs duties, forgery, cigarette trafficking, false declarations of origin in order to benefit from preferential treatment and carousel techniques in order to evade VAT payments.

Before addressing the current anti-fraud strategy, it is first necessary to describe its historical background from its origin until the creation of OLAF in 1999 and subsequently the draft Treaty on the Constitution for Europe.

The Treaty of Paris (1951), which founded the European Coal and Steel Community (ECSC) and the Treaties of Rome (1957) which founded the European Economic Community (EEC) and the European Atomic Energy Community (Euratom), established certain financial requirements for these Communities' budgets.

The Treaty of Paris specified a simplified budgetary mechanism in which the ECSC's administrative and operational expenses were to be covered by revenues derived from a tax on the production of coal and steel and loans.

In the case of the EEC and Euratom a 'Financial Requirements' heading was included, with 11 and 13 articles respectively, that regulated the budgetary process with greater precision, whereby revenues were considered to be constituted by the contributions of each Member State, set on the basis of a specific distribution criterion.

The budgetary problems experienced by the three communities were simplified following the Treaty of Brussels of 8 April 1965 that established a fusion and merged the respective executive branches, making it possible to establish a single expenditure budget for all three communities, except for the ECSC's operational expenses and Euratom's research budget.

A General Budget of the European Communities was thus established to be published in the official journal, together with the respective principles of budgetary unity and universality, with justified exceptions (operations of the European Investment Bank, Euratom's Investment Agency, the European Development Fund, and loan concession and contracting operations).

The treaties took care to foresee the possibility that the financial contributions of the Member States might be subsequently substituted by the Communities' own resources (article 201/EEC; article 173/Euratom).

By means of this provision, the Council issued its Decision of 21 April 1970 that attributed 'own resources' to the European Communities for the first time, to cover the Communities' expenditure.

The Communities' own resources are genuine revenues of a fiscal nature: agricultural levies, customs duties and a percentage (up to 1 per cent) of value added tax (VAT).

Although such revenues pertain to the European Communities, the public administrations of the Member States are responsible for collecting them.

This budgetary 'revolution' had two immediate consequences: a strengthened role for the Parliament that was granted authority over the Budget (Treaty of Luxembourg, 1970) and the creation of the European Court of Auditors (Treaty of 22 July 1975), as an independent authority for the external control of the Communities' financial activity.

These modifications resulted from the fact that the Communities' own resources derive from taxpayers in the Member States. As a result, their use in operational expenses and common policies of the Communities must be subject to rigorous independent control and to the European Parliament's power of sanction, as the body that represents taxpayers.

Own resources were used to cover the operational costs of the European Communities and also to finance the Common Agricultural Policy – around 70 per cent of the budget was applied in order to guarantee the agricultural markets – and the internal development policy (economic convergence of the Member States in terms of social, regional, industrial reconversion and environmental policy) and intervention within the fields of energy and research and cooperation with third countries.

Despite the fact that the budgets of the Communities were of a relatively limited scale, representing in 1979 only 0.8 per cent of GDP and 2.8 per cent of the total amount of national budgets,[3] the Commission and Council were already highly concerned with the need to combat the violation of financial interests.

The growing scale of common agricultural policy expenditure created successive budgetary difficulties. At the end of the 1982 financial year it was necessary to transfer the sum of 675 million ECU to the 1983 financial year in the form of an EAGGF guarantee, in addition to the authorized amount of 15,811 million ECU. The need to expand the sources of financing or to create new sources was a point of constant discussion between the Commission, Council and Parliament. In addition, with the entry of the United Kingdom into the Communities, budgetary difficulties were further aggravated because compensatory reimbursements were considered due to this Member State.

Regulation/EEC no. 1172/76, based on article 235/EEC, created an experimental seven-year financial mechanism for the compensation of

Member States who satisfied certain conditions as net contributors to the Communities.

This regulation did not, however, satisfy the insistent claims of the UK and it was therefore necessary to define mechanisms that established compensations for what were designated as 'unacceptable disequilibria' (Council Decision of 30 May 1980; agreement in Fontainebleau of 26 June 1984; agreements in Brussels of February 1988).

In order to guarantee budgetary equilibrium – which was systematically undermined during the 1980s – Decision no. 88/376/EEC of the Council of 24 June 1988 created a new financial contribution from the Member States based on their respective Gross National Product, known as the 'complementary own resource' or 'fourth resource'. This matter was later regulated by Decision no. 94/728/EC of the Council and Regulation EC no. 1150/2000 of the Council. As with the other own resources of the Communities, its ultimate source of origin was taxpayers in the Member States.

As a result of successive enlargements of the EC, a more marked difference began to be noted between Member States who were net contributors to the budget and those who were net recipients. This is perhaps the principal reason for the growing concern within the Communities' institutions to protect the Communities' financial interests.

This concern was pioneered above all by the Commission given its responsibility for budgetary execution, subject to pressures from the Parliament, Council and Court of Auditors in order to undertake actions designed to prevent and combat fraud and financial irregularities in an integrated manner,[4] with inspections to be carried out in the Member States. The Member States were responsible for around 80 per cent of the community's budgetary expenditure, in particular within the framework of the common agricultural policy and structural funds (subsidies).

THE MEMBER STATES AND THE COMMISSION IN THE FIGHT AGAINST FRAUD: THE TREATY OF MAASTRICHT

The Commission's report of 20 November 1987 on the intensification of the fight against fraud committed within the community budget was a key step in this regard. The main action lines of this report are described next.

The interventions of the Commission in the field of the fight against fraud were to be carried out in various fields and distributed across the Commission's services. The coordination of the Commission's activities in

terms of the fight against fraud was strengthened through two complementary paths that were implemented simultaneously:

- The creation of a coordination unit, with the specific responsibility
  to design, conceive, develop and manage common infrastructures,
  especially computing infrastructures, and represent the Commission
  before the Member States and Community institutions in cases of
  fraud.
- The widespread creation of anti-fraud units within all services in
  question.

This coordination unit was placed under the direct responsibility of the
President, standing alongside the General Secretariat.

The Commission was also obliged to create in all relevant Directorates-
General (DG), a unit that was clearly designated as responsible for anti-
fraud investigations as well as assuming liaison functions with the
coordination unit.

In July 1988 the Commission activated the Anti-Fraud Co-ordination
Unit (UCLAF).

On 13 April 1989, the European Parliament passed a resolution on the
prevention and repression of fraud affecting the Community Budget that
included criticism of the Council for not having invested the Commission
with sufficient powers to control the correctness of national management
of community revenues and expenditure within the Member States.

The growing concerns of the Community institutions, in particular the
Parliament, with the need to protect financial interests culminated in the
Treaty on European Union (Maastricht, 1992). In this, an addition was
made to article 209-A specifying the following:

> Member States shall take the same measures to counter fraud affecting the
> financial interests of the Community as they take to counter fraud affecting their
> own financial interests.
>
> Without prejudice to the other provisions of the Treaty, Member States shall
> co-ordinate their action aimed at protecting the financial interests of the
> Community against fraud. To this end they shall organize, with the help of the
> Commission, close and regular co-operation between the competent depart-
> ments of their administrations.

Two fundamental principles derived from this norm. First, the *principle
of analogy* between the measures adopted by each Member State in order
to fight fraud affecting their own financial interests, and the measures that
they should adopt in order to fight fraud affecting the financial interests of
the Community.

Second, the *principle of collaboration* between Member States in order to combat fraud, 'with assistance from the Commission'. The legislator intended to focus the majority of anti-fraud efforts within the administrations of the Member States, and establish a supplementary support role for the Commission. The reason for this is that the financial interests of the Community are above all the budgetary interests of the Member States themselves; that is, of their own taxpayers.

The *subsidiarity principle* was applied in this context and this matter may be considered to be integrated within the so-called *third pillar* (cooperation within the field of justice and home affairs).

These alterations to the Treaties had very important practical and legislative consequences.

In 1995 anti-fraud units pertaining to DG VI (agriculture) and DG XXI (customs) were integrated within UCLAF. As a result the latter expanded to a total of 150 staff and adopted a strategy to combat fraud committed against the community budget. This strategy was based not only on reinforcing UCLAF's autonomy and authority, in line with a recommendation from the Parliament, but also on its role in the coordination of anti-fraud policy in association with the competent Directorates-Generals, constituting 'ad hoc inter-service teams'.[5]

The European Anti-Fraud Office thus began to play an important support function to the Commission, not only for the legislative process of anti-fraud policy, but also in the execution of the respective policies of supervision and assistance to Member States, in particular in terms of the retrieval and exchange of information.[6]

At the normative level, in the wake of the Treaty of Maastricht, the Convention of 26 July 1995 (OJ C 316, of 27 November 1995) was introduced, together with Regulation (CE and EURATOM) no. 2988/95 of the Council (OJ L 312, of 23 December 1995), that defined and sanctioned the concept of financial irregularity, and Regulation (CE and EURATOM) no. 2185/96 of the Council (OJ L 292, of 15 November 1996) on controls and on-the-spot verifications, the powers of the Commission and the evidential value of inspection reports.

Additional protocols to the Convention were also published on the corruption of Community officials and agents (OJ C 313, of 23 October 1996), the incrimination of money laundering affecting the financial interests of the Community (OJ C 221, of 19 July 1997), and the protocol on the Convention on the intervention of the European Court of Justice by means of preliminary rulings (OJ C 151, of 20 May 1997).

THIRD PILLAR INSTRUMENTS IN THE FIGHT AGAINST FRAUD AND CORRUPTION

From a doctrinal perspective, rather than in terms of efficiency – given the delays in its effective entry into force[7] – *the Convention is the fundamental text for the protection of the Community's financial interests* within the framework of the third pillar. This is above all because the Convention categorized the types of financial fraud and determined their respective criminal classification.

Article 1 states:

> For the purposes of the Convention, fraud affecting the European Communities' financial interests consists of:
>
> – in respect of expenditure, any intentional act or omission relating to:
>   - the use or presentation of false, incorrect or incomplete statements or documents, which has as its effect the misappropriation or wrongful retention of funds from the general budget of the European Communities or budgets managed by, or on behalf of, the European Communities,
>   - non-disclosure of information in violation of a specific obligation, with the same effect,
>   - the misapplication of such funds for purposes other than those for which they were originally granted;
> – in respect of revenue, any intentional act or omission relating to:
>   - non-disclosure of information in violation of a specific obligation, with the same effect;
>   - the misapplication of a legally obtained benefit, with the same effect.[8]

Each Member State must take the necessary measures to ensure that the respective criminal infringements are punishable by effective, proportionate and dissuasive criminal penalties, which in the case of serious fraud, should consist of 'prison sentences'. In addition, the Member States should provide themselves with the powers, in accordance with the principle of territoriality, to cooperate in penal matters, centralizing penal procedures and facilitating related extraditions.

Subsequently, with regard to the criminal classification of the acts or omissions that affect or may affect the financial interests of the Communities, the Council approved on 27 September 1996 the first protocol dedicated to the fight against corruption involving national and Community officials with prison sentences specified in the event of more serious instances of corruption.

Finally on 19 June 1997, the Council approved a second protocol to the Convention, which specified that each Member State should take the necessary measures in order to ensure that the laundering of money related to the proceeds of fraud and active or passive corruption of public officials constitutes a penal infringement, but is not liable to a prison sentence (article 12 no. 1).

The following observations should be made on the Convention established on the basis of article k.3 of the Treaty of Maastricht (third pillar). The first is that the penal responsibility for financial fraud lies with the heads of businesses or any persons having the power to take decisions or exercise control within a business, in accordance with the principles defined in the national legislation of each Member State, without expressly consecrating the principle of the penal responsibility of corporate bodies (article 3).

Emphasis is then placed on the competency and cooperation between Member States in investigations within judicial procedures and in the execution of sanctions related to financial fraud (articles 4 and 5) without addressing the role of the Commission.

The Convention also attributes powers to the Council to define the regime of information exchange in this field for Member States – between each other and between them and the Commission (article 10 no. 2).

Finally, the intervention of the Court of Justice in the resolution of any disagreement between Member States regarding the interpretation or application of the Convention is only possible if the Council is unable to find any solution within a six-month period (article 8 no. 1).

The additional protocols to the Convention provide further clarifications to these questions. The consecration of the principle of the penal responsibility of corporate bodies is established in the second protocol of the Convention, not only for money laundering but also for financial fraud and corruption (article 3). The same protocol also establishes the regime of cooperation in this field between the Commission and Member States, in particular through technical and operational assistance that the national authorities may need in order to facilitate coordination of the respective investigations or to exchange information (article 7).

In relation to the intervention of the European Court of Justice, the protocol approved by the Council on 29 November 1996 established that the Member States may accept the Court's power to decide, by way of preliminary rulings, questions on the interpretation of the Convention and its first protocol (corruption).

The legal framework of the penal protection of the financial interests of the Communities was thereby completed, whereas its implementation was dependent on the conclusion of the complex process of ensuring that the framework entered into force in all Member States.

The system of Community control and sanctions for financial irregularities was established within the framework of each common policy.

In order to render effective the fight against fraud affecting the financial interests of the Communities it was necessary to create a common legal framework for all Community policies, until the PIF Convention enters into force. This common framework had to define the concept of irregularity subject to sanctions and the respective sanctions, procedural rules for its application, forfeiture deadlines, observance of the 'ne bis in idem' principle and the responsibility of corporate bodies.

Neither article 209-A of the Treaty of Maastricht nor any other norm of the treaties facilitated the adoption of such material or horizontal measures that guaranteed the immediate protection of the Communities' financial interests. For this purpose, the Council adopted Regulation no. 2988/95, of 18 December in order to respond to the need for such a common legal framework, invoking article 235 of the Treaty of the EC[9] and article 203 of the Euratom Treaty.

The Regulation did not provide a concept of fraud affecting the Communities' financial interests, but only of irregularity within the framework of expenditure and revenues.

According to article 1 no. 2: ' "Irregularity" shall mean any infringement of a provision of Community law resulting from an act or omission by an economic operator, which has, or would have, the effect of prejudicing the general budget of the Communities or budgets managed by them, either by reducing or losing revenue accruing from own resources collected directly on behalf of the Communities, or by an unjustified item of expenditure.'

Such irregularities may lead to the application of administrative penalties and measures to their respective authors, whether individual persons or corporate bodies, that range from the reimbursement of the amounts unjustifiably received to fines or the withdrawal of benefits or advantages (articles 4 and 5).

Although the provisions of the sixth fundamental consideration of the Regulation did not contemplate fraud, it may be concluded that such irregularities 'include fraudulent actions as defined in the Convention'.

As a result, respecting the 'non bis in idem' principle, it was foreseen that the respective pecuniary sanctions could be suspended 'if criminal proceedings had been initiated against the person concerned in connection with the same facts' in the Member State in question (article 6).

This Regulation, applicable to all sectors within the framework of the first pillar (except for VAT)[10] does not prejudice the application of rules on the control of frauds and irregularities provided for in the respective sectoral rules (article 5 no. 1 (g), article 6 no. 1, article 8 no. 2 and article 9 no. 2).

This is the case applied in Regulation no. 1552/89 of the Council (customs duties and agricultural levies), Regulation no. 1258/99 of the

Council (EAGGF-Guarantee), Regulation no. 4253/88 and Regulation no. 1260/99 of the Council (Structural Funds) and Regulation no. 1831/94 of the Commission (Cohesion Fund).

Article 10 of Regulation no. 2988/95 foresees approval of the supplementary general provisions in matters of on-the-spot inspections and checks by the Commission, without prejudice to controls to be performed by the Member States. These provisions were approved by Regulation no. 2185/96 of the Council, on 11 November.

The legislator's concern that such inspections or checks should not conflict with those undertaken by the Member States is manifested in the provisions of both Regulations. In these Regulations there is a clear intention to respect the principles of subsidiarity, proportionality and loyalty in the relations between Community institutions and the Member States. This is because, as stated in the second fundamental consideration of Regulation no. 2185/96, 'the protection of the financial interests of the Communities is primarily the responsibility of the Member States'.

As a result, on-the-spot checks and inspections to be carried out under the authority and responsibility of the Commission, are only justified in the conditions specified in article 2; that is,

- for the detection of serious or transnational irregularities or irregularities that may involve economic operators acting in several Member States, or
- where, for the detection of irregularities, the situation in a Member State requires on-the-spot checks and inspections to be strengthened in a particular case in order to improve the effectiveness of the protection of financial interests and so to ensure an equivalent level of protection within the Community, or
- at the request of the Member State concerned.

Such inspections should guarantee that other similar inspections are not being carried out 'at the same time in respect of the same facts' with regard to the economic operators concerned (article 3), and that there is 'close cooperation with the competent authorities of the Member State concerned' (article 4).

Finally, and understandably, the principle was established of identical value for the reports drawn up by the Commission's inspectors and national administrative inspectors, which may enable them to constitute 'admissible evidence in administrative or judicial proceedings of the Member State'. For this purpose, the Commission's inspectors should guarantee that when 'drawing up their reports, account is taken of the procedural requirements laid down in the national law of the Member State concerned' (article 8 no. 3).

SPECIAL REPORT NO. 8/98 OF THE EUROPEAN COURT OF AUDITORS AND THE RESOLUTION (BÖSCH) OF THE EUROPEAN PARLIAMENT

Although a regulatory framework had been established for the fight against financial fraud in the Member States, with the participation of the Commission, no such framework had been established for the fight against corruption within community institutions.

The second protocol of the Convention together with the Convention itself was very slow to be adopted by the Member States and enter into force. This protocol foresees the application of prison sentences for passive and active corruption affecting the Communities' financial interests, practised by a Community official or national official from one of the Member States.

The absence of a regulatory framework for the fight against corruption in the Communities' institutions, or even of guidelines within the field of the respective administrative investigations was emphasized by Special Report no. 8/98 of the European Court of Auditors,[11] on UCLAF. Point 6.5 of this report expressly stated the following:

> Although a number of cases of corruption could be expected in an organisation of the size of the Commission, no standard procedure for handling such cases has been adopted. Despite the fact that some cases were several years old, procedures for investigating such cases were improvised on a case by case basis. No clear guidelines exist as to how the administrative investigations have to be carried out. Questions remain as to what the powers of the officials of UCLAF and the Security Office are in terms of searching premises, the sequestration of property and documents and questioning officials and what the rights and obligations of the persons suspected are. Furthermore, and perhaps more seriously, it is not clear at which stage national prosecuting authorities have to be notified and thus when the important change from the sphere of an administrative enquiry to a judicial investigation takes place.[12]

Perhaps as a result of this criticism, in May 1998 UCLAF was transformed into a 'task force', reporting to the Secretary-General. A decision of the Commission (July 1998), granted this 'task force' investigative powers to focus primarily on cases of corruption within the Commission, with greater independence of activity in conformity with the express request of the Parliament in a resolution of 31 March 1998.

In October 1999, the European Parliament approved the Bösch Resolution[13] on the independence and role of UCLAF, which responded to the observations of Special Report no. 8/98 of the Court of Auditors. This Parliamentary Resolution laid the foundations for the creation of the European Anti-Fraud Office (OLAF), the parameters of which served as a precursor of the current OLAF, created in 1999 as a substitute for UCLAF.[14]

The Resolution stated that 'the Commission's policy in cases of corruption that occur within its own ranks continues to lack clarity and force', making it 'indispensable that UCLAF is empowered to conduct passive investigations to be applied to all European institutions', in accordance with 'clearly defined rules and procedures'. And it expressly stated that 'the protection of the Union's financial interests requires the development of a European penal space and the creation of a European Public Prosecutor'.

The Resolution invited the Commission to present a draft joint decision of the European Parliament, Council, Court of Justice and Court of Auditors, on the creation of a European Anti-Fraud Office (OLAF).

The principal power to be attributed to the Anti-Fraud Office was defined as 'powers to fight corruption and internal fraud in all European Union institutions that have adhered to this decision'.

The European Parliament was also concerned with establishing regulations for the 'question of co-operation between the Union's institutions and national judicial authorities'. For this purpose the resolution foresaw the creation within OLAF of a unit of specialists delegated by the national public prosecutors that would prepare the processes and transmit them to the national judicial authorities.

The Bösch Resolution of the Parliament was also highly critical of the activities of UCLAF in the field of combating financial fraud, echoing, with some alarm, the observations and recommendations of Special Report no. 8/98 of the Court of Auditors. These observations focused on both normative and organizational issues and the results of UCLAF's activities.

In relation to the normative framework the report clearly recognized that while the Convention and protocols in the framework of the third pillar were not ratified, the powers of the Commission and thus of UCLAF in the fight against financial fraud were somewhat circumscribed. In addition, the provisions in the field of the relationship with Member States were complex and difficult to be applied.

Cooperation between the Member States and the Commission/UCLAF was affected by the manner in which the provisions on the privileges and immunities granted to European Union staff were to be applied. In addition, in the inspections undertaken in the territory of the Member States, UCLAF was faced with considerable difficulties related to national legislation. It was confronted by a wide variety of procedures and systems in the 15 Member States, with various investigation bodies in each. UCLAF also revealed significant shortcomings in terms of organization and results.

Despite the fact that Regulation no. 2185/96 obliged UCLAF's inspectors 'to respect the procedural rules specified in the legislation of the Member State in which they are intervening', the audit carried out by the European Court of Auditors revealed an absence of full information in this regard. This explains why UCLAF at this time only carried out five missions within the framework of the regulation.

Additional factors were the lack of high-quality information contained in the databases (PRE-IRENE and IRENE), and a lack of coordination between UCLAF and the other Directorates-General of the Member States in terms of accessing and sharing information.

The national investigation services did not have access to databases, thus posing a clear risk of overlapping investigations by UCLAF and the Member States on the same case. As a result the Bösch Resolution considered that 'the results obtained to date by UCLAF in the fight against fraud continue to be well below their expectations and the goals set by the Commission', and noted 'insufficiency in quantitative and qualitative terms of the staff' of this organization (130 agents, of which only 30 may pursue investigations).

The Resolution also urged the Commission to foresee 300 staff positions in OLAF's organization structure (the office to be created) preferably to be filled by 'qualified investigators and specialists in the penal procedures of the respective services of the Member States'.

CORRUPTION AND UCLAF

In March 1998, mainly because of the pursuit of the Commission's anti-fraud policy, Parliament raised serious obstacles to the discharging execution of the 1996 budget.

The main issue in question concerned grave irregularities detected by the Court of Auditors in the MED programmes intended to implement projects spanning countries located on both sides of the Mediterranean.

The Commission was criticized for not initiating disciplinary proceedings against the officials responsible for these irregularities, and for not having informed the judicial authorities of Belgium, France and Italy of possible criminal acts.[15]

As a result, the European Parliament established as one of the conditions for discharging the 1996 budget, the need to take measures to overcome 'the failure to attribute democratic responsibilities in the struggle against fraud within European institutions'.

A period of major political upheaval was thus initiated, resulting from the tension between the European Parliament and Commission in relation to the policy to fight financial fraud and corruption.

The Bösch Resolution of the European Parliament of 26 October 1998 is a significant expression of this political tension, that intensified during the first half of 1999.

In the session of 14 January 1999, the European Parliament approved a resolution whose measures included:

- Requesting the constitution of a commission of independent experts, under the aegis of the Parliament and Commission, charged with examining the manner in which fraud, bad management and nepotism are detected and handled by the Commission;
- Urging the Commission to implement, as soon as possible, 'the proposal of the President of the European Council to constitute a high-level group of representatives of the European Parliament, the Council and Commission to analyse and approve the proposals to establish as an urgent priority, a new anti-fraud agency, that should operate independently of the Commission's political control'.
- Exhorting the Inter-governmental Conference to contemplate the creation of a European public prosecutor for crimes against the Union's financial interests.

The Committee of Independent Experts, also known as the committee of 'Wise Men',[16] presented its first report on 15 March 1999.[17] This report examined six specific dossiers (Tourism, MED programmes, ECHO, Leonardo da Vinci, Security Service and Nuclear Security), and the Committee concluded that the Commission and/or certain Commissioners bear responsibility for delays in the final decisions on certain dossiers (in the case of Tourism, the positive response to the request to remove immunity from three senior officials was delayed for over two years) or for lack of suitable control in the execution of high-risk programmes (such as MED) or consent in the hiring of personnel in breach of regulations (the ECHO case). The Committee also emphasized the ambiguity of UCLAF's situation within the Commission, procedural delays and the lack of disciplinary procedures in particular for senior officials.

The report's conclusions led to the resignation of the Commission presided by Jacques Santer.

In turn, the intense work carried out by the High-Level Group[18] resulted in the creation of the European Anti-Fraud Office (OLAF), by means of the Decision of the Commission on 28 April 1999, to substitute for the Anti-Fraud Co-ordination task force and assume all its attributes. This was followed by approval of Regulation no. 1073/1999 of the European Parliament and Council of 25 May 1999.

This Regulation of the Parliament and Council invoked article 280 of the Treaty that established the European Community (Amsterdam), one of whose innovations was the provision that the Council by means of a qualified majority, after a proposal from the Commission, in co-decision with the Parliament and after consulting the Court of Auditors, 'shall adopt the necessary measures in the fields of the prevention of and fight against fraud affecting the financial interests of the Community with a view to affording effective and equivalent protection in the Member States'.

This represents norms that may be directly applied within the Member States, in line with the framework of the first pillar, that grant to the Commission/OLAF powers to intervene in the respective territories.

THE EUROPEAN ANTI-FRAUD OFFICE AND THE ANTI-FRAUD AND CORRUPTION STRATEGY

This normative framework of the new European Anti-Fraud Office represented profound innovations in terms of organization and competencies, some of which were already foreseen in the Bösch Resolution of the Parliament in October, 1998.

OLAF was placed under the leadership of a Director designated by the Commission, after receiving the consent of the European Parliament and the Council, for a five-year renewable mandate. This designation was chosen from a list of candidates with the necessary qualifications after a call for applications published in the Official Journal.

The Director is empowered to make nominations and establish contracts to employ staff within the organization, under the terms of legislation applying to the staff and other agents of the Communities. The staff positions attributed in this manner are listed in an annex to the Commission's permanent staff.

OLAF's budgetary allocations are consigned within a specific budget heading of Part A of the Union's budget, in a separate annex, following a draft budget proposal prepared for this purpose. The Director is responsible for the execution of this budgetary heading and the specific anti-fraud policy headings within part B of the respective budget.

The Commission's decisions on OLAF's internal organization are only applied to the extent that they are compatible with the Office's regulatory framework. There are also significant changes in terms of the framework of the Office's competencies, above all in terms of the investigative function.

OLAF began to exercise the Commission's competencies specified in the Regulations of the Council nos 2988/95 and 2185/96 in the field of external administrative investigations within the Member States or even in third countries in the fight against fraud and corruption. The Office was also empowered to provide support from the Commission to Member States, and to act as the direct interlocutor with respective police and judicial authorities.[19]

OLAF undertakes activities of conception and development of anti-fraud methods, preparing the Commission's regulatory and legislative initiatives.

The area where the legislator introduced the greatest degree of innovation was in the field of internal investigations, in the wake of the crisis that occurred between the Parliament and the Commission. Article 1 no. 3 of Regulation no. 1073/1999 expressly states:

> Within the institutions, bodies, offices and agencies established by, or on the basis of, the Treaties (hereinafter 'the institutions, bodies, offices and agencies'), the Office shall conduct administrative investigations for the purpose of:
>
> - fighting fraud, corruption and any other illegal activity affecting the financial interests of the European Community,
> - investigating to that end serious matters relating to the discharge of professional duties such as to constitute a dereliction of the obligations of officials and other servants of the Communities liable to result in disciplinary or, as the case may be, criminal proceedings, or an equivalent failure to discharge obligations on the part of members of institutions and bodies, heads of offices and agencies or members of the staff of institutions, bodies, offices or agencies not subject to the Staff Regulations of officials and the Conditions of employment of other servants of the European Communities ('the Staff Regulations').

It is worth underlining the main lines of action in the field of internal and external investigations. First, OLAF exercises this power, 'with total independence', and the Director may not request or accept instructions from the Commission, from any government or from any other office, body or agency (article 3 of the Decision). If the Director considers that a measure taken by the Commission calls his independence into question, he shall be entitled to bring an action against the institution before the Court of Justice.

Second, OLAF's powers are exercised under the 'regular control' of a Supervisory Committee, in order to reinforce the Office's independence, without however interfering with the conduct of investigations in progress.[20] The Supervisory Committee is composed of 'five independent outside persons', appointed by common accord of the European Parliament, the Council and the Commission, with a three-year mandate that may be renewed once.

Third, the Director is responsible for carrying out investigations from the initial decision to open investigations through to drawing up the final report and making pertinent recommendations on the next steps to be taken.[21]

Particular care was taken when drawing up this normative regime to maintain respect for the principles of subsidiarity and proportionality, with the regime emphasizing the fact that investigations do 'not affect the powers of the Member States to bring criminal proceedings'.[22] Neither is there any reduction in the powers and responsibilities of the Member States to take measures to combat fraud affecting the financial interests of the Communities, given that OLAF's external investigations are only justified in the cases typified in article 2 of Regulation no. 2185/96 of the Council (see Note 11).

On the other hand, understandably, when drawing up the respective reports 'account shall be taken of the procedural requirements laid down in the national law of the Member State concerned', constituting 'admissible evidence in the respective administrative or judicial proceedings'.[23]

Finally, despite the various mechanisms intended to avoid duplication of procedures (by OLAF and the Member State) on the same facts, the office has the faculty to 'forward to the competent authorities of the Member States concerned, information obtained in the course of external investigations'.[24]

INTERNAL INVESTIGATIONS

As already stated, the most significant alteration introduced by this normative framework concerns internal investigations and their eventual disciplinary and penal consequences. This alteration is perfectly understandable because of both the permanent dissatisfaction of the Parliament in this field and its successive recommendations, and also the criticism made of the Commission in the first report of the Committee of Independent Experts.

In this regard, Special Report no. 8/98, in point 6, had already established a clear correlation between the need to allocate to UCLAF the responsibility to handle cases of corruption involving officials of the Commission and of other Community institutions.

International investigations will be carried out by OLAF within Community institutions, bodies and offices as a result of serious facts that may constitute a failure to comply with the obligations of officers and agents of the Communities, and may thus be liable to disciplinary proceedings and possibly penal proceedings. Such internal investigations may even concern a member or manager of the Communities' institutions, bodies or offices.

Internal investigations should observe the norms of the Treaties, in particular the Protocol on privileges and immunities, as well as having regard for the Staff Regulations of the Communities' officials and agents. These Staff Regulations should be modified, however, 'in order to specify the rights and obligations of officials and other agents in matters of internal investigations'.[25]

For this purpose, OLAF was granted significant powers of investigation and duties with persons who are subject to an internal investigation:

- The Office shall have the right of immediate and unannounced access to any information held by the institutions, bodies, offices and agencies, and to their premises. The Office shall be empowered to inspect the accounts of the institutions, bodies, offices and agencies. The Office may take a copy of and obtain extracts from any document or the contents of any data medium held by the institutions, bodies, offices and agencies and, if necessary, assume custody of such documents or data to ensure that there is no danger of their disappearing,
- The Office may request oral information from members of the institutions and bodies, from managers of offices and agencies and from the staff of the institutions, bodies, offices and agencies.[26]

The duties are associated with observance of the principle of the right to reply, so the persons involved have the right to express their views on the facts concerning them and are subject to the principle that the conclusions of an investigation must be based solely on elements which have evidential value.[27]

The legislator's policy measure to grant powers to OLAF to carry out internal investigations within institutions, bodies, offices and agencies had far-reaching consequences. As a result, the regulation included a considerable number of precautionary measures, requiring institutional coordination on the norms to be observed when carrying out such investigations.

Indeed the legislator took special care that such internal investigations were to be carried out with due regard for 'the decisions adopted by each institution, body, office and agency'. The institutions consult each other on the rules to be laid down by such decisions, which should specify:

a) a duty on the part of members, officials and other servants of the institutions and bodies, and managers, officials and servants of offices and agencies, to cooperate with and supply information to the Office's servants;
b) the procedures to be observed by the Office's employees when conducting internal investigations and the guarantees of the rights of persons concerned by an internal investigation.[28]

Hence the European Parliament, Council and Commission approved the Inter-institutional Agreement on 25 May 1999, creating a common regime for the pursuit of internal investigations by OLAF, adopting an internal decision in accordance with the model annexed to the Agreement.[29]

The Agreement and model of internal decisions have two fundamental principles. All officials and equivalent staff of each institution are obliged to cooperate in full with the agents of OLAF, including having an obligation to inform superiors without delay of 'evidence giving rise to a presumption of the existence of possible cases of fraud, corruption or any other illegal activity detrimental to the interests of the Communities'. In turn, when a manager, official or servant may be implicated, they have the right to be informed as rapidly as possible, and in any event must be given 'the possibility to express his views on all the facts which concern him' before respective conclusions may be drawn up.

The European Parliament, Council and Commission appealed to other institutions, bodies, offices and agencies to adhere to the inter-institutional agreement. This appeal was expressly rejected by the EIB and ECB, and the respective decisions were refuted in the Court of Justice and were annulled by the decision of 10 July 2003.

It was thus clearly established that the latter organizations are also subject to internal investigations to be carried out by OLAF, and could not restrict such investigations into their own internal services as specified in the annulled decisions.

Internal investigations have been, and continue to be, the principal concern of the European Parliament whenever the latter analyses the Commission's reports on the fight against fraud and corruption.

In quantitative terms, internal investigations currently represent less than half of OLAF's activity. In qualitative terms, they have merited the priority recommended by the Parliament and are adopted in OLAF's pluri-annual programmes ('zero tolerance' in relation to allegations of corruption in European institutions).[30]

THE EUROPEAN PUBLIC PROSECUTOR'S OFFICE AND THE TREATY OF NICE

The Regulation of OLAF should be considered a beginning rather than an end in terms of resolving the problems of the institutionalization of the fight against violation of financial interests of the Union and corruption within the Communities.

In terms of the normative framework it was still necessary to resolve the problem of criminalization of financial fraud and corruption after the Convention of 1995 when the additional protocols had still not yet entered into force. In parallel with this problem, work was still underway for the creation of an independent European Public Prosecutor's Office which would exercise prosecuting activities before the corresponding jurisdictions of the Member States in matters of the protection of community financial interests.

This proposal was incorporated within the Communication of the Commission of 29 September 2000 directed to the Inter-governmental Conference on institutional reforms.[31]

The Commission's Communication was based on in-depth preparatory work, undertaken at the request of the Commission and European Parliament by a group of experts from all the Member States on the penal protection of the Communities' financial interests.

This work, known under the designation of 'Corpus Juris'[32] recommended the creation of a unified community judicial space through harmonious insertion within the national systems of a European Public Prosecutor's Office and assistant prosecutors in each Member State charged solely with penal proceedings and prosecution. Judgement and the final decision would remain in the hands of national judicial bodies.

Nonetheless, the Commission's communication was not accepted by the Heads of State and Government meeting in Nice, either because they did not have time to analyse the proposal or because they wanted the practical implications of the creation of the European Public Prosecutor's Office to be studied in greater depth.

In order to overcome these abortive attempts and in particular in order to substitute the instruments of the third pillar (the PIF Convention) that had not yet entered into force, the Commission, on 23 May 2001 presented a draft Directive on the penal protection of the financial interests of the Communities.[33]

To this effect, articles 29, 47 and 280 of the Treaty of the European Union established the primacy of Community law in the adoption of measures within the field of the protection of the Community's financial interests, that essentially concern the first pillar.

Article 280 no. 4 of the Treaty of Amsterdam clearly establishes that the measures of the Council 'shall not concern the application of national criminal law or the national administration of justice within the Member States'.

As a result, the draft Directive returns to the articles of the PIF Convention and the additional protocols that are not covered by no. 4 of article 280, in particular the classification of the crimes of fraud, corruption and money laundering, applicable sanctions and cooperation between the Member States and the Commission.

This was why in fundamental consideration no. 14, the Member States were urged to ratify these third-pillar instruments in order that the provisions on 'powers, judicial co-operation, transfer and centralisation of criminal proceedings, extradition and execution of sentences may also enter into force'.

The legislative procedure of this Directive is still in progress, despite the repeated insistence of the European Parliament to the Commission of the urgent need to conclude this process.

THE EUROPEAN PUBLIC PROSECUTOR: FROM CORPUS JURIS TO THE COMMISSION'S GREEN PAPER

Approval of the said Directive and entry into force of the PIF Convention and respective protocols may contribute towards the effectiveness of the fight against financial fraud and corruption in the Union and thus the effectiveness of the activities of OLAF. However, they do not yet represent the measures required to 'afford effective and equivalent protection in the Member States, in the fields of prevention and fight against fraud affecting the financial interests of the Community', as defended in Article 280 of the Treaty of Amsterdam.

The Directive or Convention neither confer suitable legitimacy on OLAF to carry out criminal investigations, nor control the legality of its own procedures in this function, nor above all the necessary guarantees of the presumed authors of facts or omissions typified as crimes.

Only by establishing the judicial and organizational architecture delineated by 'Corpus Juris' will it be possible to support the creation of the European Public Prosecutor's Office for the criminalization of the violation of the financial interests of the Community.

The need for the creation of a European Public Prosecutor's Office continues to be at the forefront of the Commission's concerns, even after the frustrating experience of the Treaty of Nice in this regard, and is perhaps of even greater concern to the European Parliament.

The need for the creation of a European Public Prosecutor's Office has been repeatedly emphasized by OLAF's Supervisory Committee in its successive opinions, as an indispensable guarantee of OLAF's independence and of the rights and defence of persons subject to its investigations.[34]

In its Action Plan for 2001–03 the Commission addressed its global anti-fraud strategy, where one of the four key objectives was to strengthen the penal judicial dimension of the fight against fraud and corruption. In order to implement this objective, in 2002 the Commission relaunched the public debate on this question by issuing a Green Paper[35] on the creation of the European Public Prosecutor's Office charged with the penal protection of the financial interests of the Community.

The Green Paper addressed the debate on the proposal, already made by the Commission on 29 September 2000, of 'integrating in the treaty, only characteristics that are essential to the position of the European Public Prosecutor's Office (nomination, dismissal, mission, independence), and remitting to the secondary committee law for the definition of the rules and modalities required for its operation'.

This was intended to 'overcome the fragmentation of the European criminal law enforcement area', to move beyond the cumbersome and inappropriate traditional methods of judicial cooperation between Member States, and to respond to the lack of judicial follow-up to administrative investigations carried out by OLAF, strengthening the organization and effectiveness of investigations within Community institutions. All these measures conformed with the objectives of the Tampere European Council to 'create a genuine common European judicial space'.

The Green Paper also aimed at ensuring that the Convention charged to prepare revision of the Treaties in 2003 (the project to formulate a Constitution for Europe) would also consider the proposal to create a European Public Prosecutor.

The principal lines of the proposal to create a European Public Prosecutor's Office are specified in the preparatory work contained in the Corpus Juris and the subsequent studies on its viability in the national systems.[36]

Corpus Juris classifies eight types of criminal infringements liable to prison sentences of up to five years and/or a fine for individuals and a fine of €10 million for corporate bodies with complementary sanctions.

Most of these criminal infringements coincide with those described in the PIF Convention. One example is fraud affecting the financial interests of the Communities and comparable offences, money laundering and receipt of the proceeds of infringements and corruption. In addition, association of malefactors, fraud in public contracts, misappropriation of public funds, abuse of office in the management of public funds and disclosure of secrets pertaining to one's office, constitute new types of crime that the Commission adopted in the Green Paper in the wake of Corpus Juris.

The regime of criminal liability is based around the classic principles of penal law: legality, personal culpability, proportionality of penalties and judicial guarantee.

In relation to criminal procedure, Corpus Juris establishes a mixed regime combining national and community components.

The European Public Prosecution Service – Public Prosecutor and delegates in the Member States – exercise their powers of investigation throughout the territory of the European Union with identical powers in the 15 Member States.

National jurisdictions will determine the definitive judgement on the basis of their own judicial system, to be effective throughout the European judicial space.

This regime is essentially based on the principle of territoriality: the set of territories of the Member States of the Union constitutes a single judicial space for the purposes of investigation, judgement and execution of all jurisdictional decisions, including the final sentence concerning 'euro crimes'.

On the basis of the principle of territoriality other principles may be identified on which the system is structured:

- The principle of indivisibility and solidarity of the European Public Prosecution Service, including the delegates of the European Public Prosecutor's Office in each Member State.
- The principle of the exclusive power of the Public Prosecution Service to direct and coordinate the investigation of such euro crimes before national authorities or OLAF.
- The principle of subjection to the control of the national judge of the respective Member State in terms of guarantees of fundamental rights (preventive imprisonment, searches, seizures, telephone tapping, etc.).[37]
- The principle of mutual recognition of jurisdictional acts by the Member States: jurisdictional decisions taken in one Member State must be recognized in all others.
- The principle of *non bis in idem*, which imposes on all national authorities recognition of the force of the case judged under the penal judgements carried out under another national jurisdiction concerning the same crimes or facts.

The legitimacy and effectiveness of OLAF as an instrument in the fight against financial fraud and corruption depend on its suitable integration within the organizational structure of the European Public Prosecutor. With this objective in mind, the European Parliament and the Commission itself have insisted on the complete restructuring of OLAF since its creation in 1999.

OPERATIONS OF OLAF

We will now address the installation and operations of OLAF, its articulation with the Commission and its directorates-general, its form of intervention in other Community institutions and the role played by the

Supervisory Committee. For this purpose we will concentrate solely on the investigative function related to anti-fraud and corruption.

After a lengthy bureaucratic process of co-decision between the European Parliament and the Council, the Commission designated the first Director of OLAF, chosen from a list of candidates, established with the favourable opinion of the Supervisory Committee. On 1 March 2000, the designated Director assumed duties, and a total of 300 staff[38] was planned for OLAF, to be hired gradually until 2002.

It was quite natural that the first priorities of the new organization were to regularize the 'legacy' of UCLAF in terms of information (IRENE database), human resources, internal organization and pending investigations, and this was demonstrated in OLAF's first activities report (1 June 1999/ 31 May 2000).

Another significant aspect was the Office's concern with establishing an efficient database as an instrument of analysis of information and structuring of an 'intelligence' service that would support day-to-day activities.

The question of human resources and their implications for OLAF's internal organization aroused from the outset the thorny question of the Office's real budgetary and administrative autonomy in relation to the Commission. This was mentioned in the first activity report of the Supervisory Committee for the period July 1999 to July 2000. The report explicitly states that 'the dependence which still exists in terms of recruitment, transfer and dismissal of staff and that results from the close connection between the Office and administrative structure of the Commission has almost paralysed the activity of OLAF'.[39]

This connection with the Commission results in an ambiguity of OLAF's legal status, in which the office is attributed with operational independence in the investigative function, above all in investigations in which Community staff or agents are implicated.[40] This ambiguity is accentuated by the fact that OLAF has been given inter-institutional powers in terms of internal investigations – powers that were contested by the EIB, the ECB, the Committee of the Regions and the group of deputies of the European Parliament. This contestation has been resolved in part by means of intervention of the Court of Justice (see Note 20), but the ambiguity is also manifested by the fact that there is a lack of clarification regarding the frontiers or the articulation between the investigations of OLAF and the administrative investigations directed by other services of the Commission confronted with administrative or financial irregularities or disciplinary processes involving its staff or agents.

Ambiguity is also found in terms of cooperation with the judicial authorities of the Member States, where OLAF's role continues to be less than clearly defined. As a result, OLAF's investigations not only lack internal procedural rules they also do not take sufficient account of the procedural norms of the Member States in order to produce effects on the respective judicial authorities.

The latter have tended to consider OLAF as a normal service of the Commission and, as a result, in its first activity report, the Supervisory Committee identified the need to 'adopt measures without delay relating to OLAF's internal organisation, such as the creation of a magistrates unit, in order to enhance the legitimacy of its investigations and foster the emergence of a European legal culture'.

OLAF structured its internal organization chart around three directorates and gradually hired its staff – permanent employees and temporary agents.

Directorate A is principally responsible for 'Policy, Legislation and Legal Affairs', with regard to 'the preparation of the Commission's legislative and regulatory initiatives, in the light of the objectives of the fight against fraud'.

Directorate B, 'Investigations and Operations', is essentially responsible for investigations, and coordination and assistance to national authorities and Directorate C, 'Intelligence'.

A magistrates unit was also created, recruited from national magistrates (one for each Member State), intended to ensure that the investigations and final reports were presented in the respective jurisdictions in an admissible manner given the associated procedural regime.[41]

The positions of Directors B and C and the magistrates unit were only filled in 2002 due to a series of bureaucratic obstacles.

All these ambiguities continue to exist and were subject to recommendations in the most recent activity reports of the Supervisory Committee and its opinions submitted to the European Parliament, the Council and the Commission.

Article 15 of Regulation no. 1073/1999 stated that in the third year after its entry into force, 'the Commission shall transmit to the European Parliament and the Council a progress report on the Office's activities, accompanied by the Supervisory Committee's opinion, together, where appropriate, with proposals to modify or extend the Office's tasks'.

ASSESSMENT OF OLAF

The Commission only presented its progress report in April 2003,[42] and this report expressly refrained from a quantitative analysis of the investigations and trends in terms of fraud and referred instead to the previous reports of OLAF. Neither does the progress report contain any proposal to modify Regulation no. 1073/1999 except in terms of the obligation of Member

States to inform the Community institutions of the steps taken following OLAF's investigations (Recommendation no. 6).

Nonetheless, the Commission proposed to take legislative initiatives on external investigations within the field of direct expenditure, cooperation/ assistance in the field of transnational VAT and widening of the administrative sanctions of the common agricultural policy to other fields (Recommendations nos 4 and 12). It also invited the IGC/Convention to include the European Public Prosecutor's Office in the Constitutional Treaty in order to guarantee control of OLAF's operational activities and respect for judicial guarantees (Recommendation no. 13). In addition the Commission recommended that OLAF should reformulate its investigation procedures manual (Recommendation no. 2), develop its strategic and operational 'intelligence' function (Recommendation no. 5), conclude the protocols of agreement with other services of the Commission (Recommendation no. 7), conclude the memorandums of understanding in order to share disciplinary powers with other institutions, bodies, offices and agencies (Recommendations nos 8 and 9), and establish an investigation policy and priorities (Recommendation no. 11).

Part III of this report reaffirmed the hybrid status of OLAF resulting from the independence of its investigative function and its connection to the Commission. The report also confirmed the persistence of ambiguities and insufficiencies within OLAF, in line with the repeated statements of the Supervisory Committee.

The Supervisory Committee in its 'complementary' opinion to the Commission's report emphasized that OLAF was instituted within an evolving legal framework. As a result, it questioned whether it was appropriate to 'widen the Office's function' without concluding whether such a provision was viable or not, stating the difficulty of 'making an assessment due to the continued absence of a programme of activities for the Office (with a definition of priorities) and of real procedural rules for investigations, which are in the process of being drawn up, as well as by the absence of a clear concept of the role of the judicial advice unit'. In this manner it corroborated the similar recommendations made to OLAF in the Commission's report (Recommendations nos 2 and 11).

After reiterating the persistence of ambiguities of OLAF, emphasized in previous reports and opinions, the Supervisory Committee concluded that it is still too early to alter the Regulation. Before such an alteration may be made, it will be necessary to carry out an appraisal of the effectiveness of its structures (magistrates, intelligence, platform of services) by means of a management audit in 2004. In the meantime, the development of OLAF's investigations of Eurostat and their disclosure in the media caused a crisis in the Commission.

The Eurostat case, from 2000 onwards, originated from various investigations concerning subsidies and contracts with companies suspected of management and budgetary irregularities, which implied official transmission of information of a penal character to the judicial authorities of Luxembourg and Paris and the adoption of administrative writs against very senior officials within Eurostat.

The investigations confimed the criticism that had previously been made of OLAF's status and functioning. The lengthy time periods involved in decisions to open investigations and their actual conclusion, the lack of articulation with other disciplinary, penal, administrative and audit procedures, the absence of clarity in the distinction between internal and external investigations, the lack of norms regulating the various stages of the investigation, and the communication difficulties between OLAF and the Commission.

It was the latter factor that sparked the crisis, given that the Commission was only informed at a late stage of the implication of the investigations of community officials. This was especially relevant in terms of the information transmitted by OLAF to the national judicial authorities and knowledge of such information by the media.

The media impact of this case led the Commission, on 9 July 2003, to create a task force 'to take responsibility for the internal and external aspects of the investigations currently managed by OLAF', which was clearly seen as interference in the Office's operational independence.

The Eurostat case had equally significant political repercussions within OLAF itself. At the beginning of August 2003, a revised manual was adopted and a protocol of agreement was drawn up concerning a code of conduct, in order to guarantee prompt exchange of information between OLAF and the Commission in matters of internal investigations. It was also decided to ensure prior transmission to the Supervisory Committee of all information destined for the national judicial authorities.

THE EUROSTAT CASE, THE EUROPEAN PARLIAMENT AND REFORM OF OLAF

The Eurostat case had a significant impact on the European Parliament. It coincided with the submission by the Commission of the assessment report of the activities of OLAF (article 15 of Regulation no. 1073/1999).

On 18 November 2003, President Romano Prodi made a state of the Union speech before Parliament, in which he expressly referred to the Eurostat case and the reform of OLAF. This reform involved reformulation of the Office's legal framework (i.e. of Regulation no. 1073/1999), so going against the flow of the position taken in the Commission's report. Prodi identified the main lines of reform as follows:

- strengthened operational autonomy, whereby certain horizontal tasks not connected to the investigation function could be reintegrated within the administrative services of the Commission;
- legislative consecration of the principle of opportunity or discretionary action, in order to make it possible to establish priorities within its activities;
- clarification of the flows of information between OLAF and Community institutions or bodies;
- modifications in the Regulation in terms of the essential aspect of the protection of the rights of defence in investigations.

And he concluded with an announcement of draft legislation in this direction to be presented to the European Parliament, and also stated that 'in the perspective of a European Public Prosecutor, OLAF should have complete autonomy within a clear political framework'.

The European Parliament subsequently analysed the aforementioned assessment report of OLAF, leading to a Resolution[43] on the Commission's report that was advanced and profoundly critical.

It was critical in terms of the action of OLAF in the Eurostat case, adopting comments contained in the opinion of the Supervisory Committee. In symphony with President Prodi's speech, it invited the Commission to present legislative proposals based on article 280 of the EC Treaty in order to introduce improvements in the OLAF regulation. These alterations should include the safeguard of the rights of those being investigated, the preparation of procedural rules for investigations, the information to be provided to institutions and strengthened independence and powers for the Supervisory Committee.

The Parliament's Resolution also included specific recommendations to OLAF on its internal organization and programme of activities, with priorities for 2004, and requested a report from OLAF to be provided by May 2004 on the 150 pending cases inherited from UCLAF. Significantly, it was stated that there were 2300 pending cases related to structural funds, customs, external aid and direct expenditure, some of which had been pending for over two years. Finally, the European Parliament underlined that it 'understands that OLAF should be seen as an independent authority in terms of investigations that co-operates with Europol, Eurojust, the European Judicial Network and in the future may co-operate with the European Public Prosecutor'.

Draft legislation is currently being prepared in order to modify

Regulation no. 1073/1999. This legislation contemplates, in particular, reinforcement of OLAF's control mechanisms, respect for the rights of those being investigated, the regime for the transmission of information to institutions and national authorities and widened powers for the Supervisory Committee in such matters.

THE CONSTITUTION FOR EUROPE, THE EUROPEAN PUBLIC PROSECUTOR'S OFFICE AND OLAF

The Treaty of Amsterdam consecrated a set of norms concerning the creation of an area of freedom, security and justice in the European Union, involving judicial cooperation between the Member States.

The Tampere European Council, in October 1999, considered that this judicial cooperation would include mutual recognition of the decisions of the judicial authorities of each Member State even in penal matters, a decision which presupposes consecration of the principle of reciprocal confidence of the Member States in the respective criminal justice systems.

These principles were incorporated within the Convention of 26 July 1995 concerning the protection of the financial interests of the Communities and the respective additional protocols. The principle of mutual recognition of judicial decisions and the respective criminal justice systems would apply to all phases of penal proceedings. As a consequence, the Decision of the Council of 28 February 2002[44] created Eurojust, as an indispensable instrument for such judicial cooperation.

In relation to the fight against financial fraud, this Decision contained two main action lines.[45] First, the general power of Eurojust covers the crimes of fraud and corruption together with any penal infringements affecting the financial interests of the European Community and money laundering, and the proceeds of these crimes (article 4 no. 1 (b)). Second, Eurojust may intervene within the framework of investigations and penal proceedings that implicate two or more Member States in relation to crimes within its area of competency (article 3 no. 1).

As underlined in the fundamental consideration no. 8 of this Decision 'the powers of Eurojust do not prejudice the powers of the Community in matters of protection of the Community's financial interests'. In turn the Framework Decision of the Council on 13 June 2002[46] created the European arrest warrant, intended to substitute for previous extradition instruments used in relations between Member States.

This mechanism also applies to the crimes of corruption and fraud, including fraud affecting the financial interests of the European Communities in the sense given by the Convention of 26 July 1995, and to the money laundering of the proceeds of these crimes and counterfeiting of the euro (article 2 no. 2).

As already emphasized, the effective system for the protection of the Union's financial interests, in addition to criminalization of the respective infringements, also presupposed the creation of a European Public Prosecutor's Office which, supported by the investigations of OLAF, would introduce the subsequent formal charges in the jurisdictions of the Member States.

After the failure of inclusion of this system in the Treaty of Nice it was even suggested to create by means of secondary Community law a European Public Prosecutor's Office solely for the internal investigations of OLAF.[47]

The set of questions related to the European Public Prosecutor's Office were always connected with the protection of the financial interests of the Union and the fight against corruption affecting these interests, together with the integration of OLAF within this strategy – one only needs to look at Corpus Juris and the Green Paper published by the Commission. Nonetheless, the draft Treaty establishing a Constitution for Europe refocused this question in terms of wider parameters.

Article III–321, under the sub-heading 'combating fraud', specifies that the Union and the Member States shall counter fraud and any other illegal activities affecting the Union's financial interests through the adoption of measures that afford 'effective protection in the Member States'. And that the coordination of the actions of the Member States should be organized 'in co-operation with the Commission'. This is a strengthened reaffirmation of the principles of the analogous nature of the financial interests of the Union and the Member States, of their effective protection and collaboration between the Member States and the Commission that formed the basis of the current article 280 (Treaty of Amsterdam).

In effect, it was also foreseen that a law or European framework law would set the measures necessary for combating fraud affecting the financial interests of the Union in the Member States.

Article III–174 refers to Eurojust, with its current powers of coordination of national authorities, including actions concerning infringements affecting the financial interests of the Union.

Article III–175 admits the possibility that a European law may establish a 'European Public Prosecutor's Office' from Eurojust, in order to fight serious crime with a cross-border dimension as well as crimes affecting the interests of the Union. The European Public Prosecutor's Office shall be responsible for investigating such crimes and exercise the functions of prosecutor in the competent courts of the Member States in relation to such offences.

It is now not only the strategy to fight financial fraud and corruption, and the respective anti-fraud instrument – OLAF – that justifies the need to create a European Public Prosecutor's Office. The underlying reason is the creation of an area of freedom, security and justice in the European Union, consecrated in the Treaty of Amsterdam and reinforced in the Tampere European Council, and the effectiveness of the fight against serious crime with a cross-border dimension. Thus the European Public Prosecutor's Office is no longer intended for combating crime against Europe but instead within Europe.

We wait to see the role that will be played by OLAF within this new European system. The Resolution of the European Parliament of 4 December 2003 that formed the basis of the legislative process in progress to modify Regulation no. 1073/1999 stated that OLAF will cooperate in the future with the European Public Prosecutor's Office.[48]

The final word on this will rest with the European Parliament that will be elected in the forthcoming elections and with the new European Commission.

NOTES

1. Annual Report for 2001 of the Commission – OJ C 295 of 28 November 2002.
2. Internet site: europa.eu.int/olaf.
3. Daniel Strasser, 'Les Finances de L'Europe', Edições Labor (Brussels), 1980, page 337. In 1977, the MacDougall Report, prepared at the Commission's request, predicted that the Community would dedicate between 5 per cent and 10 per cent of its GDP to its expenses.
4. Since 1970, inspection units have been created in various Directorates-General in order to combat financial fraud, in accordance with regulations of sectorial control. These units have supervisory powers in the Member States (external inspections) and operate in cooperation with the respective research authorities.
5. Communication of the Commission of 4 November 1992, subscribed by Commission President, Jacques Delors.
6. The European Anti-Fraud Office developed a database on fraud and irregularities called IRENE. In October 1997 this database included information on 25,615 cases, over half of which were in the framework of the EAGGF guarantee. Another database was also set up, called PRE-IRENE, that was restricted to the cases investigated by UCLAF, as an instrument of internal management, see Annex III of Special Report no. 8/98 of the Court of Auditors (Tribunal de Contas), OJ C 230, of 1 June 1999.
7. The Convention only entered into force after notification to the General Secretariat of the Council of adoption by the last Member State, which took place on 17 October 2002, together with the first protocol and the protocol on the Convention's interpretation by the Court of Justice. The second protocol on money laundering has not yet been ratified by the various Member States (see Bulletin of the EU 10-2002).
8. Curiously this formula is the detailed development of the formula adopted in the protocols attached to the draft Treaties of the Commission on this matter in 1976, which were not approved at the time by the Council. These projects already foresaw the

9. Article 308 of the Treaty of the European Union.
10. See no. 12 of Annex I of Special Report no. 8/98 of the Court of Auditors.
11. OJ C 230 of 1 June 1999.
12. The European Court of Auditors in its Special Reports no. 1/96 – 'Aid programmes in the Mediterranean region MED', and no. 3/96 – 'Contracts in the Commission's tourism service indicate instances of corruption'.
13. Resolution A4-0297/98, OJ C 328 of 26 October 1998.
14. Decision of the Commission of 28 April 1999 (OJ L 136/20 of 31 May 1999) and Regulation no. 1073/1999 of the European Parliament and Council of 25 May 1999 (OJ L 136 of 31 May 1999).
15. Commission's Report on Budgetary Control, A4-0097/98, of 18 March 1998.
16. This Committee was composed of the President, A. Middelhoek (President of the European Court of Auditors), I.-B. Ahlenius (Sweden's Auditor-General), J.A. Carrillo Salcedo (Member of the European Court of Human Rights), P. Lelong (President of the French Court of Auditors) and W. van Gerven (Professor of Law and ex-Attorney of the European Court of Justice).
17. Available at the European Parliament's website.
18. This Group, also known as the Schöder Group, comprised the President of the Council (Schöder), the President of the Budgetary Control Committee of the European Parliament (Theato) and Commissioners van Miert, Monti and Gradin from the European Commission. In relation to the creation of OLAF, see J.A.E. Vervàele, in *European Journal of Crime, Criminal Law and Criminal Justice*, 3/1999, page 331.
19. Article 3 of the Regulation of the Council no. 1073/1999.
20. Article 11, nos. 1 and 2 of the Regulation of the Council no. 1073/1999.

Under the terms of nos. 7 and 8 of this article, the Director shall forward to the Supervisory Committee each year the Office's programme of activities, its investigations and results thereof, the reasons for which it has not yet been possible to wind up any investigation within nine months, and of the expected time for completion, cases where the institution concerned has failed to act on the recommendations made by it and cases requiring information to be forwarded to the judicial authorities of a Member State.
The Supervisory Committee shall adopt at least one report on its activities per year and may submit reports to the Community institutions on the results of the Office's investigations and the action taken thereon.

21. See Article 5, no. 1 of the Decision of the Commission; and Articles 5, 6 no. 1, 9 no. 1 and 12 no. 3 of the Regulation of the Council no. 1073/1999.
22. Article 2 of the Regulation of the Council no. 1073/1999.
23. Article 9, nos 2 and 4 of the Regulation of the Council no. 1073/1999. This provision reaffirms the regime of the judicial value of these reports specified in Article 8 no. 3 of the Regulation (EURATOM, CE) no. 2185/96.
24. Article 3 of Regulation no. 2185/96 and Article 6 of Regulation no. 2988/1999; Article 10, no. 1 of Regulation no. 1073/1999.
25. Fundamental consideration no 10 and Article 14 of Regulation no. 1073/1999. Reform of the Staff Regulations, although repeatedly announced in the activity plans of the Commission has not yet been approved.
26. See Article 4 no. 2 of Regulation no. 1073/1999.
27. Fundamental consideration no. 10 and Article 4 nos 5 and 6 (b) of Regulation no. 1073/1999.

28. Article 4 nos. 1 and 6 of Regulation no. 1073/1999.
29. OJ L 136 of 31 May 1999.
30. See OLAF's fourth activities report (June 2002/June 2003), www.europa.eu.int/olaf <http://www.europa.eu.int/olaf>. During this period, 64 new processes were registered, and 49 per cent of internal investigations concerned tenders/subsidies procedures.
31. Previously, on 19 January 2000 the European Parliament had made a similar appeal to the Inter-Governmental Conference – OJ C 304/126 of 24 October 2000.
32. Corpus Juris that establishes penal provisions for protection of the financial interests of the European Union, under the direction of Delmas-Marty, *Económica*, Paris, 1997. The test of Corpus Juris is also available on the Internet (<http://www.law.uu.nl/wiarda/corpus/indexi.htm>). In the wake of these recommendations, the experts completed more recently an important comparative study analysing the need, legitimacy and viability of 'Corpus Juris', and the impact that a European Public Prosecutor's Office might have on national systems of repression: *Application of Corpus Juris in the Member States*, Delmas-Marty/J.A.E. Vervåele, *Intersentia*, Utrecht, 2000.
33. OJ C 240 E, of 28 August 2001.
34. Activities Report, OJ C 360 of 14 December 2000.
35. The site for consultation of the Green Paper is as follows: http.europe.eu.int/olaf/livre vert.
36. See note 32. The work of Delmas-Marty/J.A.E. Vervåele closely follows this point.
37. OLAF's Supervisory Committee in its Opinion no. 2/2002 on the Green Paper foresaw for this purpose 'the creation of a preliminary European chamber, in accordance with the model of jurisdiction created by the Statute of Rome for the International Court of Justice', as a result of the unit of application and interpretation of Community law and equity in the determination of the Court of judgement.
38. UCLAF had 139 staff members, of which 87 were allocated to operational units.
39. JO C 360 of 14 December 2000.
40. Opinion no. 2/2002, annexed to the first activity report of the Supervisory Committee.
41. Initially the magistrates unit was placed in Directorate A, but from the beginning of 2002 it started to report directly to the Director-General in order to emphasize the horizontal nature of its activity.
42. COM (2003), 154, final version, available at: europe.eu.int/eur-lex.
43. www 3.europarl.eu.int/ (minutes of 4 December 2003).
44. OJ L 63 of 6 March 2002.
45. In light of the powers of Eurojust created by this Decision and in the perspective of its articulation with those of OLAF in the same field, a protocol of understanding was signed between both organizations.
46. OJ L 190 of 18 July 2002.
47. Recommendation of the European Parliament, referred to in the first Activity Report of OLAF's Supervisory Committee and Opinions no. 5/99 and no. 2/2000, annexed.
48. See Note 31.

8. The coordination of internal controls: the single audit – towards a European Union internal control framework

Vítor Caldeira

INTRODUCTION

The European Union (EU) is a unique organization due to its political and legal context, scale and complexity. Its budget is subject to many layers of procedures both within the European Institutions and Member (or beneficiary) States. Management is complicated by the large number and varied nature of the schemes, the millions of beneficiaries, and the involvement of many different bodies in Member States often representing different administrative cultures.

The effectiveness of the audit systems and control procedures over EU expenditure has been a cause of concern for a number of years (Harlow, 2002). Meanwhile, the European Commission has developed a series of fundamental reforms[1] aimed at improving the quality of financial management.

This reform process has led to major changes in the European Commission environment, namely the decentralization of responsibilities for the use of funds to those managing them (i.e. authorizing officers) and the replacement of the Financial Controller's role with an internal audit function. An important reform of the Financial Regulation, which governs the management and control of the EU budget, has also been achieved. The financial management and control systems for agriculture and structural measures were strengthened too during the 1990s, in particular by setting out the procedures and checks that need to be undertaken by Member States as part of their responsibilities for the operational management of those European financial instruments.

Despite these advances, both the European Parliament[2] and the Council have expressed concerns about a lack of coordination of the various controls and checks at the different administrative levels. In practice, this means that some beneficiaries can be subject to checks on the same expenditure by different inspectors and auditors, whereas other beneficiaries are not being checked at all. As such, the idea of a single audit concept was introduced, with the aim of providing an audit framework applicable to all Community funds, in which checks would be coordinated to ensure adequate coverage with minimum overlapping, and allowing reliance to be placed on checks done at a lower level in the audit chain.

This chapter aims to discuss what is meant by single audit in the particular context of the European Union, based on the current EU control and audit arrangements and on the best-known single audit experiences. It takes account of the potential impact of the Commission's administrative reform on internal controls and proposes key attributes for the development of 'a more efficient and effective system of internal control for European Union revenue and expenditure' (Caldeira, 2002) as the basis to evolve towards an EU internal control concept and framework.

WHAT IS MEANT BY 'SINGLE AUDIT'?

The Concept

The term 'single audit' needs a clear common understanding because there are different perceptions of what it means according to different experiences.

Underlying the concept of a single audit is the desire to avoid uncoordinated, overlapping controls and audits, with some auditees subject to several audits and others subject to none. It also concerns the development of an integrated internal control structure in which checks carried out at higher levels in the system can rely on checks carried out at lower levels.

In broader terms, single audit can be defined as 'a name which covers a way of thinking about a situation where one entity is subject to many audits, and there is by implication a requirement to rely on the work of other auditors if the audits are not to be repetitious' (Ball, 2002).

In the European Union environment there is a perceived need for the audit resources applied to the internal control and audit of public finances to be organized more coherently and cost-effectively. There are, however, other matters to be taken into account in the European Union context, such as those examined hereafter. It is therefore preferable to address single audit in terms of an internal control concept allowing for a more efficient and effective system of internal control in the European Union architecture.

The Experiences of the United States and the Netherlands

Two of the most well-known experiences are the *Single Audit Act* in the United States of America (USA), and the single audit approach followed in the Netherlands. Let us look at those systems.

United States of America

Around one-sixth of the US Federal budget[3] is expended by non-federal entities (NFEs).[4] Such organizations may receive multiple grants for different areas. In the past, this resulted in a number of audits of the same organization, sometimes overlapping in time, and often covering the same material. This inflated the overall audit cost and placed an unnecessary burden on auditees.

The Single Audit Act of 1984 tackled the problem by providing that only one audit need to be undertaken on the organization as whole (e.g. on the basis of its annual financial statements) – replacing the need for individual audits of individual funds – and establishing uniform audit standards.

The objectives of the Single Audit Act (GAO-AIMD, 1996) were to:

- improve financial management of state and local governments receiving federal financial assistance;
- establish uniform requirements for audits of federal financial assistance provided to state and local governments;
- promote the efficient and effective use of audit resources; and
- ensure that federal departments and agencies, to the extent practicable, rely on and use audit work done pursuant to the act.

The single audit is intended to provide a cost-effective audit of NFEs. Efficiencies can be considerable when an organisation-wide, or single audit, is conducted in lieu of multiple audits of individual Federal programs. The parties involved in the audit process know beforehand what is expected and what the products of the audit will be. Furthermore, repeated exposures to a structured audit process promote discipline in an auditee's accounting practices.

The auditor provides an opinion as to whether the auditee's financial statements are presented fairly, thus providing a tool to assess the financial condition of the auditee.

A risk-based audit approach assures audit coverage to high-dollar, high-risk Federal programs and provides opportunities for the auditing of small-dollar, high-risk programs.

Single audit reports are not intended to provide detailed audit coverage of all the Federal awards or provide detailed financial information for individual awards. To do so would be cost prohibitive. (Grants Management Committee, 2001)

The main characteristics of the application of the US single audit model can be summarized as follows:

- a single audit is required for all state and local government entities receiving more than a specified dollar threshold of federal assistance (300,000 dollars after the Single Audit Act Amendments of 1996) in a financial year. Organizations with annual expenditure of less than this threshold are required to make their records available for review or audit;
- recipient organizations are required to maintain effective internal controls and comply with all applicable rules and regulations;
- it is the recipient organization's responsibility to arrange for an audit (including selection of auditor), ensure it is properly completed, submit the report when required and take corrective action on audit findings;
- the cost of the single audit is funded by the federal grant;
- the audit is conducted in accordance with Government Auditing Standards and the auditor must: (1) provide an opinion on the financial statements and schedule of expenditure of the Federal grant; (2) gain an understanding of the internal controls over Federal programmes and test them; and (3) provide an opinion on compliance with programme requirements;
- on receipt of the Single Audit Report the federal awarding agency has six months to issue a management decision on each audit finding. This specifies the corrective action needed, including repayment of funds. The auditee has the right to appeal;
- to ensure single audits are carried out to the required standard, the work papers can be subject to a quality control review by Federal agencies.

The Netherlands

The single audit concept in the Netherlands was developed in the context of an action programme aimed at modernizing and strengthening the whole infrastructure for financial control and internal audit. This comprehensive action programme covered internal control procedures, separation of duties, financial controls, information systems, recast of the financial regulatory framework, establishment or strengthening of internal audit departments, and speeding up of accounting procedures. The implementation of this programme took a period of approximately ten years (1986–96) during which two distinct phases can be identified.

The first phase concerned the audit of government ministries by the external auditor, the Netherlands Court of Audit. This involved reliance by the Netherlands Court of Audit on the work of the internal auditors of the ministries, having first set up common standards and guidance for their operation. The second phase covered a lower level within the control chain whereby the ministry auditors relied on the work of the auditors of local authorities over the use of government funds managed by them. The ministry issued terms of reference indicating the issues the regional or local auditor should cover in his opinion.

The first phase was introduced as part of a wide-ranging improvement in the quality of financial control and audit of ministries, including the implementation of an adequate system of internal control procedures. The central audit service of the Ministry of Finance played a key role in monitoring the ministries. Considerable improvements were achieved, including provision of timely and efficient information flows and adequate compatible computerized accounting and information systems. Particular attention was paid to establishing strong and effective internal audit units in each ministry and the requirement to provide an annual audit opinion was formalized. The opinions were based on financial audits, which themselves were based on risk analysis. Internal audit standards were established and promulgated which were compatible with the standards of the Netherlands Court of Audit. The Netherlands Court of Audit also established standards for the review of the work of the internal audit department.

The second phase concerned the lower tier of public financial management in the Netherlands, namely regional and local authorities. These organizations have their own accountability structures, including local audit and discharge procedures. The area of concern for single audit was the central government funds managed by these bodies, such as specific purpose grants, which represent around 20 per cent of the national budget. The previous arrangement was for audit certificates to be obtained for all grants, however, as with the US experience, this resulted in a multitude of uncoordinated reporting and audit requirements by the various ministries responsible for the various grants, with the associated burden on the auditees.

A Cabinet decision of 1989[5] set the objectives of the Dutch single audit policy for lower tier levels as follows:

- streamlining of audit activities;
- establishing efficient and effective information flows;
- obtaining a sufficient view about the legality/regularity and effectiveness of financial management for shared management tasks;
- dissolving the impediments to decentralization and deregulation.

Single audit at this level revolves around the need for the local authority or other body to produce only one set of financial statements annually, and that the audit certificate provided on these financial statements includes verification of the compliance of the central government grants with their respective obligations. The audit at the lower level is done in a way that also meets the requirements of those at a higher level.

An important result of single audit in the Netherlands was to highlight the need for coherent, practical and applicable legislation governing the use of national funds. As such the single audit had a corresponding effect of stimulating an improvement in the clarity, effectiveness and relevance of legislation. A further recent development has been the move towards financial statements that concentrate on achievement of policy objectives and performance indicators, in addition to presenting basic financial accounting data.

Relevant Points for the EU Context

In terms of relevance to the European Union context some parallels can be identified. From the US model the following should be noted:

- the US structure is simpler than that of the European Union. Federal departments deal directly with the implementing organizations, making a much flatter management and control structure. Single audit is therefore more restricted and easier to define and operate as no intermediary organizations are involved;
- the US approach includes no common standards on the internal controls to be applied, although examination of these is an integral part of the single auditor's remit. The scale (in terms of number of beneficiaries and relatively low value of claims) in the EU context requires specific consideration of this aspect;
- there is no specific consideration made of the work of internal auditors (other than presumably an evaluation of their place within the internal control structure as a whole);
- for much of the EU budget (e.g. agriculture) there are many more individual beneficiaries, very few of which will receive significant grants. For Structural Funds there are more individually significant beneficiaries although not many manage multiple grants;
- the US experience is more akin to the EU directly managed expenditure. The use of a standardized audit approach and particularly standard reporting documentation would be of specific interest;
- selection of auditor by the auditee introduces an element of risk (underqualified or insufficiently independent auditors), however this risk can be managed by comprehensive terms of reference, detailed reporting and the review of working papers;

- the particular attention paid to corrective action indicates the positive and dynamic nature of the process;
- funding of the audit through the Federal grant significantly adds to the transparency and control over the process.

The Dutch experience also raises some relevant aspects to consider:

- the single audit concept is just an audit concept and, as such, doesn't directly cover the definition and application of control procedures;
- the administrative structure is somewhat more complex than for the USA, although less so than for Community income and expenditure;
- the Dutch single audit concept places the Netherlands Court of Audit above the process. The Netherlands Court of Audit has taken effective steps for reviewing the work of other auditors in terms of reliance;
- implementing the Dutch single audit has not been a quick or easy process, despite being introduced in a relatively small national context;
- the Dutch single audit concept requires considerable responsibility and workload to be placed on the internal audit capabilities of the ministries, and the availability of sufficient resources to perform the corresponding tasks.

Although important lessons can be learned from these or other experiences,[6] the single audit concept must be seen in its particular context of application. As said before, it is preferable to address single audit in the European Union in terms of the need for a more efficient and effective internal control framework for EU revenue and expenditure. For that reason it is worthwhile focusing on the EU current control framework as a starting point for further reflection.

EU CURRENT CONTROL FRAMEWORK

It is of prime importance to provide an adequate level of control over the EU budget in order to obtain reasonable assurance that income and expenditure are legal and regular, and comply with the principles of economy, efficiency and effectiveness. Oversight and control involve both the European Union and the Member States' institutions and administrations. Our analysis is focused only on internal control and external audit within the immediate Community environment.

Internal Control

Many and varied participants both within the European Commission and Member States are present in the European Union internal control framework.

The Commission is responsible in cooperation with Member States for the implementation and control of the budget,[7] and therefore for developing and implementing effective control systems to provide assurance that financial management is sound. Over 80 per cent of the Community budget is managed in partnership with Member (or beneficiary) States. Partnership means that while the Commission retains overall responsibility for the budget, the Member (or beneficiary) States are responsible for the day-to-day administration and control of these funds, following rules established by the Union. Administration involves the identification and selection of beneficiaries, and making payments thereto. The remainder of the budget is managed directly by the Commission[8] including the selection of, and payments to, beneficiaries or suppliers.

The Commission's internal audit function helps management ensure that its procedures are being followed and its objectives met. This function is performed by the Commission's central Internal Audit Service (IAS) and by the different Directorates-General's (DGs) internal audit capabilities. The IAS undertakes audits on issues concerning both the institution as a whole and individual areas of interest, and provides technical support to the internal audit capabilities.

The Commission is organized in Directorates-General that are responsible for implementing specific policy areas and the corresponding parts of the EU budget. Included within the DGs are control units that check that expenditure is being implemented correctly both within the Commission and in Member States, and internal audit capabilities that help the management of the Directorate-General to ensure that internal controls are operating effectively.

The administration of the EU budget is complex. Different control arrangements are foreseen for specific budgetary areas covering revenue (own resources) and expenditure (agriculture, structural measures, pre-accession aid, internal policies, external actions and administrative expenditure).

Own resources are the revenues by which the EU budget is financed. In 2002, they amounted to 79.8 billion euros. Over 90 per cent of own resources derive from the Gross National Product (GNP) and Value Added Tax (VAT) bases involving monthly transfers from Member States. The remainder of own resources represent customs duties and agricultural and sugar levies. These are collected by Member State administrations (e.g. customs) that are required to operate appropriate controls to ensure completeness and accuracy of collection. The Commission DGs operate supervisory controls to check that Member States are meeting their obligations. A 'Joint Audit Initiative' has existed within the traditional own resources field since the mid-1990s. It covers cooperation between the Commission and the customs' internal audit functions in the majority of Member States. This initiative has resulted in the preparation, on a voluntary basis, of common audit plans and tools, with particular emphasis on assessing the adequacy of control systems covering the identification and payment of traditional own resources. This involves the internal audit service of the Member State undertaking audit procedures agreed between itself and the Commission. The cost of the checks is borne by the Community budget through the retention by Member States' administrations of 25 per cent of customs duties collected.

Agricultural expenditure, with payments of 43.5 billion euros in 2002, represents over 50 per cent of the EU budget. The expenditure involves many millions of relatively small payments to millions of individual farmers through a wide range of schemes. Payments are made through agencies established and financed by Member States, following rules established by the Commission. Paying agencies are subject to an independent audit each year by a certifying body, which certifies whether the financial claims to the European Commission are accurate, and if the required control systems are in place and the necessary checks have been carried out. The paying agencies are required to undertake a number of checks within the integrated administrative and control system (IACS), which covers the payments based on declared area or numbers of animals. IACS comprises both administrative checks of claims, and on-the-spot inspections of beneficiaries. Expenditure not subject to IACS, such as production and processing aid and export refunds, is subject to checks by Member State bodies based on risk analysis and subject to the monetary amounts involved.[9] The cost of the checks is borne by the Member State.

Structural measures expenditure,[10] with payments of 23.5 billion euros in 2002, represents 28 per cent of the EU budget. This expenditure involves payments for eligible projects within the framework of operational programmes, and often involves reimbursement of costs to public bodies engaged in construction or training projects. The expenditure is managed by Member State administrations (managing and paying authorities) that select projects and make payments to beneficiaries.[11] Member States are responsible in the first instance for ensuring the financial control of EU expenditure. In the second half of the 1990s the European Commission issued a regulation[12] defining the administrative and control requirements on structural measures expenditure in order to address criticisms about the quality of management. These introduced the requirement for an independent body to provide a closure statement on the accuracy and legality and regularity of expenditure presented to the Commission for reimbursement. Such statements are largely based on an inspection of a defined value (5 per cent) of underlying expenditure intended to verify the effectiveness of the management and control systems, as well as the transactions themselves. In November 2002 the Commission made a proposal to the Structural Funds Technical Group entitled '*contrat de confiance*'. This proposal does not add new regulatory requirements but is based on effective coordination of Community and national controls; the presentation by the Member States of an adequate control strategy; and provision of annual reports detailing the results of control activities. As a counterpart the Member States are promised less checking by the Commission, and a reduction in the time that supporting documentation must be held. The cost of the checks is borne by the Member State.

Pre-accession aid is the other budgetary area that is largely co-managed with the beneficiary states. Expenditure, which totalled 1.8 billion euros in 2002, is aimed at helping the countries prepare for accession to the Union[13] by financing investment projects as well as institution building measures such as twinning. Management and control of this expenditure are undertaken by agencies within the countries concerned, which are homologated by the European Commission. The cost of the checks is borne by the beneficiary State.

Internal policies are directly managed by the European Commission and comprise the co-financing of actions carried out by private or public organizations. Payments in 2002 amounted to 6.6 billion euros. The Commission selects these actions, generally following an evaluation by independent external experts or with the involvement of Member States. In most areas the Commission has a direct contractual relationship with the beneficiaries. The co-financing takes place through the reimbursement of costs incurred and claimed by the beneficiary. During the course of an action the Commission makes financial and non-financial checks, including *ex post* financial audits. From the fifth RTD framework programme (1998–2002) the Commission mandated independent auditors to carry out part of these audits on its behalf based on standard guidelines. From the sixth framework programme (2003–06) the cost statements for indirect RTD actions have to be accompanied by an audit certificate certifying the eligibility and reality of the costs claimed. However the Commission will still be required to check that the costs were necessary for undertaking the action. The cost of the checks is borne by the EU budget.

External actions are directly managed by the European Commission and comprise payments made to finance eligible development aid projects outside the Union, mostly in the developing world. Payments in 2002 amounted to 4.4 billion euros. In the context of decentralization much of the expenditure is increasingly managed by the European Commission delegations that are responsible for making payments and checking projects. Other expenditure is channelled through non-governmental organizations (NGOs) and some expenditure is paid directly by the Commission's central services. Some projects are subject to independent audit of the expenditure declarations. The cost of the controls is borne by the EU budget.

Administrative expenditure is managed directly by the European Commission or by the other EU institutions and bodies involved. The expenditure, some 5.2 billion euro in 2002, largely comprises payment of salaries and other staff-related costs, as well as accommodation costs. This expenditure is checked by the institutions' services involved, and the cost is borne by the EU budget.

External Audit

The European Court of Auditors (ECA) is the external audit institution of the European Union and therefore not an element of internal control. The ECA is responsible for providing independent oversight of the financial management and control of Community funds and reports to the discharge authority (European Parliament and Council).[14] For this purpose, the ECA checks that the financial statements are complete and accurate, that the underlying transactions are legal and regular, and that the funds have been soundly managed. The ECA pays particular attention to evaluating control systems and making recommendations for corrective action.

Each Member State has a National Audit Institution (NAI) (NAO, 1996) responsible for the independent external audit of their respective state budgets and, as such, they are outside the EU internal control framework. The NAIs have no formal role in the external audit of the EU budget. However, the EC Treaty requires them to cooperate with the European Court of Auditors in undertaking its duties.[15] In some cases the NAIs have chosen to take on the function of certifying bodies for the agricultural paying agencies,[16] which is a specific task done within the remit of internal control of the EU budget. The national mandates, rights and obligations of the NAIs in terms of the audit of EU funds vary widely between different Member States. While in practice most NAIs do not audit EU funds directly, they are often responsible for auditing compliance with national conditions of the national funds used for co-financing EU-funded projects (Flizot, 2002).

Weaknesses in the Current Arrangements

The European Court of Auditors has identified many instances of poor control leading to errors and irregularities or inefficient and/or ineffective use of funds in its annual and special reports. While recent progress has been made, the quality of the systems of administration and control over Community income and expenditure remains variable, as illustrated by the most recent findings presented in the ECA's annual report concerning the financial year 2002.[17]

For own resources, agriculture, structural measures and pre-accession aid, the systems differ in conception and implementation and many aspects are left to the sole responsibility of the Member States.

In respect of traditional own resources the Member States are required to implement an adequate standard of checks, however this standard is not always defined or detailed. There are some coordinated audits between the Commission and the Member States, but these remain voluntary arrangements only.[18]

For agriculture nearly 60 per cent of the expenditure is subject to the Integrated Administrative and Control Systems (IACS), which has taken many years to establish. The ECA has found IACS to be effective in respect of arable area payments, however animal payments remain at higher risk. The other agricultural payments not covered by IACS present higher risks and are subject to less effective control systems. Even when systems are judged as satisfactory, the ECA notes many instances where improvements are necessary.[19]

For structural measures the ECA has found that the conception of the systems relating to the 2000–06 period has improved, compared with the previous one. In particular, the Commission's supervisory and control systems have improved during 2002, although important weaknesses remain in those governing the areas of shared management within Member States.[20]

For pre-accession aid the Commission is overseeing the establishment of adequate systems in the countries concerned. The ECA found problems with both the systems in place and the Commission's supervision and control functions.[21]

The Commission itself is responsible for the control of direct expenditure. In respect of the various internal policies the controls are a mixture of on-the-spot checks and more detailed financial and technical audits. The Commission and external audit firms undertake both these audits. There is a need to reinforce the quality of the audits carried out by the latter and to improve the regulatory framework. Indeed, the nature and complexity of the rules in the RTD area increase the risk of error without this risk being adequately managed by the control systems.[22]

For external actions, audits undertaken by external audit firms on programmes, projects and NGOs are increasingly used. However, again the coverage is small and the procedure needs to be adequately managed. The European Court of Auditors has identified a lack of coherent control strategy for the area in general.[23]

The current control framework has evolved over time, with no clearly defined common objectives. As such it is difficult to:

- establish systems to the required quality;
- define the level of resources needed;
- judge the results they give; and
- provide a baseline for subsequent audit.

This results in systems of internal control procedures that vary in terms of approach and intensity between different parts of the EU budget and between, and within, Member States.

It is sometimes considered that internal control systems should guarantee or assure the legality and regularity of transactions, raising expectations that they should prevent, detect and correct all irregularities. This is unrealistic due to the disproportionate cost of undertaking detail on-the-spot checks imposed by the nature of the expenditure and the large number of geographically dispersed payments.

Four main sources foresee and impose checks on EU income and expenditure:

- the EC Treaty which gives the European Commission overall responsibility for implementing the budget, in cooperation with Member States;
- the EU Financial Regulation which governs how Community funds are to be administered;
- specific Council and Commission regulations for particular budget areas; and
- Member States' rules and practices.

With insufficient coordination the different control functions may be undertaking the same work, resulting in wasted effort, undue inconvenience to the auditee and a poor image of the management and control of EU funds. Certain categories of expenditure may fall outside any effective control remit. Central level checkers are unable to rely on those at a more local level, as inspectors and auditors are reluctant to make their work available for review and use by others.

As explained before, in the areas of shared management (representing over 80 per cent of the budget) the majority of the costs of undertaking controls are borne by Member or beneficiary States. However, the benefit of these controls accrues to the EU budget. This may result in little natural incentive for Member States to devote sufficient resources to controlling EU funds, and explains why the Commission needed to resort to defining the type and intensity of control procedures in regulation.

As no system can reasonably be expected to assure absolute correctness of all transactions, the extent and intensity of checking need to make an appropriate balance between the overall cost of operating those checks and the overall benefits they bring. The benefit can be considered in terms of reducing or containing the incidence of error, irregularity and ineffective use of funds.

Within the current framework no information is available on the cost of controls borne by either Member States or the Commission or on the benefit they bring. Furthermore the fact that much of the cost is borne by the Member States but the benefit accrues to the EU budget results in a lack of transparency and makes it difficult to undertake informed management of the balance between the two.

The detailed checks of underlying transactions are required by the regulatory control frameworks to be undertaken on both a risk and a random basis. However there is a fundamental incompatibility between the purposes of these two approaches as each has very different objectives, and when insufficiently defined in the rules this results in confusion and reduced effectiveness.[24] Even when clearly defined there are problems in implementation, such as in the case of IACS where random testing revealed a higher rate of error than the risk-based testing.[25]

Both the European Commission and the Member States have a high level of decentralization of control procedures, but in practice there is not always consistency in basic matters such as approach, extent, timing, coverage and follow-up. As a consequence, there are significant differences between the quality of checks.

Independent audits of claims or cost statements are used in some areas of the EU budget. The terms of reference setting out how the work is to be undertaken and reported must be improved. Furthermore there are not always standard procedures used for the selection of the auditors.[26]

Publicity about checks is also unsatisfactory, and varies between different schemes and Member States. As a result, beneficiaries often have little perception of the risk of being checked or its consequences, which is likely to reduce the deterrent effect of the system. Furthermore the application of penalties to deter beneficiaries from making incorrect applications is used within agricultural expenditure but not in other budgetary areas.

THE EUROPEAN COMMISSION ADMINISTRATIVE REFORM

General Overview

The Commission's wide-ranging administrative reform programme[27] is focused on implementing improvements in management in general and financial management in particular.

The key principles of the reform are simplification, decentralization and the assumption of greater responsibility by department heads. Rules governing expenditure have been simplified, making them easier to administer and the centralization of the *ex ante* financial control authorization has been replaced by authorization at the level of spending departments. Since 2001 each Directorate-General has had to produce an annual activity report covering financial management for the year, including a declaration by the Director-General attesting that adequate internal controls are in place and resources have been used for their intended purpose. A central Internal Audit Service has been created, together with internal audit capabilities within each Directorate-General. A revised Financial Regulation has been issued and fundamental accounting reform is ongoing.

Along with these measures significant efforts have been made to improve the systems of internal control, taking into account the extent and quality of the control procedures themselves as well as instilling a control culture throughout the organization. This process has been centred on a set of 24 internal control standards[28] that are intended to provide a framework for the control environment and internal control systems. The standards are general in nature. Many of them apply to the control environment and background rather than setting out the approach and objectives of individual controls. Furthermore the standards do not cover the controls to be applied in Member (and beneficiary) States.

The internal control standards were inspired by the COSO[29] framework. An important element of this framework is that it recognizes that internal controls provide reasonable, and not absolute, assurance on the reliability of financial statements, the legality and regularity of transactions and the soundness of financial management. It also recognizes that an effective control framework goes beyond the individual control procedures to take into account the wider issues of the control culture and environment of the organization.

Key elements of the reform process in terms of the control framework are the Director-General's annual activity reports and declarations produced for each Directorate-General. These include a self-assessment about the implementation of the internal control standards, and are intended to provide reasonable assurance that the control procedures put in place give the necessary guarantees concerning the legality and regularity of the underlying transactions.

Impact of Commission's Administrative Reform

Because, as explained before, not all the areas of the EU budget are subject to the same management model, the impact of the Commission's administrative reform varies, according to the area in question.

For own resources, the management is delegated to Member States in relation to the basis of assessment and recovery. In this case, the reform is only concerned with supervision of the management and control arrangements put in place by Member States.

Regarding expenditure, and in accordance with the provisions of the new financial regulation,[30] four different scenarios are foreseen:

- *direct management* – the Commission has sole responsibility for implementing actions on a centralized basis. In this case, the reform affects all the procedures for the management and control of relevant expenditure;
- *shared management* – the Member States' authorities are responsible for operational management (e.g. agriculture and structural measures expenditure) and the Commission must verify that the national administrations' application of the Community regulations has been compliant. In this case, the reform deals only with Commission activities that are related to supervising implementation;
- *decentralized management* – the Commission may leave to the beneficiary states the implementation of certain operational aspects of expenditure once it has performed an *ex ante* control (e.g. preaccession aid). In these circumstances, the reform's impact on most of the management procedures is similar to the one that occurs when the Commission calls on the services of a proxy in a centralized management context;
- *joint management* – the Commission may entrust certain operations to international organizations. In this case, the reform's impact is limited to the Commission's responsibility to ensure that appropriate accounting, audit, control and procurement procedures exist for the programmes managed jointly with those organizations.

The results achieved in the first two years of the reform of the Commission's internal controls show that the effects of the reform are only beginning to be felt.

Despite the satisfactory progress that has been made as regards the reform actions dealing with the regulatory framework, namely those linked to the new financial regulation and its implementing rules, there are others where special and important efforts must be developed, in particular those related to the effective application of the internal control standards and the implementation of a new accounting system.[31] Another aspect that demands further improvement is the Directors-General annual activity reports and declarations. Indeed, while they are in a position to arrive at an opinion on the systems within the Commission, they are unable to do so for systems in Member States in areas of shared management.[32] Furthermore, the Commission has experienced difficulties in employing staff with the necessary financial experience, and instilling an adequate management and control culture within the organization.[33]

ATTRIBUTES OF AN EFFECTIVE AND EFFICIENT EU INTERNAL CONTROL FRAMEWORK

In order to ensure that the European Union budget is subject to effective and efficient internal control, it is fundamental to evolve towards a comprehensive and coherent system – a *European Union Internal Control Framework* – that provides a rational basis for developing existing and new systems to a common standard while aiming for the transparent and optimum use of resources.

For this purpose, it is important to consider the attributes linked to the objectives to achieve, and the conditions for the proper functioning of this framework, its structure and application, as well as those linked to the cost–benefit relation of the control procedures. The roles and responsibilities of the Community and Member State institutions directly or indirectly involved are also a key point to address, even if this framework concerns only internal control over the Community budget.

Objectives

It is vital that the objectives of the EU internal control framework are clearly and comprehensively defined and disseminated. These objectives should define:

- the scope (the entirety of the EU budget);
- the purpose (legality, regularity and sound financial management);
- those involved (all levels of administration from the European Commission through to those paying the final recipients);

- what it comprises (a common standard of controls);
- to what end (to ensure a cost-effective control over the EU budget);
- with what constraints (zero risk of irregularity is not realistic or economic);
- to what extent (appropriate balance between cost and benefit); and
- how (transparent control chain).

The system's efficiency should be achieved by ensuring that controls are undertaken to a common standard, that they are coordinated to avoid unnecessary duplication and that the overall benefit is in proportion to the overall cost. Control procedures should not repeat controls on some operations to the detriment of checking of others. By undertaking checks to a common standard, maximum use can be made of local level control procedures by those at a central level. Efficiency should also be a key element for the use of the human and financial resources required to implement control procedures.

Control procedures are only effective for improving financial management if complete and timely corrective action is taken on errors or weaknesses identified. In this sense, the EU internal control framework should include procedures to ensure that appropriate action is taken such as recovery of funds, or remedying of management and control weaknesses.

In brief, we can say that the *first attribute* of the EU internal control framework is that it should set out the basis for a comprehensive and coherent internal control system for the European Union, providing reasonable assurance that income and expenditure are raised and spent in accordance with the legal provisions, and managed so as to achieve value for money.

Conditions

The EU internal control framework should be a Community system by conception and purpose, albeit implemented by both the European Commission and the Member States. Controls should be undertaken to a common standard, and the work done, results and supporting documents made available to central-level controllers to allow quality review. This is a basic requirement for an effective and transparent control chain where reliance is placed on controls undertaken at a local level, and emphasizes the EU internal control framework as a Community system rather than the work of individual control units or organizations.

The purpose of controls over legality and regularity is to ensure that rules and regulations covering Community income and expenditure are complied with. The rules and regulations should minimize the scope for differing interpretations and not impose requirements that cannot be subsequently verified by controllers or auditors. The more demanding and difficult the requirements, the greater the risks that they will not be followed, either by design or accident. Well-designed rules and regulations contribute to the achievement of the policy objectives set, decrease the risk of error, simplify the controls required and reduce the number and cost of controls necessary for a defined level of risk. Furthermore, legislation could include an incentive for beneficiaries to make accurate claims by extending the use of penalties to all areas of the budget.

A *second attribute* for the EU internal control framework to be effective and efficient is thus that the legislation underlying policy and processes should be clear and unambiguous, sufficient to secure the proper use of funds but not unnecessarily complex. Controls should be undertaken in an open and transparent way, allowing the results to be used and relied on by all parts of the system.

Structure

An effective structure is necessary to enable the EU internal control framework to operate in a way that maximum synergy can be achieved. Without prejudicing the necessary flexibility to accommodate the differences between budgetary areas and the different constitutional and administrative traditions existing in Member States, a chain model could be envisaged, comprising different control levels in Member States and at the European Commission.

Within Member States, the chain may have three control levels:

- *primary controls*, which are those undertaken at local level by the paying organization on the grant application or claim; they will generally comprise administrative checks, together with checks of reality on the spot for claims considered at risk;
- *secondary controls*, which will be undertaken by a functionally separate control unit or organization, and will obtain evidence that the primary systems and controls are operating effectively, and then undertake risk-based checking of transactions in line with the tolerable risk; and
- *high-level controls*, which will be undertaken by Member State central-level control bodies, and will examine the operation of the primary and secondary controls, providing assurance that the control work undertaken at the local and intermediate levels is to the required standard and quality, and thereby allows reliance to be placed on that work.

At the European Commission's level, the DGs' control and audit units will perform supervisory controls on the operation of the EU internal control framework. The intensity of these supervisory controls will be linked to the risk of each budget area and to the evaluation of the working of the EU internal control framework, namely at Member State level.

Both Member States' high-level controls and the Commission's supervisory controls should ensure that appropriate action has been taken to address the weaknesses identified in the different management and control systems.

An independent audit certificate should accompany expenditure claims over a defined threshold, and report on the basis of common standards of approach and content. Beneficiaries should be required to provide a certificate from an independent auditor attesting to the reality, accuracy and compliance with relevant rules and regulations of cost claims. Management of the process needs to take into account the fact that the auditors are selected, engaged and paid by the beneficiary but report to the European Commission, either directly or indirectly, through Member States. Furthermore, by certifying reality and legal aspects the task goes beyond the usual remit of private sector auditors, thus requiring well-defined and supervised terms of reference. The Commission in cooperation with the Member States, by overseeing the homologation and selection of auditors, and reviewing their findings and reports should manage this process.

Given the cost involved this procedure should be used for all claims, or annual series of claims by a beneficiary, over a certain threshold. For direct cost actions the threshold is likely to be lower than shared management expenditure where smaller claims should be more economically controlled by the 'standard' procedures. By making the cost of this certificate eligible for reimbursement by the EU grant in question, the Commission obtains information on the cost of control, and allows better management of the process.

In order to optimize the use of resources, the *third attribute* of the EU internal control framework should be a transparent chain of control procedures undertaken to a common standard at different levels, with each level having specific defined objectives, which take into account the work of the others.

Application

One of the most important elements of the EU internal control framework will be the definition of the minimum requirements or characteristics of the systems administering and controlling Community revenue and expenditure. This will require an analysis and common definition of the basic building block components of systems and control procedures. For the legality and regularity of transactions, aspects to be taken into account include administrative checks, segregation of duties, record keeping, checking of input, control accounts, reconciliation and on-the-spot checks. Controls to ensure value for money may contain some similar elements at the level of transactions but will require a greater emphasis on higher-level procedures and policy review at the Commission's level.

An effective control system requires that controls be undertaken to common standards of method, coverage and quality no matter who undertakes them, and at whatever location. This includes checks on transactions as well as the examination of systems. Rules are required on how the controls are to be undertaken, as well as how the work should be documented. This latter aspect is essential for ensuring openness and transparency in the process.

The common standard should be applied through the use of a common approach to documenting, evidencing and reporting all aspects of the process, including the reason for selection of the transaction or system; objective of the checks; description of the checks undertaken; supporting documentation; results; reaction of those controlled; and follow-up. This information should be maintained in central databases, with access available to all participants in the control process subject to appropriate security safeguards.

One of the key elements of the EU internal control framework is the concept of reliance being placed by central level controllers on controls undertaken by others in the control chain. This requires the central level to have access to the local-level work undertaken as a basis for obtaining assurance that it was done to the common standard.

Control systems should use sampling for clearly defined purposes: risk-based samples should be used to identify and correct irregularities; representative sampling should be used to confirm the effectiveness of the systems. A logical use of sampling within the EU internal control framework would be for primary and secondary-level checkers to use risk-based techniques to identify and correct transactions with error based on the acceptable risk fixed for the budgetary area. The central-level checkers would then use random representative sampling to estimate the actual level of remaining error in the population, in order to confirm compliance with the parameters set.

The EU internal control framework should be accompanied by an effective and coordinated information approach in order that beneficiaries are clearly aware of its objectives and consequences. The more beneficiaries are aware of the existence of an effective system of controls, the greater the efforts they may make to ensure that claims are legal and regular.

The *fourth attribute* for the EU internal control framework should be the definition of minimum requirements for control systems at all levels within the process, taking into account the specific characteristics of the different budgetary areas. Moreover, control procedures should be implemented and documented to a common standard, and the work done and results recorded in a common database and made available to others in the control chain as a basis for placing reliance on them.

Costs and Benefits

Any control system is a trade-off between the cost of operating the defined intensity of checks on the one hand, and the benefit these procedures bring on the other. In the EU context the benefit should take into account containing the risk of error (and thereby wrongly used funds) to a tolerable level. It is likely that the level of tolerable error or irregularity would vary between different budgetary areas, depending on both the cost of controls as well as the inherent risk of transactions containing errors or irregularities (taking into account their nature, and the administrative and legislative backgrounds).

In practice it is highly unlikely that the desired cost–benefit balance would be achieved immediately, but would require fine-tuning over a number of years, taking into account information on costs, and the results and effectiveness of different types and intensities of checking.

The system should record information on the cost of operating controls as well as the benefit in terms of the residual risk of irregularity. To operate effectively the EU internal control framework will require full information, particularly on the cost of operating the controls, and their benefit.

If the EU internal control framework procedures were financed by the EU budget it would facilitate the provision of cost information and provide for greater transparency.

The *fifth attribute* of the EU internal control framework requires specific and open agreement on the intensity of controls by making an appropriate balance between the cost of controlling a particular budgetary area compared with the benefits they bring.

Roles and Responsibilities

Finally, the *sixth attribute* of the EU internal control framework should be a clear understanding of the roles and responsibilities of all the relevant parts and actors directly or indirectly linked to it: European Institutions and Member States' authorities.

According to article 274 of the EC Treaty the European Commission is the institution responsible for the execution of the EU budget, in partnership with Member States. Thus the Commission would be responsible for implementing and monitoring the internal control systems established by the internal control framework, working jointly with Member States in respect of the shared management areas, which cover over 80 per cent of the EU budget. Primary, secondary and high-level controls would be the responsibility of Member State administrations and the Commission should provide assurance that they are operating effectively (supervisory controls).

The EU budgetary authorities (Parliament and Council) should be responsible for establishing the cost–benefit balance inherent within the application of this framework for each different policy area, based on a detailed proposal of the Commission taking into consideration the costs to be devoted to checking income and expenditure, and the risks to be tolerated. It is likely that different budgetary areas will be subject to different levels of balance based on the nature, type and risks of the transactions concerned.

The external auditors – the European Court of Auditors (as the EU independent external auditor) and the Member States' National Audit Institutions – are not, by definition, a direct element of the EU internal control framework. They have, however, a professional interest in its effective running and their tasks would include the audit of its application, providing an independent overview of financial management, including the functioning of internal control systems. Furthermore, international auditing standards[34] require auditors to assess the reliability of internal control when determining the approach and extent of testing, and to make use of the work of other auditors where feasible. This latter aspect requires the other auditors' work to have been undertaken to an acceptable professional standard and be available for review and scrutiny.

For the European Court of Auditors there is a need

> to take into account, and benefit from as much as possible, the internal control systems when carrying out its external audit function. The present audit policies and standards adopted by the Court stated this clearly. The Court, therefore, while at all times maintaining its independence, has every interest in ensuring that its viewpoint on the control and audit system is communicated effectively, and in indicating where improvements in the system should take place. Placing more emphasis on the examination, evaluation and audit of the systems performance as a whole would be the perspective for the Court, primarily through the audit of the functioning of the Commission. This would include the Commission's own internal management, how it met its responsibilities of ensuring that the whole system works effectively, and its establishment and monitoring of indicators which could enable to demonstrate whether or not this is the case. (Caldeira, 2002)

The ECA's professional responsibilities include the audit of internal control systems, and therefore the establishment and implementation of the EU internal control framework. The ECA's audit assessments of the adequacy and effectiveness of control systems will be judged objectively against the baseline set out by this framework.

CONCLUSION

Developing a more effective internal control system in the European Union along the lines outlined above will be considered unrealistic. It may, however, be both realistic and necessary to introduce some of the key elements or attributes identified for the EU internal control framework, which will improve the current situation considerably. A Union of 25 Member States makes this need more pressing. Thus the establishment of a coherent and comprehensive system of internal controls over the EU budget, based on an EU internal control concept and framework to be applied at all levels of administration in the institutions and Member States alike, should be a priority in the context of the protection of the financial interests of the EU.

The EU internal control framework should provide reasonable, but not absolute, assurance[35] on the legality and regularity of transactions, and compliance with the principles of economy, efficiency and effectiveness. The cost of the controls should be in proportion to the benefits they bring. The system should comprise a logical chain structure[36] where controls are undertaken, recorded and reported to a common standard, allowing reliance to be placed on them by all in the system. Many of the building blocks for implementing such a framework are fully or partially in place in the current systems, whereas others will need to be introduced.

To establish and implement a coherent and comprehensive system of internal controls will require the active participation of all parties involved in the financial control of the EU budget. Both improved legislation and work practices are also needed as a level of openness and transparency over the management and control of the EU budget. This will demand considerable commitment from both the institutions and the Member States of the European Union.

NOTES

1. In particular the Commission's White Paper 'Reforming the Commission' (COM (2000) 200 final of 5 April 2000). The initiatives taken under the Commission's programme 'SEM 2000', and the reforms linked to 'Agenda 2000' were the first steps in this direction.

2. See European Parliament Resolution on the discharge for the financial year 2001, point 48 (OJ L 158 of 17 June 2002).
3. The equivalent of 300 billion US dollars.
4. This concept covers state, local government, universities or non-profit organizations.
5. The single audit policy in the Netherlands is formally laid down as a Cabinet's opinion and has as such been discussed with the Tweede Kamer (Parliament's second chamber). There is no legislative act as is the case in the USA. The following policy documents are of prime relevance: letter of the State Secretary of Home Affairs of 7 April 1989 – government's first opinion on single audit, in Tweede Kamer, 1988/1989, 21 8000, VII, no. 33; and letter of the State Secretary of Home Affairs of 8 November 1996 – government's second opinion on single audit, in Tweede Kamer, 1996/1997, 21 8000, VII, no. 33, herdruk.
6. Other experiences in the current EU Member States or abroad (e.g. Canada, New Zealand) can be mentioned. By way of example, we can refer to the current control structure around Structural Fund expenditure in Portugal. The objective of the control structure is to ensure an adequate level of control over EU expenditure for which management is shared but for which the Commission retains ultimate responsibility for sound management. In Portugal, the control framework is established by national control system legislation designed to implement Community requirements. The internal controls are arranged around three levels:

    - the first level concerns the internal audit capabilities within the operational management units responsible for administering the expenditure to final beneficiaries;
    - the second level concerns internal audit or 'inspections' at an intermediate level such as regional administration which covers *inter alia* the functioning of the internal audit at the first level; and
    - the third level comprises the Inspection General of Finance, a central organization responsible for financial control over all state income and expenditure, including coordination of controls at a lower level.

    The purpose of the controls is to cover all aspects of existence and legality and regularity of transactions, as well as recovery of overpaid amounts. The controls are based on risk-based samples of transactions selected by each of the three levels. These controls are subject to a common audit methodology and they are coordinated within the framework of the national internal control system, aimed at ensuring that beneficiaries are only inspected once, and that there is coverage over all areas.
7. Article 274 of the EC Treaty states that the Commission is responsible for implementing the EU budget and that 'Member States shall cooperate with the Commission to ensure that appropriations are used in accordance with the principles of sound financial management'.
8. The management of external actions is currently undergoing a decentralization of management from central Commission services to its delegations.
9. Council Regulation (EEC) 4045/89 (OJ L 388, 30 December 1989, p. 18).
10. These include namely the European Regional Development Fund (ERDF), the European Social Fund (ESF) and the Cohesion Fund.
11. Council Regulation (EC) 1260/99, (OJ L 161, 26 June 1999, p. 1).
12. Commission Regulation (EC) 2064/97 (OJ L 290, 23 October 1997, p. 1) and Commission Regulation (EC) 438/01 (OJ L 63, 3 March 2001, p. 21).
13. It comprises three main funds – Sapard, which relates to rural development, and PHARE and ISPA which concern structural development.
14. See article 248 of the EC Treaty.
15. See article 248-3 of the EC Treaty and declaration 18 annex to the Nice Treaty that foresees the creation of a Contact Committee of the Heads of the NAIs of the EU Member States and the ECA.
16. The National Audit Office of the United Kingdom.

17. OJ C 286, 28 November 2003, p. 1.
18. ECA annual report – financial year 2002, Chapter 3, paragraphs 3.14–3.17 (OJ C 286, 28 November 2003).
19. ECA annual report – financial year 2002, Chapter 4, paragraph 4.49 and Annex II (OJ C 286, 28 November 2003).
20. ECA annual report – financial year 2002, Chapter 5, paragraph 5.32 (OJ C 286, 28 November 2003).
21. ECA annual report – financial year 2002, Chapter 8, paragraphs 8.45–8.48 (OJ C 286, 28 November 2003).
22. ECA annual report – financial year 2002, Chapter 6, paragraphs 6.46, 6.59 and Annex II (OJ C 286, 28 November 2003).
23. ECA annual report – financial year 2002, Chapter 7, paragraphs 7.40 and 7.44 (OJ C 286, 28 November 2003).
24. See ECA Special Report 10/2001concerning the financial control of the structural funds (OJ C314, 8 November 2001).
25. ECA annual report – financial year 2002, paragraph 4.51 (OJ C 286, 28 November 2003).
26. ECA annual report – financial year 2002, paragraphs 7.24–7.27 and 8.11 (OJ C 286, 28 November 2003).
27. Commission's White Paper 'Reforming the Commission' (COM (2000) 200 final of 5 April 2000).
28. The internal control standards were adopted on 13 December 2000 (SEC (2000) 2203) and amended in 2001 (SEC (2001) 2037 of 21 December 2001).
29. Committee of Sponsoring Organization of the 'Treadway Commission'. See http://www.coso.org.
30. See article 53 of the Council Regulation 1605/2002 of 25 June 2002 (OJ L 248, 16 September 2002).
31. ECA annual report – financial year 2002, Chapter 1, paragraphs 1.108–1.110 (OJ C 286, 28 November 2003).
32. ECA annual report – financial year 2002, Chapter 1, paragraph 1.97 (OJ C 286, 28 November 2003).
33. ECA annual report – financial year 2002, General Introduction, paragraph 0.8 (OJ C 286, 28 November 2003). See also section 3.2 of the Commission's Synthesis of Annual Activity Reports 2002 (COM (2003) 391 of 9 July 2003). For an overall assessment of the reform, see the Commission's Communication 'Progress Review of Reform' (COM (2003) 40 final of 30 January 2003).
34. The distinction between external audit and internal control, as well as their relation, is set out clearly in the international audit standards and in the INTOSAI Lima Declaration of Guidelines on Auditing Precepts. For example, ISA 620 highlights the role of internal auditing as being determined by management, with objectives varying according to management's requirements. The objectives and reporting lines are within the entity being audited. The external auditor, on the other hand, is outside the entity and is appointed to report independently. The Lima Declaration provides that, as the external auditor, the Supreme Audit Institution has the task of examining the effectiveness of internal audit. If internal audit is judged effective, efforts shall be made to achieve the most appropriate division or assignment of tasks and cooperation between the Supreme Audit Institution and internal audit, without prejudice to the right of the first one to carry out an overall audit.
35. According to INTOSAI's first internal control standard, 'reasonable assurance equates to a satisfactory level of confidence under given considerations of costs, benefits and risks'. See INTOSAI Guidance for Reporting on the Effectiveness of Internal Controls in http://www.intosai.org/3_ICExpe.html.
36. The structure of individual systems will need to be adapted to take account of the specific characteristics of the different budgetary areas and also the different administrative and constitutional traditions in the Member States.

REFERENCES

Ball, Ian (November 2002), 'The Single Audit and its Preconditions – Governance, Controls, Accounting and Audit', p. 9, presented to the Verstehen Workshop 2002 – 'Single Audit in Europe?', available at http://europa.eu.int/comm/dgs/internal_audit/verstehen_en.htm.

Caldeira, Vítor (2001), 'Le contrôle des fonds structurels au Portugal', *Revue Française de Finances Publiques*, **74**, April, pp. 103–10.

Caldeira, Vítor (November 2002), 'The Single Audit – from the point of view of the European Court of Auditors', pp. 2 and 5, presented to the Verstehen Workshop 2002 – 'Single Audit in Europe?', available at http://www.eca.eu.int/EN/DISCOURS/caldeira_261102.htm.

Flizot, Stéphanie (November 2002), 'European Landscaping', summary of the presentation to the Verstehen Workshop 2002 – 'Single Audit in Europe?', available at http://europa.eu.int/comm/dgs/internal_audit/verstehen_en.htm.

Government Accounting Office, GAO-AIMD-96-77 (March 1996), *Single Audit Refinements Can Improve Usefulness*, p. 2.

Grants Management Committee, Chief Financial Officers Council (October 2001), 'Highlights of the Single Audit Process', p. 4, available at http://www.cfoc.gov.

Harlow, Carol (2002), *Accountability in the European Union*, Academy of European Law, European University Institute. Oxford: Oxford University Press, Chapter 5, 'Accountability through audit', pp. 108–30.

National Audit Office (1996), *State Audit in the European Union*. London: Commercial Colour Press.

9. Towards the coordination of financial reporting at the different levels of public administration in Europe

Vicente Montesinos Julve

Although it is at the heart of growing controversy, the fact is that globalization appears to be a sign of our times, a phenomenon deriving from the growing internationalization and interdependence of economies. Fiscal austerity, privatization and market liberalization have been, for the World Bank and International Monetary Fund (IMF), the three basic pillars of sustainable economic growth, especially in the case of developing countries (Stiglitz, 2002). However, the truth is that liberalizing mechanisms have, in many respects, not worked in the way they should have done, leading to the emergence of justified criticisms of the globalization process, especially concerning economically weaker countries.

In spite of the criticisms and controversies caused by the deficient operation and undesirable effects of liberalizing mechanisms, globalization is a phenomenon from which, for the moment, there appears to be no way back. Therefore, the mechanisms required for its proper functioning must intervene, eliminating barriers and privileges and introducing transparency and competitiveness as essential features.[1]

In this context, the availability of quality information appears to be a clear requirement: the comparability of financial information seems more necessary, the availability of analytical information becomes more urgent with a view towards the modernization of public administrations, and complete, systematic and reliable macroeconomic information is essential. Only in this way will the globalization process be really effective, in that only transparency can make reasonably just and equitable international relations possible.

In the same way, regional integration is another phenomenon characterizing our times, deriving from the need to set up expanded markets that make a better competitive position and stronger economic development possible for its members; this is the case with the European Communities or the Common Market of the Southern Cone (MERCOSUR) in the southern part of Latin America. Around these expanded markets, more ambitious political projects may also emerge, as is happening with the European Union.

Focusing on the European case, the setting up of an integrated monetary system within the European Economic and Monetary Union has made it necessary to design policies for convergence and stability within the Euro zone, whose guiding principles are stable prices, solid public finances and monetary conditions, and a stable balance of payments. From the financial point of view, these conditions take shape in the short-term maintenance of the public deficit below 3 per cent of GNP and a public debt of no more than 60 per cent of the country's GNP, as laid down in the Stability and Growth Pact (SGP).

This scenario has a significant influence on the area of accounting of public bodies, although this is uneven depending on the country and the level of administration we are looking at. The deficit and debt are quantified in accordance with national accounting criteria, as included in SEC 95. This involves the generalized use of accrual criteria and the incorporation into the public administration sector of bodies whose income from the market does not cover 50 per cent of their costs, regardless of the legal form they take. Figure 9.1 shows the expression of the various

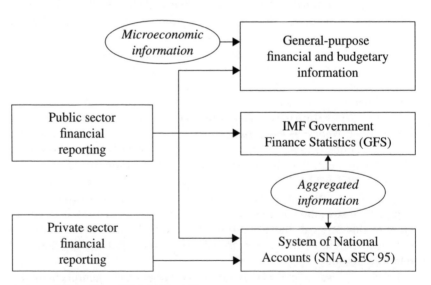

Source: Adapted from IFAC (2000), p. 88.

Figure 9.1   Public sector financial information systems

information systems made up of data from public sector bodies: micro-economic ones leading to the presentation of financial and budgetary accounts for each body, and macroeconomic systems including aggregate magnitudes, such as those structured in Systems of National Accounts and International Monetary Fund government statistics.

This quantification of deficit and debt also requires that, in the micro-economic financial information from public bodies, established magnitudes are drawn up and presented in accordance with national accounting system criteria. This will make it possible to draw up more reliable macroeconomic accounts for the public sector and compare the contribution of each body to the aggregate amount, as well as verifying whether the generally established criteria and targets are being met at an individual level. In our case, these are the public deficit and debt limits for Economic and Monetary Union (EMU) Member States.

When national accounting criteria are also introduced into the accounting of individual public bodies, they must consider four areas or subsystems, properly coordinated and integrated with one another, when they prepare the information necessary for turning in their accounts and taking decisions properly. These four areas are as follows:

1. The area of budgetary information, which is the traditional one and, until recently, practically the only one attended to by public bodies;
2. Financial/asset information, collected by the financial information subsystem and intended to present a faithful image of assets, the financial situation and results;
3. Information in accordance with national accounting methodology, with a double facet: aggregate accounts, and the incorporation into microeconomic accounts of certain magnitudes, such as deficit and debt, established in accordance with System of National Accounts (SNA) criteria (included in ESA 1995 for the European sphere);
4. Finally, analytical information and management indicators referring to effectiveness, economy and efficiency and the impact of the management of public bodies.

Regional integration, therefore, has a special influence in the area of approximation between micro- and macroeconomic accounting and an equally positive effect should be expected concerning microeconomic accounting harmonization, although this effect is proving less significant in the European sphere than might have been expected or at least desired. Ultimately, comparability of public accounting information is an essential instrument for proper decision-making and transparency in the actions of public sector bodies.

In addition, the principles of good governance and market efficiency proposed for supranational areas are factors which, at least in the medium and long terms, should drive the other aspects we mention, such as the development of analytical accounting and management indicators.

In this environment, we can better understand the importance, significance and scope of efforts to develop international public accounting standards and it would be logical to expect determined support from national governments for their implementation, ensuring comparability that would improve transparency and make it possible to detect and eliminate inefficiencies. Because of this, it seems that the first consequence of globalization and regional integration in the field of public accounting may be the development and implementation of common standards for public bodies, regardless of the country or geopolitical region where they carry on their activities.

Figure 9.2 shows, in schematic form, the socioeconomic factors driving the development of public accounting information and the main ways in which the reforms undertaken in it are taking shape.

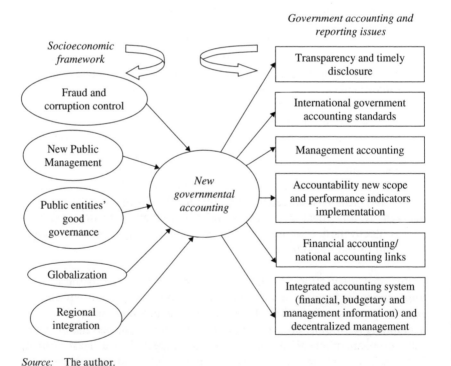

Source: The author.

Figure 9.2   The new governmental accounting

TOWARDS INTERNATIONAL HARMONIZATION OF FINANCIAL REPORTING BY PUBLIC BODIES

An important feature of international trends in public sector financial reporting is the implementation of significant reforms in most countries' public sector accounting models. The extent of these reforms has been rather varied and they have even reached the financial reporting objectives and the registration procedures in use.

A common characteristic of all the reforms undergone in most countries is the interest in providing public sector accounting with broader content. The final objective is to make information more useful for decision-making. Thus a quite generalized modification arises in the traditional notion of public sector accounting, which in most countries has always been orientated towards the rendering of accounts and legal control, under the influence of budget regulations and public resource management.

Briefly, the following features of the reforms undertaken can be highlighted:

- Double entry accounting, according to generally accepted accounting principles, moving towards the private accounting model. Australia and New Zealand lead this initiative to make both accounting systems converge.
- Attention to the budgetary procedure, integrated as a subsystem of the public sector information management system or independently designed, tending gradually towards the full accrual basis of accounting.
- Closer links between public sector accounting and national accounts criteria. The objective is to make comparisons and reconciliations easier and safer.
- Development of public financial reporting adapted to New Public Management (NPM) principles and methodology. Information is orientated towards decision-making and responsibilities are assigned with a view towards the rendering of accounts. In most countries, the reforms are part of a wider process of change and modernization of public management, with the final objective being to control public expenditure and improve the quality of public administration.
- Harmonization of accounting systems, with an international focus that requires the development of worldwide standards. Documents and pronouncements by the Public Sector Committee of the International Federation of Accountants (IFAC-PSC) are the most important result of this process.

- Accounting information systems as a tool for both internal management and external accountability.

Even though different institutions are working on governmental accounting harmonization, as is the case with the International Organization of
Supreme Audit Institutions (INTOSAI), their pronouncements have very
limited influence. In the case of the European Federation of Accountants
(FEE), support for the IFAC International Public Sector Accounting
Standards (IPSASs) is considered as the best policy for governmental
accounting harmonization in Europe.[2]

Moreover, IFAC accounting projects are closely coordinated with those
of the International Accounting Standards Board (IASB) in the development of standards for business accounting. This circumstance gives a
pre-eminence to IPSASs on any other pronouncements on governmental
accounting, as the most effective way of building up international standards. The aim is not to divide efforts, but to focus them on a single set of
pronouncements, with common roots in international business accounting
standards issued by IASB. Therefore, the only international governmental
standards we will consider hereafter are IFAC-PSC's IPSASs.

The standards attempt to enhance the comparability of financial
statements around the world, but neither the Committee nor the accounting profession has the power to require compliance with IPSAS. Moreover,
IPSASs do not override the regulations of general purpose financial statements in a particular jurisdiction. Each regulatory body has to decide about
the adoption of IPSASs, and the Committee strongly encourages their
adoption and the harmonization of national requirements with them. The
success of the Committee's efforts is dependent on the recognition and
support for its work from many different interest groups acting within the
limits of their own jurisdictions.

Up to February 2004, 20 standards had been issued, all of them based
on the corresponding IASB standards (Figure 9.3). The Committee has
also issued two guidelines, 14 studies and a Cash Basis IPSAS ('Financial
Reporting under Cash Basis of Accounting').

Another important international project on the harmonization of
financial reporting is the convergence of IPSASs with national accounts
systems[3] as a result of the cooperation of the IFAC-PSC, IMF, Organization
for Economic Cooperation and Development (OECD), Eurostat, European
Central Bank, Australian Accounting Standards Board, UK Treasury and
UK Office of National Statistics. A task force has been set up on the convergence of these systems, with the aim of promoting convergence of
the requirements of IPSASs, GFSM 2001 and ESA 1995 where appropriate,
and making recommendations for the revision of SNA (scheduled for 2008).

IPSAS 1	Presentation of financial statements
IPSAS 2	Cash flow statements
IPSAS 3	Net surplus or deficit for the period, fundamental errors and changes in accounting policies
IPSAS 4	The effects of changes in foreign exchange rates
IPSAS 5	Borrowing costs
IPSAS 6	Consolidated financial statements and accounting for controlled entities
IPSAS 7	Accounting for investments in associates
IPSAS 8	Financial reporting of interest in joint ventures
IPSAS 9	Revenue from exchange transactions
IPSAS 10	Financial reporting in hyperinflationary economies
IPSAS 11	Construction contracts
IPSAS 12	Inventories
IPSAS 13	Leases
IPSAS 14	Events after the reporting date
IPSAS 15	Financial instruments: disclosure and presentation
IPSAS 16	Investment property
IPSAS 17	Property, plant and equipment
IPSAS 18	Segment reporting
IPSAS 19	Provisions, contingent liabilities and contingent assets
IPSAS 20	Related party disclosures

Source: The author.

Figure 9.3   International Public Sector Accounting Standards (IPSASs)

If we analyse IPSASs, we can see that their main characteristics are the pressure of business accounting standards and the influence of the Anglo-Saxon tradition.

With respect to the first characteristic, it is becoming increasingly clear that reliable, clear and comprehensible information on accounting is a *sine qua non* for the smooth operation of the financial market, as the International Organization of Securities Commissions (IOSCO) showed when it adopted international accounting standards for quoted companies in 2000. IFAC accounting projects are closely coordinated with those of the IASB in developing standards for business accounting. This responds to the interest in approximating the public accounting system to the business accounting system so homogeneity can be achieved both between the two types of bodies and between bodies in different countries. This is a very important decision in the international context of public accounting, which has already been adopted by many regulatory bodies at national level. However, there are academics and professionals who think that public administrations have characteristics justifying accounting systems different to those of the business sector and they therefore criticize the position adopted by the IFAC (Chan, 2002). As a consequence of the close links between public bodies and business accounting standards, IFAC-PSC is adapting its standards to IASs and it is certain (at the time of writing) that a process to harmonize IPSASs with IASs, which were improved in 2003, will take place in the next few months.

On the other hand, the pre-eminence of the Anglo-Saxon tradition may be due to the composition of the Committee, as well as to the important influence the culture of these countries has traditionally had in the international accounting context, both in the private and in the public sector. So IPSASs have not yet taken into account some aspects of the continental European model, which may be important in establishing international standards. Neither have they yet considered some specific features that government bodies may have, such as differences in the sources of incomes, the treatment of infrastructure assets, budgetary reporting and the meaning that can be attributed to the results. Some of these issues, however, are included in IFAC-PSC projects and future developments, as in the case of the ITC[4] on *Revenue from Non-Exchange Transactions (Including Taxes and Transfers)* which deals with the recognition and measurement of revenue from non-exchange transactions and the project on the consideration by IFAC-PSC of the published budgets of public sector bodies.[5]

These two main characteristics raise an essential question regarding the international harmonization of governmental accounting standards: can or should the IFAC accounting principles and standards set up by IPSASs be considered as the only generally accepted international accounting principles? In fact, public bodies – the OECD, NATO and the European Commission – have recently been striving to bring their accounting systems into line with international standards. However, even when IFAC is developing an active policy before national governments and international institutions to achieve real government Generally Accepted Accounting Practices (GGAAP) and the introduction of IPSASs in the medium term, it is still too early to consider IPSASs as the effective generally accepted international rules for public bodies, as governmental practices and traditions are still very diverse in the international context.

ACCOUNTING AND BUDGETING SYSTEMS OF CENTRAL GOVERNMENTS AND DECENTRALIZED JURISDICTIONS IN EUROPE

There are two types of accounting system in the international environment: commercially driven systems and government-driven systems. Belonging to the first category are those built under the British influence, with a strong effect from professional regulation (as is the case with Australia, New Zealand, the United Kingdom and Ireland) and the systems of American influence, where the requirements of stock exchange control bodies are fundamental (Canada, the USA). As far as the second category is concerned, the government-driven systems are all characterized by the significant role played by public bodies in accounting regulation. Among those systems, those based on the existence of a Chart of Accounts, as is the case in France, Belgium and Spain should be highlighted.

In the European framework, accounting standardization begin in the 1960s, using Community Directives (Fourth Directive, concerning companies' annual accounts, and the Seventh Directive, regulating consolidated accounts) for this process. From the second half of the 1980s a stagnation of the European standardization process could be observed, which then underwent a complete change of direction from the second half of the 1990s, in order to ultimately approximate to international standards. This process involved a major change after stagnation, with the introduction of commercially driven IAS/IFRS[6] into a government-driven system as the European Accounting Framework. This fundamental change will finally be carried out by means of regulations as normative support, characterized by their direct application in the Member States. This is different from Directives, whose application requires the prior adoption of national legislation: the Regulations passed in 2002 represent the starting point of the normative part of this new step, which will result in the adoption of IFRSs for the consolidated accounts of listed groups before 1 January 2005. It should be emphasized that the new scheme requires the practically automatic introduction of standards issued by a professional private body in the public legal standards of the Union and its Member States.

Special emphasis will be necessary in the field of enforcement mechanisms, as the FEE has undertaken to stress in a specific document, in order to prevent, and thereafter identify and correct, material errors or omissions in the application of IFRSs in financial information and other regulatory statements issued to the public. These mechanisms could be organized on a proactive or a reactive basis and be applied to listed companies, public interest companies and other companies using IFRSs. For the establishment of these mechanisms, the principle of subsidiarity should be followed, with the possibility of adopting two models: on one hand a securities regulator (Commission des Opérations de Bourse, COB; Commissione Nazionale per le Società e la Borsa, CONSOB; Comisión Nacional del Mercado de Valores, CNMV) or, on the other, a review panel, made up of stakeholders for this specific purpose, as in the case of the UK.

As in the case with business accounting, governmental accounting systems can be classified as continental or Anglo-Saxon in nature. The continental accounting tradition can be associated with the family of German and Roman legal systems, while the Anglo-Saxon accounting tradition is normally linked with the 'common law' legal system family (see Salter and Doupnik, 1992).

Continental accounting systems have a macroeconomic basis, connected with a more bureaucratic design of accounting principles and standards, which have been established by public bodies as legal or administrative rules. The main objective of financial statements within this tradition is the fulfilment of legal and administrative rules when reporting financial information. This is the case with Germany, France, Belgium, Spain, Italy and Portugal, in Europe, and most of the economically influential countries in Latin-America, such as Argentina, Brazil, Chile and Colombia (see Montesinos and Vela, 1996, 2000).

In continental European countries, the budget has been traditionally almost the only element in governmental accounting and there has been a lack of business accounting influence until recently. In the same way, accountability has not really been developed, as financial statements are prepared because of compulsory legal requirements. Hence, they are more oriented towards internal departments of the public administration itself (closed accountability approach) than towards a broader range of mainly external users (open accountability approach). Little attention has been paid to effectiveness, efficiency and financial indicators. External audit has not been sufficiently developed and in some cases, such as in Spain (Montesinos, 2000), very few municipalities have periodic independent external audit (in fact, of the large Spanish towns and cities, only Barcelona has an independent annual audit).

On the other hand, Anglo-Saxon accounting systems have a microeconomic basis, connected with a non-bureaucratic design of accounting principles and standards, set up by private professional accounting bodies. The main objective of financial statements is faithful representation of the body's real economic and financial position, in such a way that transactions and events are accounted for and presented in accordance with their financial substance and not merely their legal form. This is the tradition of the United Kingdom and Ireland in Europe, and the USA, Canada, Australia and New Zealand in the rest of the world. Unlike continental countries, the Anglo-Saxon European countries have reported to users in a more open way (open approach), including non-financial information. Business accounting has had a relevant influence. External and independent audits have a very long tradition in these countries.

This duality of accounting models remains and becomes even more pronounced, if possible, among public bodies than it is in the business field (see IFAC, 2000). Therefore, while globalization in economies has strongly fostered harmonization of business accounting, European public administration accounting has not evolved in a similar way, so substantial diversity still exists.

So a European governmental accounting model does not yet exist and the systems in continental and Anglo-Saxon countries are the two models we can describe in Europe, bearing in mind that, when grouping the different systems into these two models, only their basic characteristics are taken into consideration.

Moreover, the majority of practitioners and academics involved in public sector management agree that governmental accounting must be reformed in Europe and that important decisions are necessary. It is also true that all national reforms are moving towards the introduction of accrual accounting and the accounting practices generally accepted in the business sector. The EU institutions are also adapting their accounting system to these principles.

As shown in Figure 9.4, most European countries and the European Commission have accounting reforms in progress, moving through accrual basis models. In some cases, as with central government in Switzerland, Spain, Finland and Sweden, and local government in France, Finland, the Netherlands and United Kingdom, the reform process has been completed. However, very important jurisdictions, such as central government in Germany, Italy and the Netherlands, have not yet started it. These processes have developed at different dates in 'waves', as shown in Figure 9.4; the most important changes took place in the 1990s, but after 2000 there is a wider application of accrual, and therefore harmonization becomes a more realistic target for European governments and institutions (see Lüder and Jones, 2003, pp. 19–21).

Europe, then, still lacks clearly defined and truly generally accepted accounting standards. In these circumstances, auditors cannot refer their opinions on financial statements to unambiguous and specific accounting and reporting principles, irrespective of the country or region where the audited public body is established or its activities are going on. Unless clear and uniform standards are available, governmental financial statements will hardly be useful for users and it will be rather difficult to operate with confidence and financial safety in a proper European public sector.

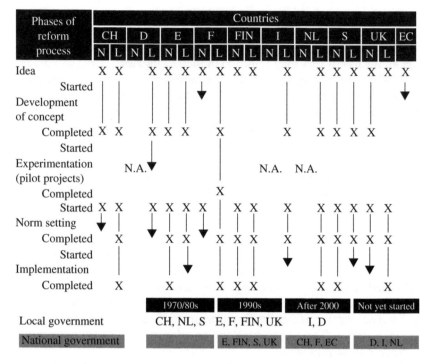

Phases of reform process	Countries																			
	CH		D		E		F		FIN		I		NL		S		UK		EC	
	N	L	N	L	N	L	N	L	N	L	N	L	N	L	N	L	N	L	N	L

```
Idea                    X X     X X X X X X X       X   X X X X X X
        Started
Development
of concept
        Completed X X     X X X       X           X       X X X X
        Started
Experimentation   N.A.                          N.A.   N.A.
(pilot projects)
        Completed                 X
        Started  X X     X X X X   X X       X     X X X X X
Norm setting
        Completed  X     X X     X X X       X     X X X X X
        Started
Implementation
        Completed  X       X       X X X           X X           X
```

	1970/80s	1990s	After 2000	Not yet started
Local government	CH, NL, S	E, F, FIN, UK	I, D	
National government		E, FIN, S, UK	CH, F, EC	D, I, NL

Note: N = National; L = Local; CH = Switzerland; D = Germany; E = Spain; F = France; FIN = Finland; I = Italy; NL = The Netherlands; S = Sweden; UK = United Kingdom; EC = European Communities.

Source: Lüder and Jones (2003), pp. 20–21.

Figure 9.4 Phases and dates of accrual accounting reform

Accounting harmonization is now an essential requirement for the effective coordination of audit and public expenditure control functions, not only within the European Union, but in the wider economic and political area of the European and Mediterranean countries.[7]

Even though governmental accounting harmonization may be considered less important than the case of business accounting, because no international market information requirements arise, as we have discussed there are other important reasons supporting the importance of comparability for governmental information, especially for countries belonging to the European Union.

Governmental accounting harmonization can therefore generate outcomes similar to those in the business sector, as accounting diversity in public bodies leads to a lack of comparability of financial information and makes interpretation of financial statements difficult even for users aware of accounting principles and practices – and much more so for non-expert users of public bodies' financial reports.

The IFAC international public sector accounting standards (IPSASs) are now bursting strongly onto the European scene. Ultimately, these standards are currently the most important factor in the realm of international accounting harmonization for public bodies, as the other variables traditionally considered have not really worked as a useful tool for approaching public sector financial reporting in Europe.

In this context, we consider that it is of paramount importance to be aware of current developments in public sector accounting in the international arena. This is why projects for international cooperation in the fields of public sector micro- and macroaccounting are, in our opinion, the most useful and relevant way – in fact the only way – to achieve financial transparency and the fair comparability of European financial reporting, by both national governments and European institutions. Active involvement of European countries and institutions in these international projects, such as the IFAC, OECD, IMF, and United Nations (UN) World Bank[8] ones, becomes not only a challenge, but a real necessity and an essential tool for improving the governance, accountability and efficiency of the public sector in Europe.

Adaptation of national accounting norms to international standards should be done according to national legal procedures; unlike standards for listed companies, there is not a European jurisdiction for adopting accounting rules for national governments at central, regional or local levels. As different procedures and regulatory bodies exist in European countries, the process becomes more complex and its implementation takes longer (see Figure 9.5 for central government norm and rule-setting processes). Even though these characteristics are barriers to harmonization, the reform of European institutions' accounting systems to meet IPSASs will no doubt foster the adaptation of Systems of National Accounts to international standards as the best deal for the effective harmonization of public sector financial reporting in Europe.

ACCOUNTING AND BUDGETING IN EUROPEAN INSTITUTIONS

Components of the System

Budget and financial accounting are the two components of the information system in the European Communities. Traditionally, budgetary information occupies a primary position in the system, with the objective of

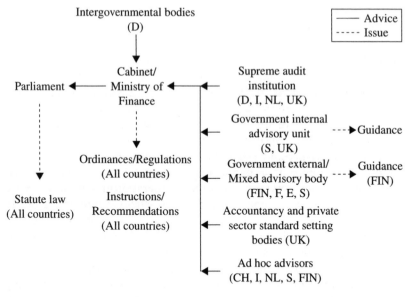

Source: Lüder and Jones (2003), p. 42.

Figure 9.5   Norm and rule setting for national governments in Europe

demonstrating that the established expenditure limits have been respected, as well as reporting the budgetary result. In addition to this, accounting information is prepared in order to allow an evaluation of the Commission's financial management and make public the net worth of the EU's institutions.

Budgetary information encompasses the European budget and its implementation, both revenues and expenses, reporting the origin and application of resources. This information is basically drawn up on a modified cash basis, as a result of the recognition of budgetary rights and obligations.

The aim of the financial accounting area is fair presentation of the economic and financial position of the European Communities. Using the double-entry method, the general accounts are prepared on the modified accrual basis of accounting, although they are moving closer to full accrual accounting. Specifically, the annual balance is obtained using the modified accrual basis, because the general method is to record the operations when the payment is made or the revenue is received, although appropriations carried over are considered as expenditure when calculating the balance for the year. However, the balance sheet shows the European Union's assets and liabilities, including fixed assets.

General Framework and Main Objectives of Reform of the System

In recent years, a lively controversy about the soundness of the European institutions' accounting system, with particular reference to the Commission, has hit the headlines. It has been argued that the accounts system is outdated, lacking the proper safeguards, and out of line with the most basic accounting principles. All of this has happened in an atmosphere of distrust and denigration of the accountancy profession and the activities of audit firms, following the scandals in major corporations such as Enron, WorldCom and Xerox, and the extraordinary measures taken in the USA in response to the scepticism with which investors now treat information in companies' financial statements.

The gravity and the scale of accounting fraud and impropriety in these large companies has no parallel in public institutions in the West – or at any rate no one has been able to prove that comparable situations exist in the public sector. So it would be wrong and misleading if the crisis of confidence in the mega-corporations were to be extended to accounting and auditing in public bodies. However, the failure of the Santer Commission revealed the need to undertake in-depth reform of the financial and monitoring mechanisms used by the EU institutions, and this reform is doubtless being carried out in the awareness that there is a need to make up for lost time.

The reform of the accounting and budgetary system is a project that began in 2000, based on a preliminary study ordered by the DG Budget (Montesinos et al., 2000). The modernization of the accounting system addresses three principal objectives:[9]

- compliance with recently developed and internationally accepted accounting principles for the public sector, as stated by the IPSAS and IFRS;
- integration of the financial and accounting systems held on different computer platforms; and
- improving the functioning of the present system, in particular concerning security and consistency between data from different sources.

The guiding principle for the implementation of the system, from an operational point of view is 'decentralized implementation, centralized information', which means an integrated accounting system where data are entered only once and events are recorded as soon as they occur.

Recent years have therefore seen the gradual introduction of reforms and improvements, the aim being to get ever closer to the idea of an 'accurate record' of the Commission's economic and financial situation. Thus the information content of the accounts is both expanding and improving, the quantification of risks and commitments has been modified (in 2001, for the first time, 15,300 million euros of pension commitments were recognized), off-balance sheet transactions are set out more clearly, and so on.

The Legal Framework for the Reform: The 2002 Financial Regulation

A significant issue which is worth mentioning because of its importance in the field of financial reporting is undoubtedly the adoption of the new Financial Regulation, concerning the European Communities budget and accounts, by Council Regulation.[10] According to this Regulation, the 2005 annual accounts should be drawn up on a full accrual basis, as required by IPSASs. This means a new phase will then begin for the financial reporting of European institutions, with more relevant data for economic decisions and management evaluation, allowing a broad comparability of its information as a result of adopting international accounting standards.

Budgetary rules, accounting and control, both internal and external, are the main subjects of the Financial Regulation. The most important innovations are undoubtedly managers' direct responsibility for the substance of the statements they issue and the data they provide for incorporation into the general information, collectively prepared and presented by the Commission; accounting harmonization with generally accepted principles; and the new role of internal control, adapted to administrative reform and the newly designed managers' responsibilities.

The Financial Regulation clearly defines the powers and responsibilities of the authorizing officer, the accounting officer and the internal auditor, in accordance with Article 279(c) of the Treaty. Decentralization of responsibilities is one of the features of the new framework, as recommended by New Public Management principles and trends. This decentralization implies deep changes in the scope of functions and responsibilities of authorizing officers and internal auditors.

Authorizing officers are made fully responsible for all revenue and expenditure operations carried out under their authority and must be held accountable for their actions, including, where necessary, the use of disciplinary proceedings.

The empowerment of authorizing officers requires changes in old control mechanisms. Previous centralized controls, and in particular the advance approval of revenue and expenditure operations by the financial controller, must be removed, with the check by the accounting officer considered a valid discharge.

The accounting officer retains his or her traditional responsibilities and continues to be responsible for the proper execution of payments, the collection of revenue and the recovery of receivables; treasury management is also among the officer's functions. From the accounting and reporting point of view he or she has the most important responsibility, as the person responsible for keeping the accounts and drawing up the institution's financial statements.

Finally, the reform of the internal control system is very far-reaching, and an Anglo-Saxon model has been adopted. The internal auditor is not involved in financial operations and performs his or her duties independently, in accordance with international audit standards, verifying the proper functioning of the management and control systems put in place by the authorizing officers. Unlike the previous continental financial control system, the internal auditor does not exercise control over operations ahead of the decisions by the authorizing officers.

Each institution establishes its own internal audit function and appoints an internal auditor, different from the accounting and authorizing officers. This internal auditor will be answerable to the institution for verifying the proper operation of budgetary implementation systems and procedures. He or she will issue recommendations for improving the conditions for implementing operations and promoting sound financial management.

Reporting on the European Budget and its Implementation

Based on the principles shown in Figure 9.6, the European budget will be implemented without material changes to the current system. The recognition of revenue and expenditure will be done on a modified cash basis: revenue is recognized when collected and expenditure when payments are made or the amounts are committed. The distinction between differentiated and non-differentiated appropriations is retained by the new Financial Regulation, in spite of the existence of critical warnings on its usefulness and appropriateness for budgetary management. Differentiated appropriations will consist of commitment appropriations and payment appropriations, and decisions on carryovers of commitment and payment appropriations will be taken by each institution.

The budget comprises a summary statement of revenue and expenditure, and separate sections subdivided into revenue and expenditure statements for each institution. The expenditure for the Commission section will be classified on the basis of three criteria: economic (what resources), organic (who spends them) and functional (what is the spending for). A title will correspond to a policy area and a chapter will, as a rule, correspond to an activity. Economic classification will allow clear links between budgetary figures and financial accounts, while the differentiation of current and capital items in budgets makes the assignment of transactions to revenues

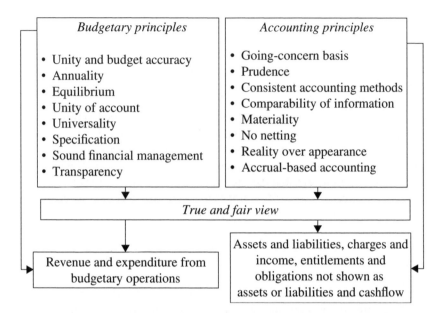

Budgetary principles	Accounting principles
• Unity and budget accuracy • Annuality • Equilibrium • Unity of account • Universality • Specification • Sound financial management • Transparency	• Going-concern basis • Prudence • Consistent accounting methods • Comparability of information • Materiality • No netting • Reality over appearance • Accrual-based accounting

True and fair view

| Revenue and expenditure from budgetary operations | Assets and liabilities, charges and income, entitlements and obligations not shown as assets or liabilities and cashflow |

Figure 9.6   The main principles and objectives of budgetary and financial reporting

and expenses for the year's income, or to assets, liabilities or equity, easier in the financial position statement.

The European budget is implemented by the Commission according to the following methods:[11]

1. centralized management, that may be carried out directly by Commission departments or indirectly by delegation to bodies governed by Community law or by national public law;
2. management shared with Member States or on a decentralized basis with third countries receiving external aid; or
3. joint management with international organizations.

When implementing the budget on a centralized basis and indirectly by delegation, the Commission may entrust tasks of public authority and in particular budget implementation tasks to (a) agencies governed by Community law (executive agencies); (b) bodies set up by the Communities; and (c) national public sector bodies or bodies governed by private law with a public service mission providing adequate financial guarantees and complying with the conditions provided for in the implementation arrangements.

When the budget is not implemented directly, but rather under indirect, shared, decentralized or joint management, coordination of the control systems and full comparability of information are especially important. In order to enhance this coordination and to safeguard comparability, the following provisions are inserted into the Financial Regulation:

1. For indirect budget management, decisions entrusting executive tasks to bodies and agencies will include all appropriate arrangements for ensuring the transparency of operations carried out, and must comprise:
   - transparent procurement and grant-award procedures which are non-discriminatory and exclude any conflict of interest;
   - an effective internal control system for management operations;
   - accounting arrangements for these operations and procedures for the presentation of the accounts which will enable the proper use of Community funds to be ascertained and the true extent of this use to be reflected in the Community accounts;
   - an independent external audit;
   - public access to information at the level provided for in Community regulations. The importance of compliance with international standards strongly relies on the provisions of the new legal framework, when, according to the Financial Regulation, the Commission may accept that the audit, accounting and procurement systems of the national bodies are equivalent to its own, with due account taken of internationally accepted standards.

2. When shared or decentralized management operates, the Commission will apply clearance-of-accounts procedures or financial correction mechanisms which enable it to assume final responsibility for the implementation of the budget. The Member States and third countries will also conduct regular checks to ensure actions to be financed from the Community budget have been implemented properly.

3. Where the Commission implements the budget by joint management, certain implementation tasks will be entrusted to international organizations. These organizations will, in their accounting, audit, control and procurement procedures, apply standards offering guarantees equivalent to internationally accepted standards.

Financial Reporting and Accountability

The Community's accounts will comprise:

1. the financial statements and reports on implementation of the budget of the European bodies and institutions; and

2. the consolidated financial statements and reports on implementation
    of the budget of the European bodies and institutions.

And the accounts of the institutions and bodies will be accompanied by a
report on budgetary and financial management during the year.

The accounts must comply with the rules, be accurate and comprehensive and present a true and fair view of (see Figure 9.6):

- the assets and liabilities, charges and income, entitlements and
  obligations not shown as assets or liabilities and cash flow; and
- the revenue and expenditure from budgetary operations.

Figure 9.6 shows the generally accepted accounting principles (GAAP) in
accordance with which the financial statements must be presented.

Accrual is undoubtedly the principle most emphasized by the reform. In
accordance with the principle of accrual-based accounting, financial statements will show the charges and income for the financial year, regardless of
the date of payment or collection.

The financial statements will comprise the balance sheet, the economic
out-turn account, the cash-flow table and the statement of changes in
capital. The annex to the financial statements will supplement and
comment on the information presented in the statements and will supply all
the additional information prescribed by internationally accepted accounting practices, where such information is relevant to the Communities'
activities.[12]

The accounts are consolidated using the full consolidation method.
Investments in associated bodies, as in the case of the European Investment
Fund, are reported using the equity method. They cover the accounts of the
European Parliament (including the Ombudsman), the Council, the
Commission (including the Publications Office and the Joint Research
Centre), the Court of Justice, the Court of Auditors, the Economic and
Social Committee and the Committee of the Regions. Operations not
included in the budget are not entered either in the consolidated revenue
and expenditure account or the balance sheet, with the sole exception of
lending and borrowing operations.

Before 1 May, the European Commission submits its Annual Accounts
to the European Parliament and to the Court of Auditors. The Court of
Auditors submits a Statement of Assurance (declaration on the reliability of the accounts and compliance with legal provisions) before
30 November. This is published in the *Official Journal of the European
Communities*.[13]

Phases and Dates for Implementing the Reform

The reform must be implemented in a gradual way, following a process in which the improvements operate step by step, allowing time for smooth adaptation of the different elements of the organization, where the mechanisms designed originally can be modified and adapted as the process progresses and human resources skills develop in an effective way. The organizational culture as a whole is likely to require profound development in order to ensure it adapts to the new features of the reformed system. This gradual implementation is provided by the Financial Regulation, which states that the renewed accounting system will be progressively implemented, setting 2005 as the deadline for the completion of the process of changes to the system's principles, rules and procedures, which should all be working by this date. This gradual procedure for reforming the system is described in a specific communication issued by the Commission on 17 December 2002, on the modernization of the accounting system of the European Communities, focusing on the quality and broader scope of information presented by the financial statements.

Achievement of the general objective of the reform – providing reliable financial information – requires important changes on several fronts, involving (Commission of the European Communities, 2003, p. 1030):

- Adoption of generally accepted accrual-based accounting principles;
- Development of an integrated accounting system containing all the information necessary for presenting the accrual accounts;
- Development of a general accounting system based on accrual accounting and maintenance of cash-based budget accounting;
- Adoption of detailed accounting methods and valuation rules that elaborate on the accounting principles adopted;
- Improvement of the financial statements so they give an accurate picture of the financial situation in terms of assets and liabilities, budget implementation, the out-turn and the cash flow;
- Extension of the scope of consolidation.

All these changes require the implementation of specific actions until 2005, according to the timetable that has been set out. This new system, worked out in a coordinated and efficient way by 2005, is undoubtedly quite an important challenge for the European institutions. From an operational point of view, the traditional lack of coordination between the Commission's Directorates-General is one of the most significant handicaps for this coordination, as this circumstance makes data control by the accountant more difficult. A very important limitation, affecting the reliability of information, derives from the data that Member States and third countries must provide to the Commission when there is shared or decentralized management of the European funds.[14]

MANAGEMENT ACCOUNTING AND PERFORMANCE INDICATORS

A more ambitious target for public reporting and accountability in Europe is the elaboration and presentation of detailed information and reports on the management and performance of public bodies. The most important challenge in this field is to design analytical systems allowing comparisons between different bodies with similar characteristics in order to make possible a more realistic policy evaluation and even the development of 'virtual' markets for non-market services. This achievement will only be possible if harmonized databases and performance indicators become available for the European public sector, both for countries and for European institutions, policies and programmes.

Obviously, if financial comparability is not yet an available tool for decision-makers and policy-makers in Europe, comparable management data and performance indicators would seem to be an even more difficult and remote target for European countries, institutions and common policies. However, as huge amounts of European resources are managed on a decentralized or shared basis, detailed information and control systems are essential tools for the effective and efficient administration of these resources. One very important factor in implementing an information and control system for monitoring European policies is the Integrated Administration and Control System (IACS) for certain areas of Community aid, with special relevance in the case of the European Agricultural Guidance and Guarantee Fund-Guarantee Section (EAGGF-Guarantee).[15] Each Member State has to set up an integrated administration and control system, applying in both the crop and the livestock sectors. The integrated system comprises the following elements:

1. a computerized database to record the data on aid applications for each agricultural holding;
2. an alphanumeric identification system for agricultural plots;
3. an alphanumeric system for the identification and registration of animals, which enables claims to be cross-checked and controlled on the spot;

4. aid applications for area aid, forage areas and animals;
5. an integrated control system for administrative monitoring and field inspections.

The system will cover all aid applications submitted, in particular regarding administrative checks, on-the-spot checks and, if appropriate, verification by aerial or satellite remote sensing.

As the different market regulations are by nature complicated, so IACS structure is complicated in order to provide the information necessary for implementing control mechanisms in a reliable way. The Agriculture Directorate-General, the Health and Consumer Protection Directorate-General and Member States are directly involved in the implementation of IACS. The efficiency of the system mainly depends on the extent and quality of information and coordination between Member States and different Directorates involved in the implementation of the system. Figure 9.7 shows a general overview of the main IACS databases and control mechanisms.

Although the Member States are responsible for the current implementation of IACS, the role of coordination, control and enforcement of the European institutions is a critical issue for the usefulness and effectiveness of any management information system. The IACS experiment is no doubt an important reference to be evaluated for the future development of analytical information and reporting systems in Europe.

Important experiments in cost and management accounting projects and decentralized management evaluation and control are currently underway at central, regional and local levels in Europe. Municipal networks exist around Europe for benchmarking and best practice control and New Public Management criteria are increasingly widening their influence in public jurisdictions. As a result of these environmental features and circumstances, new coordinated databases and management reporting requirements are clearly felt as unavoidable challenges for sound financial and economic decision-making and policy design. It is not yet possible to present here or anywhere the specific way in which these emerging challenges and requirements will be resolved: this will be one of the most important fields for research and development of new public sector information systems over the next few years. The existence of an integrated economic and political area in Europe will no doubt be a very important stimulus to joining in the development of projects and common systems, especially between bodies closer to people, as in the cases of municipal and regional jurisdictions.

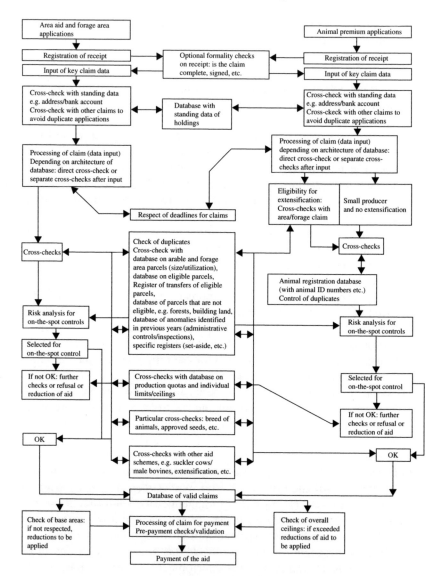

Note: In case of decentralized databases there must be cross-checks at central level, for instance cross-checks of animal numbers or areas claimed in other regions.

Source: Court of Auditors review of relevant regulations.

Figure 9.7   Overview of principal controls

THE ROLE OF EUROPEAN INSTITUTIONS IN THE PROCESS OF REFORM AND HARMONIZATION OF GOVERNMENT ACCOUNTING AND BUDGETARY SYSTEMS IN EUROPE

The existence of different governmental accounting traditions in Europe implies important accounting diversity in this field. During the last few years, many important reforms have been implemented with regard to European governmental accounting systems. However, the IPSASs issue has raised the need for discussion on how the process of setting governmental accounting standards must be carried out.

The standard-setting process affects, in the first place, the accounting of European institutions, and these institutions could also foster the process and even play a leading role in it, as, in the European context, the position of the EU institutions is quite important, especially in the case of the Commission, which essentially represents the executive power in the Union. As the adaptation of European institutions' accounting systems to IPSASs requirements is under way, this reform could constitute an important incentive for the Member States of the Union to follow this initiative.

Taking into account the current state and characteristics of governmental accounting systems in Europe and their process of convergence, we can analyse what their foreseeable development might be and the ways that are open for harmonization. In order to make this analysis, the following four topics may be considered for reflection, as main subjects for the process of harmonization and the development of alternative policies and decision-making:

1. *Scope and pace of harmonization.* European governmental accounting systems may evolve in different ways, between lack of harmonization and full development of accounting standards. According to current conditions, it would be reasonable to promote a gradual introduction of international accounting standards for national governments in Europe, in a similar way to the EU institutions, although it is difficult to be specific at the moment about the rate of the development and the stage this harmonization can reach.

   This policy would allow real comparability of public sector financial information, and reconciliation between financial reporting by public bodies and macroeconomic figures would become more feasible and reliable. Otherwise, if uniform standards were not adopted, there would be no room for a European public sector where transparency and fair financial safety could be reasonably guaranteed.

2. *Budgetary information.* A decision must be made between the inclusion or non-inclusion of budgetary reporting rules in international governmental accounting standards. The least contentious solution is to limit the impact of standards to financial reporting, as has been IFAC's policy to date, while a clear policy in this field has not yet been designed. If budgetary reporting regulation were finally excluded from accounting standards, these would then only consider financial information, and budgetary accounting and reporting, as well as their links with financial accounting, would simply be a responsibility of national governments.

    In a similar way to IFAC-PSC policy in this field, it would be realistic for European countries and institutions to use a step-by-step approach. As a first stage, standards would only deal with non-budgetary information, and working information systems with a dual structure; budgetary accounting would be regulated by standards at a second stage, normally using the accrual basis for drawing up and reporting budgets.

3. *Process management.* Another decision to be adopted is on the intervention or non-intervention of a European supranational authority when drawing up and/or introducing new common accounting standards. Either EU authorities lead (or at least support) the process, or national governments join voluntarily in a process of harmonization negotiated with the other countries, for the preparation and introduction of accounting standards according to international pronouncements.

    The most effective policy for governmental accounting harmonization in Europe would be process led, monitored or supported by European institutions. If this process were negotiated and implemented gradually, political opposition might be weak and reaching agreement among governments and institutions would be a realistic goal. The first step could be the adaptation of EU Commission accounting to international accounting standards requirements and generally accepted accounting principles, as is now under way. Once this adaptation has been made, it should be easier for the Commission to foster real accounting harmonization by EU Member State governments in a decisive way.

    Renouncing control to this leadership may be an easier decision in the short run for European institutions, but then the initiatives for approaches to Systems of National Accounts would be taken by IFAC or other organizations, and the European authorities would lose their control over the process. However, as neither the Commission nor the European Parliament are allowed by law to set up uniform obligatory accounting standards for Member States, this policy is not very likely to be implemented, and a more indirect method would then operate, through national improvements, for a gradual approach to the accrual basis and international requirements and accounting standards.

4. *European involvement in the elaboration of international standards.* Finally, Europe can play a more active and influential role in the approval and elaboration process of IPSASs and then give up issuing accounting standards by itself, except for specific adaptations of international standards. If this active involvement is not achieved, European authorities should evaluate *ex post* the suitability of adopting IPSASs, even if there is no European Union participation.

Moreover, this policy would be the most consistent with the Commission's position in the scope of business accounting, where it has renounced making further developments to its own accounting directives model.

CONCLUDING REMARKS

According to our previous considerations, it can be concluded that diversity in governmental accounting is still quite significant in Europe and very much deeper than in the business accounting field. Different political, economic and cultural traditions give rise to a wide diversity among national governments and even among regions and local authorities in the same country. These differences also give rise to opposition to reforms, as the changes required in accounting reporting appear to be very considerable.

Although the process of reform has being going on for many years, old-fashioned and inappropriate accounting systems are still operating. Significant examples are the cases of central government accounting systems in Germany, Italy and the Netherlands, where reforms for adopting accrual-based models have not yet begun.

The best way to achieve effective convergence of European governmental accounting systems is undoubtedly a very important issue. There are various options covering the stages and pace of harmonization, budgetary reporting, process leadership or monitoring, and European involvement in the preparation of governmental accounting standards. It would not seem reasonable to renounce governmental harmonization in Europe right now, as there would then be no room for a transparent and financially safe European public sector.

To achieve this target, some sort of European leadership would be necessary for the success of the harmonization process. This would guarantee a useful result in line with European needs and traditions. To do this,

European institutions should implement an active policy in this field, or at least foster cooperation by national governments, getting involved in a joint financial reporting harmonization project. So agreements on the reforms and their gradual introduction would be the basic principles. Nonetheless, deadlines should be set for the different stages in order to assure real and effective achievements.

As repeatedly recommended by European Court of Auditors, the European Communities are involved in a process of deep reforms of their accounting and budgetary information system, in order to adapt it to internationally accepted accounting principles. This experience gives the opportunity to the European institutions to become a reference for Member States, fostering the reform of their Systems of National Accounts in order to adapt them to international standards. In addition, as around 85 per cent of the European budget is implemented by shared management with Member States, harmonization of national reporting cultures and practices would provide strong support for sound accountability and transparency in public sector management, as well as for effective control of public financial policies and allocation of resources.

An ambitious target for public reporting and accountability in Europe is the elaboration and presentation of detailed information on the management and performance of public bodies. The most important challenge in this field is to design analytical systems enabling comparisons to be made between different bodies with similar characteristics, in order to make possible more realistic policy evaluation and even the development of 'virtual' markets for non-market services; this achievement will only be possible if harmonized databases and performance indicators become available for the European public sector, both for countries and for European institutions, policies and programmes. A relevant experience implementing an information and control system for monitoring European policies is the Integrated Administration and Control System (IACS) for certain areas of Community aid, with special relevance to the case of the EAGGF-Guarantee, whose system is undoubtedly an important reference to be evaluated for the future development of analytical information and reporting systems in Europe.

NOTES

1. The general principles of transparency and good practice for public bodies can be found in international codes, like that of the International Monetary Fund (2001a) and on the OECD and European Commission public management and governance websites.
2. The International Federation of Accountants (IFAC) is the worldwide organization for the accountancy profession. Founded in 1977, its mission is to develop and enhance the

profession with harmonized standards to enable it to provide services of a consistently high quality in the public interest. IFAC is made up of more than 150 member bodies from every part of the globe, representing more than 2.4 million accountants in public practice, education, the public sector, industry, and commerce.

3. The systems considered are GFS (Government Finance Statistics) and ESA 1995 (European System of National Accounts). The GFS system has been developed by the International Monetary Fund (see IMF, 2001b) and the ESA 1995 has been adopted as a Regulation by the European Union (see European Commission/Eurostat, 1996). Both are structured according to the System of National Accounts, SNA (see Commission of the European Communities, International Monetary Fund, Organization for Economic Co-operation and Development, United Nations, World Bank, 1993).

4. Invitation to Comment.

5. The IFAC-PSC has initiated a project to provide input on whether the published budgets of public sector entities are presented as general purpose financial statements and fall within the scope of the PSC's mandate; and if so, whether an IPSAS should be issued on budget reporting. The first stage of this project involves the preparation of a Research Report detailing best practice in budget formulation, presentation and reporting. The PSC will consider an updated draft of the Report at its meeting in March 2004.

6. International Accounting Standard/International Financial Reporting Standard.

7. The European Union gives support to accounting and audit reforms in the Mediterranean countries within the framework of EuroMed Market Programme.

8. The 'World Bank' is the name that has come to be used for the International Bank for Reconstruction and Development (IBRD) and the International Development Association (IDA) <http://www.worldbank.org/ida>. Together, these organizations provide low-interest loans, interest-free credit, and grants to developing countries.

9. See DG Budget, http://europa.eu.int/comm/budget/execution/execution_en.htm#reform <http://europa.eu.int/comm/budget/execution/execution_en.htm>.

10. Detailed rules for the implementation of these Council Regulations are laid down by the Commission Regulations (EC, Euratom) No. 2342/2002 of 23 December 2002.

11. The implementation methods should guarantee that the procedures for protecting Community funds are complied with, whatever the body responsible for all or part of this implementation, and must confirm that final responsibility for budgetary implementation lies with the Commission, in accordance with Article 274 of the Treaty.

12. The annual accounts of the European Communities are set out in three volumes:
Volume I: Consolidated statements on budget implementation and consolidated financial statements
Volume II: Part I: Commission – Budget implementation statements
        Part II: Commission and Euratom Supply Agency – Financial statements
Volume III: European Parliament, the Council, the Court of Justice, the Court of Auditors, the Economic and Social Committee, the Committee of the Regions and the Ombudsman.
In accordance with Article 122 of the new Financial Regulation, the report on budgetary and financial management during the year no longer forms part of the annual accounts as in the past, but accompanies the annual accounts.

13. The final accounts will be published in the *Official Journal of the European Union* together with the statement of assurance given by the Court of Auditors by 30 November 2003 in accordance with Articles 129 and 181 of the Financial Regulation.

14. Around 85 per cent of the total expenditure is implemented under shared responsibility with the Member States. In its 2001 annual report, the Court of Auditors said it could give the declaration of assurance only for 5 per cent of the 79 billion paid by the Commission, because of this circumstance. The impossibility of the Court delivering a broader declaration of assurance does not relate to the way these monies have been accounted for by the Commission, but to the way they have been spent on the ground.

15. Originally established by Council Regulations (EEC) No 3508/92 Official Journal L 017, 24 January 2004, pp. 0007–0010. The 1992 reform of the Common Agricultural Policy (CAP) significantly increased the number of beneficiaries, but also the risk of irregularity and fraud. The IASC was then introduced to deal with those risks.

REFERENCES

Chan, J.L. (2002), 'Comparative International Accounting Research (CIGAR) Methodology: Issues and Strategies', in Montesinos, V. and Vela, J.M. (eds), *Innovations in Governmental Accounting*, Boston: Kluwer Academic Publishers, pp. 23–30.

Commission of the European Communities, International Monetary Fund, Organization for Economic Co-operation and Development, United Nations, World Bank (1993), *System of National Accounts 1993*, Brussels/Luxembourg, New York, Paris, Washington DC.

Commission of the European Communities (2003), 'Modernisation of the Accounting System of the European Communities', in Lüder, K. and Jones, R. (eds), *Reforming Governmental Accounting and Budgeting in Europe*, Frankfurt am Main: Fachverlag Moderne Wirtschaft, pp. 1001–71.

European Commission/Eurostat (1996), *European System of National Accounts – ESA 1995*, Luxembourg.

European Court of Auditors (2001), 'Special Report No 4/2001 on the Audit of the EAGGF-Guarantee – The Implementation of the Integrated Administration and Control System (IACS) together with the Commission's Replies', OJ C, 31 July 2001.

International Federation of Accountants (IFAC) (2000), *Governmental Financial Reporting. Accounting Issues and Practices*, IFAC Public Sector Committee Study 11, New York, May.

International Monetary Fund (IMF) (2001a), *Manual on Fiscal Transparency*, Washington, DC.

International Monetary Fund (IMF) (2001b), *Government Finance Statistics Manual*, Washington, DC.

Lüder, K. and Jones, R. (2003), 'The Diffusion of Accrual Accounting and Budgeting in European Governments – A Cross-country Analysis', in Lüder, K. and Jones, R. (eds), *Reforming Governmental Accounting and Budgeting in Europe*, Frankfurt am Main: Fachverlag Moderne Wirtschaft, pp. 13–58.

Montesinos Julvé, V. (2000), 'External Audit in Spanish Local Authorities', in Caperchione, E. and Mussari, R. (eds), *Comparative Issues in Local Government Accounting*, Boston: Kluwer Academic Publishers, pp. 241–57.

Montesinos, V. and Vela, J.M. (1996), 'Governmental Accounting in Spain: Evolution and Reforms', in Chan, J.L. (ed.), *Research in Governmental and Nonprofit Accounting*, vol. 9, Greenwich, CT: Jai Press, pp. 219–38.

Montesinos, V. and Vela, J.M. (2000), 'Governmental Accounting in Spain and the European Monetary Union: A Critical Perspective', *Financial Accountability & Management*, **16** (2), 129–50.

Montesinos Julve, V. et al. (2000), *Study on the Preparation and Presentation of the Consolidated Accounts of the European Institutions*, available at http://europa.eu.int/comm/budget/execution/execution_en.htm#reform.

Salter, S.B. and Doupnik, T.S. (1992), 'The Relationship between Legal Systems and Accounting Practices: A Classification Exercise', in Most, K.S. (ed.), *Advances in International Accounting*, vol. 5, Greenwich, CT: Jai Press, pp. 108–26.
Stiglitz, J.E. (2002), *Globalization and its Discontents*, London: Penguin.

Website References

European Commission:
  Governance: http://europa.eu.int/comm/governance.
  Budget and accounting: http://europa.eu.int/comm/budget/execution/execution_en.htm#reform.
IFAC-PSC: http://www.ifac.org/PublicSector.
OECD Public Management: http://www1.oecd.org/puma/pubs.

Index

accountability
  executive responsibility 9–10
  external audit institutions 67–8, 69, 130–33
  financial reporting 229–30
accountability trials, Spain 111–12
accounting and budgeting systems
  European institutions
    components 223–4
    general framework and reform objectives 225–6
    legal framework for reform 226–7
    phases and dates for implementing reform 231–2
    reporting and accountability 229–30
    reporting and implementation 227–9
  international environment 219–23
  see also government accounting; public accounting
accounting officers, EU 226–7
accounts, *see* macroeconomic accounts; public accounts; state accounts
Accounts Commission, UK 17
accrual-based accounting 45, 230
Action Plan for 2001 (EC) 171
administration, *see* public administration
Administration and Accounting Act (1850) 102, 103
administrative accounting, Spain 105
agricultural expenditure 192
  poor control 195
Amsterdam 55
analogy, principle of 155
analytical systems, for comparing information 238
Anglo-Saxon model
  accounting systems 218, 220–21, 227
  state audit institutions 15

annual activity reports, Directorates-General 198–9, 200
annual reports
  of the ECA 23, 136
  three H questions, Netherlands 61
Anti-Fraud Co-ordination Unit (UCLAF) 25, 155
  Bösch resolution 161–3
  corruption and 163–5
  Special Report no. 8/98 161, 162
anti-fraud policy, origins and foundations 151–4
anti-fraud units 155, 156
approval, joint reports 141–2
Audit Commission, UK 17, 42
  cooperation with National Audit Office 36–7
  example of a report issued by 32–3
Audit Committee
  Germany 85
  Netherlands 64
audit criteria, Bundesrechnungshof 83
audit directorates, of NCA 70
audit function
  Comptroller and Auditor General 41
  Spanish autonomous communities 117
  Tribunal de Cuentas 21, 109, 110–11
Audit Groups (ECA) 135
audit reports 6
  Netherlands Court of Audit 67, 71
  Tribunal de Cuentas 110, 111
  United Kingdom 17, 31–8, 47–8, 51
  see also financial reporting
Audit Standards, Bundesrechnungshof 84
Audit and Supervision Policy Directorate (ASP) 65
audit tasks, ECA 135–6
audit traditions, diversity of 138
Audit Units, Bundesrechnungshof 81
auditees, Bundesrechnungshof 82–3

Auditor General for Scotland 16, 43
  reports issued by 34–5
Auditor General for Wales 16, 43–4
  reports issued by 35
authorization, presenting of accounts 7
authorizing officers, EU 226
autonomous communities, Spain 99,
    114–15
  coordination with Tribunal de
      Cuentas 119–24
  external control 116–17
  internal control 115–16

Beatrix, Queen 56
benchmarking 11
benefits, EU internal control
    framework 205
Bösch Resolution 161–3
Budget Act (1977) 100, 103, 105
Budget Act (2003) 100
Budget Officers, Germany 87
budgetary cycle, Spain 106–7
budgetary equilibrium, EU 154
budgetary information
  European institutions 223–4
  financial reporting 27, 236
budgetary procedures, public
    accounting information 215
budgets
  European Union 23, 138–9, 152
  legislation agreement, Germany
      79–80
  National Audit Office 50
  Netherlands Court of Audit 70
  see also accounting and budgeting
      systems; competence-based
      budgeting; outcome-based
      budgeting
'Build Your Own Audit Office'
    workshops 77
Bundesrechnungshof 19
  advisory function 84
  audit criteria 83
  auditees 82–3
  distribution of tasks,
      Landesrechnungshöfe and 91–6
  how audits and advice are put into
      effect 85
  legal bases 80–81
  organization of 81–2

powers 84
  status and functions 80–81
Burgundy, Dukes of 66
business audits, as reference for public
    audit 11
business organizations, management
    control 8

Cabinet, Netherlands 58
causal relationships, outcome-based
    budgeting 60–61
Central Audit Department,
    Netherlands 65
central government expenditure,
    audits, UK 41
central government ministries,
    Netherlands 56–7
chain model, control levels 202
Chamber of Audit for the Netherlands
    (1447) 66
Child Support Agency, example of
    report on 31–2
clearance process, Netherlands Court
    of Audit 76
closure statements, structural measures
    expenditure 193
co-financing
  EU internal control 193
  Federal Government and the Länder
      89–90
collaboration
  ECA and SAIs 142–4
  principle of 156
  public and private spheres 133–4
collegiate principle, organization of
    Bundesrechnungshof 81–2
commercially driven accounting and
    budgeting systems 219
Committee of Independent Experts
    164
Committee of Public Accounts 38, 50
  reports 51
Committee on Standards in Public Life
    44
Common Agricultural Policy 138–9,
    153
common legal framework, Community
    policies 159
common standard, EU internal control
    framework 204

Communication of the Commission
(2000) 170
comparability, financial information
211, 214, 238
compatibility, implementation of joint
reports 141
compensatory reimbursements,
member states 153–4
competence overlap, external control,
Spain 120
competence-based budgeting 102–3
competency, in fight against fraud 158
complementary own resource 154
Comptroller and Auditor General
appointments 39
auditing process
inspection rights 41, 46
value for money examinations
46–9
creation of 38
examples of reports issued by
Child Support Agency 31–2
criminal cases 33
leading to improvements in
quality of public services 34
leading to significant financial
savings 33
pre-audit 7
relations with Parliament and
Government 49–50
reporting 50–51
requirement to report to Parliament
38–9
scope, role and rights of access
40–42
Comptroller and Auditor General for
Northern Ireland 16–17
audit responsibilities 42–3
Conference of the Heads of the
German SAIs 91–2
consolidated annual accounts, Spain
107
Consolidated Fund 41
Consultative Body of Ministry Audit
Departments, Netherlands 65
Consultative Forum, UK 44
Contact Committee 140
continental accounting systems 220
contrat de confiance 193
Convention (1995)

categorization of fraud 157
introduction of 156
judicial cooperation between
member states 179
third pillar instruments in fight
against fraud 157–60
cooperation
ECA and SAIs 95–6, 139–40
in fight against fraud 158, 162, 169
NCA and other countries 78
public audit institutions, UK 36–7
supranational organizations for
12–15
cooperation agreements, German SAIs
93–5
coordination, between Spanish control
institutions 118–25
Coordination Committee, Spain 123
coordination strategies
anti-fraud policy 25, 151–81
financial reporting 26–8, 211–38
internal control 184–207
need for 24
coordination unit, fight against fraud
155
corporate bodies
NCA examination of 75
penal responsibility, financial fraud
158
Corpus Juris 25, 170, 171, 172
corruption, *see* fraud
Cortes Generales 101, 108, 113
COSO framework 198
cost–benefit analysis, UK 30
cost–benefit balance, EU internal
control framework 205
costs of external control, lack of
information on 197
Council of State, Netherlands 58
Court of Audit, *see* Netherlands Court
of Audit
criminal cases, example of a UK report
on 33
criminal infringements, Corpus Juris
172
criminal liability, Corpus Juris 172
criminal procedure, Corpus Juris
172
criminalization, financial fraud 169,
171

decentralization
  EU accounting system 226
  EU external control procedures 197
  external audit institutions 128–30
  public administration 5–6
  Spain 99–100
decentralized government, Netherlands
  57
decentralized management, EC
  administrative reform 199
Decision no. 88/376/EEC 154
Decision no. 94/728/EC 154
deficit and debt, quantification of
  212–13
departmental accounts, UK 45
direct management, EC administrative
  reform 199
Director, OLAF 165, 166, 174
directorates, OLAF 175
Directorates-General
  anti-fraud units 155
  implementation of IACS 233
  internal control framework 191, 192,
    198–9, 200, 203
discharge procedure, of the ECA 136
District Audit Agency 42
double entry accounting 105, 215, 224
duties, OLAF 168

economic theory, effectiveness and
    efficiency 3–6
economy
  Dutch 55
  UK auditing process 46
economy control 8
effectiveness
  in economic theory 3–6
  NCA strategy 69
  UK auditing process 46
effectiveness audits, Netherlands 74
effectiveness control 8
efficiency
  in economic theory 3–6
  NCA strategy 69
  UK auditing process 46
efficiency audits
  Bundesrechnungshof 83
  Netherlands 74
efficiency control 8
electoral system, Netherlands 57

enforcement mechanisms, budgeting
    and accounting 219–20
environment, management control 8
Estatutos de Autonomía 116
Eurojust 179–81
European Agricultural Guidance and
    Guarantee Fund-Guarantee
    Section 232
European Anti-Fraud Office (OLAF)
    25, 161
  anti-fraud and corruption strategy
    165–7
  assessment of 175–7
  downward trend in fraud 151
  Eurostat case and reform of 177–9
  internal investigations 166, 167–9
  operations 173–5
  support function to the Commission
    156
European Atomic Energy Community
    (EURATOM) 152
European Chart of Local Autonomy
    100
European Coal and Steel Community
    (ECSC) 152
European Commission
  audit and control procedures
    administrative reform 184,
      198–200
    internal control 191–4
  Communication (2000) 170
  fight against fraud 154–6, 160
  Green Paper on European Public
    Prosecutor's Office 171–3
  implementation of European budget
    228
European Community, *see* European
    Union
European constitution, European
    Public Prosecutor's Office and
    OLAF 179–81
European Court of Auditors 22–3
  cooperation with audit institutions
    139–40
    Germany 95–6
    Spain 124–5
    United Kingdom 37–8
  EU internal control framework
    206–7
  main features and activities 134–6

responsibility 194
singularity of 136–9
Special Report no. 8/98 161, 167
Statement of Assurance 230
uniqueness as audit institution 16
European Court of Justice, protocol
   on intervention 156, 158
European Federation of Accountants
   (FEE) 216, 219
European funds, NCA audit of 76
European institutions
   accounting and budgeting 223–32
   role in reform 235–7
European Organization of Regional
   Audit Institutions (EURORAI)
   13, 14–15
European Organization of Supreme
   Audit Institutions (EUROSAI)
   13, 14
European Parliament
   Bösch Resolution 161–3
   estimation of fraud, OLAF 151
   Eurostat case and reform of OLAF
     177–9
European Public Prosecutor's Office
   25
   Commissions' Green Paper 171–3
   constitution of Europe 179–81
   Treaty of Nice 169–71
European Union 184
   audit and control procedures
     current framework 190
       external control 194
       internal control 191–4
       weaknesses in 195–7
     EC administrative reform 184,
       198–200
     lack of coordination 184–5
     relevance of US and Dutch single
       audits 189–90
     see also internal control
       framework
   budget 138–9
     ECA Annual Report 23
     reporting and implementation
       227–9
   decisions, *see* decisions
   Dutch contribution to 76
   involvement in international
     standards 27

own resources, *see* own resources
   regulations, *see* regulations
Eurostat case 177–9
Exchequer and Audit Departments Act
   (1866) 38, 39
Exchequer and Audit Departments Act
   (1921) 39
exclusive power, Public Prosecution
   Service 173
executive responsibility, public
   managers 9–10
expenditure control mechanisms, lack
   of, EU 11
expenditure fraud 151, 157
external actions, EU 193–4
   poor control 196
external audit institutions, *see* Supreme
   Audit Institutions
external control 6
   European Union 194
   Germany
     at federal level 80–85
     at regional level 85–6
   Netherlands Court of Audit 65–78
   Spain
     autonomous communities 116–17
     competence overlap between
       institutions 120
     coordination between internal
       control and 118–19
     Tribunal de Cuentas 108–13

fairness, management control 8
Federal Budget Code, Germany 80, 84
Federal Republic of Germany
   external Wnancial control
     at federal level 80–85
     at regional level 85–6
   Federal Government and the Länder
     budget legislation agreement
       79–80
     distribution of tasks between
       87–91
     division of functions between 79
     responsibilities, expenditure and
       revenue 79
   internal financial control 86–7
   state audit institutions
     distribution of tasks between 91–6
     organization 19–20

federal statutes, granting payments, Germany 90
feedback, management control 8
financial aid, German SAIs 95
financial assistance, from Federal Government to Länder 90
financial audit
  Spain 104, 109
  United Kingdom 45–6, 53
financial competence, Federal Government and the Länder 89
financial control
  State General Intervention 104–5
  see also public financial control
financial fraud, *see* fraud
financial information systems, public sector 212–13
Financial Regulation (2002) 226–7, 229
financial reporting
  coordination of 24, 26–8, 211–38
  Netherlands Court of Audit 77
  UK National Audit Office 50–51
  see also reports
financial savings, example of a UK report leading to 33
financial statements 230
Fontainebleau agreement (1984) 154
fourth resource 154
Franco regime, control institutions under 103
fraud
  anti-fraud policy 152–4
  classic examples and categories 152
  corruption and UCLAF 163–5
  estimated amount 151
  European Public Prosecutor's Office Commission's Green Paper 171–3
  Treaty of Nice 169–71
  member states and the EC in fight against 154–6
  public control coordination 24, 25
  Special Report no. 8/98 and the Bösch resolution 161–3
  third pillar instruments 157–60
  see also European Anti-Fraud Office
'From Policy Budget to Policy Accountability' 18, 59–60
  consequences for auditing 71–2
Full Session, Tribunal de Cuentas 108–9

full study phase, value for money reports 47

General Budget of the European Communities 152
general policy objectives, Dutch budget 62
General Public Accounts Plan (1994) 115–16
General Senate, Bundesrechnungshof 82
General-Rechen-Kammer 80
Generally Accepted Accounting Practices (GAAP) 218, 228
German model, state audit institutions 15–16
Germany, *see* Federal Republic of Germany
globalization, need for quality information 211
goal realization audits 74
good governance, NCA strategy 68–9
government
  legislative control over executive 131
  value of criticizing administration 132
  see also parliamentary and government relations
government accounting 219, 220
  harmonization 222–3
  reforms 221, 222
  role of European institutions 235–7
  reporting issues 214
  standards 221
  United Kingdom 44–5
  see also accounting and budgeting systems; public accounting
Government Accounting Reform Operation 59, 64
Government Accounts Act (2001) 18, 59, 61, 64, 72, 75
Government Resources and Accounts Act (2000) 39, 41
Government of Wales Act 44
Green Book of Audit 11
Green Paper (EC 2002) 171–3
guarantees, audit of, Netherlands 75

Hague, The 55
harmonization
    government accounting 222–3
    role of European institutions
        235–7
    public accounting 27, 28, 215–18
health authority, public audit, UK 42
High Councils of State, Netherlands
    66–7
high-level controls, chain model 202
High-Level Group 164
horizontal group, ECA 135
House of Representatives, Netherlands
    57, 58, 67, 68, 75

identical value, principle of 160
imperfect information, economic
    agents 3–4
Indemnity Acts, Netherlands 71
independence
    Bundesrechnungshof 81
    Landesrechnungshöfe 85
    Netherlands High Councils of State
        66–7
    public control 13–14
independent audit certificates 203
Independent Expert Committee 25
indirect budget management 229
indivisibility, principle of 173
information, on performance 10
information approach, EU internal
    control framework 204
information exchange, fight against
    fraud 158
information provision, public control
    7
information systems, public accounting
    212–13
inspection checks, fight against fraud
    160
inspection rights, UK auditing process
    41, 46
institutional architecture, of the ECA
    137–8
institutional design, economic policy
    5–6
institutional relationships, ECA and
    SAIs 140, 142–4
institutional watchdogs, Netherlands
    58

institutions, *see* public control
    institutions
Integrated Administrative and Control
    System (IACS) 192, 195, 232–3
integrity, NCA 72
intelligence service, OLAF 174
Inter-institutional Agreement (1999)
    168–9
internal audit, NCA reliance on 71
Internal Audit Service (IAS) 191
internal auditors, EU 227
internal control 6
    European Union
        current framework 191–4
        see also internal control
            framework
    Germany 86–7
    Netherlands
        Audit Committee 64
        Audit and Supervision Policy
            Directorate 65
        Ministry Audit Departments 64
    Spain
        autonomous communities
            115–16
        coordination 118
            between external and 118–19
        State General Intervention
            102–8
internal control framework 200
    application 203–5
    conditions 201–2
    costs and benefits 205
    need for 24, 26
    objectives 200–201
    roles and responsibilities 205–7
    structure 202–3
internal control offices, Germany 87
internal control standards 198
internal investigations, OLAF 166,
    167–9
internal policies 193
International Accounting Standards
    Board (IASB) 216, 217
International Federation of
    Accountants (IFAC) 27, 216, 217,
    218, 223
International Organization of
    Securities Commissions (IOSCO)
    217

International Organization of Supreme
  Audit Institutions (INTOSAI)
  12–14, 216
international principles, public
  accounting, Spain 105
International Public Sector
  Accounting Standards (IPSASs)
  27, 28, 216, 217, 218, 223
international quality standards
  10–11
Intervención General del Estado, *see*
  State General Intervention
intervention procedure, Spain 104
intervention protocol, European Court
  of Justice 156, 158
investigative powers
  OLAF 168
  UCLAF 161–2, 162–3
irregularities, in expenditure and
  revenues 159, 163

joint activities, Federal Government
  and the Länder 89–90
Joint Audit Initiative 192
joint audits, ECA ands SAIs 140–42
joint management, EC administrative
  reform 199
judicial cooperation, member states
  179–81
judicial decisions, mutual recognition
  173, 179
judicial function, Tribunal de Cuentas
  21
juridical powers, Netherlands Court of
  Audit 65
jurisdictional function, Tribunal de
  Cuentas 109, 111–12

Länder
  and Federal Government
    agreement on budget legislation
      79–80
    distribution of tasks between
      87–91
    division of functions between 79
    separation of responsibilities,
      expenditure and revenue 79
Landesrechnungshöfe 80
  audit procedures 86
  competence 85–6

distribution of tasks,
  Bundesrechnungshof and 91–6
legislation 85
organization 86
Latin American and Caribbean
  Organization of Supreme Audit
  Institutions 13
Latin model, state audit institutions
  16
Law on Budgetary Principles (1969)
  19, 79–80, 86
Law of Procedure (1988) 21
leadership, European harmonization
  237–8
legal entities, Dutch regularity audits
  75
legal status, OLAF 174
legislative competence, Federal
  Government and the Länder 88
Liaison Officers, SAIs and ECA 140
Lima Declaration 13–14
loans and guarantee audits,
  Netherlands 75
local audits, Netherlands 77
Local Authorities (Separation of
  Powers) Act (2002) 77
local entities, Spain 99, 100
local government, audit (UK) 42

Maastricht Treaty (1992) 25, 134,
  155–6, 158, 159, 170
macroeconomic accounts, public sector
  213
management accounting 232–4
management control
  business organizations as pioneers of
    8–9
  three Es 7–8
management statements, Dutch
  budgets 64
market failures, economic activity of
  the state 2
MED programmes, irregularities 163
media, UK auditing process 52
member states
  compensatory reimbursements
    153–4
  and EC in fight against fraud 154–6,
    157–8
  judicial cooperation between 179

microeconomic financial information, public bodies 213
ministers, Dutch 56–7, 58
Ministry Audit Departments, Netherlands 64
Consultative Body 65
regularity audits 70–71
mission, ECA 23, 135
mission statement, NCA 68
monarchy, Netherlands 56
Municipal Councils, Netherlands 57
Municipal Executives, Netherlands 57
mutual recognition, judicial decisions 173, 179

national accounting, Spain 105–6
national accounting criteria 213, 215
National Audit Act (1983) 39, 40, 41
national audit institutions, *see* Supreme Audit Institutions
National Audit Office 16
auditing process
financial audit 45–6
impact of work 52–3
media 52
overseas work 51–2
relations with Parliament and Government 49–50
reporting 50–51
value for money 46–9
cooperation with
Audit Commission 36–7
European Court of Auditors 37
historical development 38–9
staff, recruitment remuneration and qualifications 40
structure 39–40
see also Comptroller and Auditor General
National Loans Fund 41
National Ombudsman, Netherlands 58
neoclassicism, origin of state functions 3
Netherlands
central government ministries 56–7
decentralized government 57
economic and general information 55
electoral system 57

external control, *see* Netherlands Court of Audit
institutional watchdogs 58
internal control
Audit Committee 64
Audit and Supervision Policy Directorate 65
Ministry Audit Departments 64
political environment 58
public expenditure control
'From Policy Budgeting to Policy Accountability' 59–60
operation accounting reform 59
outcome-based budgeting 61–4
single audit 187–90
state structure 55–6
Netherlands Court of Audit 17–19, 58
audit activities 70–76
background information 65
cooperation with other countries 78
historical development 66
independence 66–7
organization 68
procedures 76
relations with Parliament and Government 67–8
reporting 77
staff and other resources 70
strategy 68–9
structure 70
support for local and provincial authorities 77
tasks and responsibilities 59
New Institutional Economy 3
New Public Management (NPM) 9, 215, 233
'non bis in idem' principle 159, 173
non-financial improvements, due to UK auditing process 53
Nordic model, state audit institutions 16
normative framework, OLAF
innovations 165–7
internal investigations 167–9
introduction of 164–5
Northern Ireland Audit Office 42–3

on-the-spot inspections 160
Operation Accounting Reform, Netherlands 59, 64

operational relationships, ECA and
SAIs 140
ordinary financial control, under
IGAE 105
Organic Act (1982) 21, 22, 108, 109,
116–17, 118
outcome targets, Dutch budget 62
outcome-based budgeting
defined 60–61
Netherlands 18, 61–4
outcomes, in outcome-based budgeting
61
outputs, outcome-based budgeting 60
overseas work, UK auditing process
51–2
own resources 191–2
EC administrative reform 199
Joint Audit Initiative 192
main categories of fraud 152
poor control 195
provision to cover Communities
expenses 153

parliamentary control, public money
(UK) 38–9
parliamentary and government
relations
Netherlands Court of Audit 67–8
Tribunal de Cuentas 112–13
UK National Audit Office 49–50
parliamentary responsibility,
Netherlands 17–18
partnerships
management of EU budget 191
NCA examination of 75
see also public–private partnerships
paying agencies, audit of 192
penal protection, financial interests,
draft directive 170–71
penal responsibility, corporate bodies
158
performance audits
government departments 10
Netherlands
importance attached to 72
of outputs and outcomes 73–4
policy evaluation 73
reporting 77
selection of 74–5
United Kingdom 46–9

performance indicators 232–4
permanent financial control, under
IGAE 104
PIF Convention 159, 170, 171
policy agenda, Dutch budget 62
policy articles, Dutch budget 62
policy evaluation systems, Netherlands
73
policy paragraph, Dutch budget 62
policy-implementation gaps, Dutch
performance audits 74–5
political decisions,
Bundesrechnungshof 83
political environment, Netherlands 58
post-audit control 7
powers
Bundesrechnungshof 84
public sector auditors, UK 36
see also exclusive power;
investigative powers; juridical
powers
pre-accession aid 193
poor control 195
pre-audit control 6–7
pre-audit units, Germany 20, 86–7
preliminary study phase, value for
money reports 47
prevalence, principle of 121
primary controls, chain model 202
private companies, NCA examination
of 75
private corporations, concern about
control of 130
process management, financial
reporting 27, 236
Prodi, R. 177–8
property criterion, presenting of
accounts 7
proportional representation, Dutch
electoral system 57
proportionality, principle of 166
Provincial Councils, Netherlands 57
Provincial Executives, Netherlands 57
proximity principle 100
Prussia, independent audit body (1714)
80
public accountability, *see*
accountability
public accounting
diversity of, Europe 26

harmonization 215–18
need for identical accounting criteria
   24
regional integration 211–13
Spain 105–6, 115
standards 214
see also budgeting and accounting
   systems; government
   accounting
public accounts
   criteria for presenting 7
   United Kingdom 45
public administration
   decentralization of 5–6
   expenditure, EU 194
   Federal Government and the Länder
      activities 89
      powers 88–9
   financial reporting 211–38
Public Administrations Act (1992) 122
Public Audit Forum 44
public audit, United Kingdom
   characteristics 30–38
   devolved audit institutions 42–4
   government accounting system 44–5
   organization 16–17
   see also National Audit Office
public control
   basic principles to be followed 13–14
   coordination, *see* coordination
      strategies
   European Union, *see* European
      Union
   evolution of the content of 8–12
   external, *see* external control
   information provision 7
   internal, *see* internal control
   management control 7–8
   post-audit 7
   pre-audit 6–7
   sequence of process 8
   Spain 101
      external 108–13
      internal 102–8
   see also public audit; public
      expenditure control; public
      financial control
public control institutions
   administrative structures 5–6
   Spain

autonomous communities 114–17
   coordination between 118–25
   under Franco regime 103
supranational
   EURORAI 13, 14–15
   EUROSAI 13, 14
   INTOSAI 12–14, 216
   see also Supreme Audit Institutions
public expenditure control,
   Netherlands
   Accounting Reform Operation 59
   'From Policy Budgeting to Policy
      Accountability' 59–60
   outcome-based budgeting 61–4
public financial control, Germany
   19–20
   external
      at federal level 80–85
      at regional level 85–6
   Federal Government and the Länder
      budget legislation agreement
         79–80
      distribution of tasks between
         87–91
      division of functions 79
      responsibilities, expenditure and
         revenue 79
   internal 86–7
public interest, example of a UK
   report issued in 32–3
public limited liability companies,
   NCA examination of 75
public management, reform 9
public managers, responsibilities 9–10
public policies, evaluation of 11
public resources, sound economy of 4
public sector auditors
   features of, UK 35–8
   training 13
public services, UK
   example of reports leading to
      improvement in quality 34
   recommendations leading to non-
      financial improvements 53
public–private partnership 133–4
publicity, about checks 197

qualifications, National Audit Office
   staff 40
Queen's Commissioner, Netherlands 57

Rechnunungshöfe 80
recruitment, National Audit Office 40
reforms
    EU accounting and budgeting 28,
        225–6
    legal framework 226–7
    role of European institutions
        235–7
    EU audit and control procedures
        198–200
    European Anti-Fraud Office 177–9
    government accounting 221
    public accounting 215–16
    public management 9
Regional Audit Offices,
    Bundesrechnungshof 82
Regional Budget Codes, Germany 80
regional external audit institutions,
    ECA relationship with 144–5
regional integration, public accounting
    information 211–13
regularity audits
    Bundesrechnungshof 83
    NCA
        consequences of VBTB 71–2
        systematic approach 70–71
Regulations
    (no. 1073/99) 164, 166, 175–6, 177,
        181
    (no. 1150/00) 154
    (no. 1172/76) 153–4
    (no. 1258/99) 159–60
    (no. 1260/99) 160
    (no. 1552/89) 159
    (no. 1831/94) 160
    (no. 2185/96) 156, 160, 162
    (no. 2988/95) 156, 159, 160
    (no. 4253/88) 160
    see also Financial Regulation
Reichenhaller Erklärung 94
relationships, ECA and SAIs 140–47
remuneration, National Audit Office 40
reporting, *see* financial reporting
reports
    principle of identical value 160
    Special Report no. 8/98 161, 162,
        167
    'Wise Men' (1999) 164
    see also annual reports; audit
        reports; joint reports

Resolution of the European
    Parliament (2002/2211-INI) 151
resource allocation, management
    approach 8–9
responsiveness, NCA strategy 69
revenue, Federal Government and the
    Länder 91
revenue fraud 151, 157
*Revenue from Non-Exchange
    Transactions (Including Taxes and
    Transfers)* 218
reviews, UK value for money reports
    48
Rotterdam 55
RTD framework programmes 193
Rules of Procedure Act 120, 121

sampling, EU internal control
    framework 204
Scotland Act (1998) 43
secondary controls, chain model 202
securities markets, need for
    transparency 130
Select Committee on Public Monies
    (1857) 38
Senate, Netherlands 57, 58
shared management
    costs of external control 197
    EC administrative reform 199
    EU accounting and budgeting 229
single audit
    concept 185
    Netherlands 187–90
    relevance for the EU context
        189–90
    United States 186–7
Single Audit Act (1984) 186
socioeconomic public accounting
    information 214
solidarity, principle of 173
Spain
    decentralization 99–100
    public control 20–22
    audit institutions
        autonomous communities
            114–17
        coordination between 118–25
    expenditure 101
    external 100, 108–13
    internal 100, 102–8

transfer payments from European Union 102
Spanish Constitution (1931) 114
Spanish Constitution (1978) 99, 101, 114
Special Report no. 8/98 161, 162, 167
Stability Plan 11–12
staff
  National Audit Office 40
  Netherlands Court of Audit 70
  Northern Ireland Audit Office 43
  Tribunal de Cuentas 110
Staff Regulations, internal investigations 167–8
standardization, accounting 219
standards
  government accounting 27, 214, 221
  see also Audit Standards; internal control standards; International Public Sector Accounting Standards; international quality standards
state accounts, Spain 103, 106–8, 111, 113
state activity, economic theory 3–4
state audit institutions, *see* Supreme Audit Institutions
State Expenditure Committee, Netherlands 67
State General Intervention 20, 100
  cooperation between Tribunal de Cuentas and 118–19
  history and function 102–3
  intervention and financial control 104–5
  public accounting 105–6
  reform of 100
  relations with
    European Court of Auditors 125
    Tribunal de Cuentas 101–2
  state accounts 106–8
State Sector General Accounts 107
state structure, Netherlands 55–6
Statement of Assurance (ECA) 230
States General, Netherlands 57, 58, 67, 68, 75, 77
strategic planning process, UK auditing 47
Structural Actions 138–9
Structural Funds Technical Group 193

structural measures expenditure 192–3
  poor control 195
studies, value for money 47, 48–9
subsidiarity principle 100, 156, 166, 219
Supervisory Committee (OLAF) 166, 171, 174, 176
support directorates, of NCA 70
supranational political integration, external audit institutions 128–30
supranational public control institutions 12–15
supremacy, of Tribunal de Cuentas 120–23
Supreme Audit Institutions
  audit of government performance 10
  changing boundary between public and private spheres 133–4
  cooperation with ECA 139–40
  demand for transparency and accountability 130–33
  different models 15–16
  EU internal control framework 206
  external control, EU funds 194
  public control task 6–7
  supranational political integration and decentralization 128–30
  see also individual institutions
Swedish Audit Office 16
systematic approach, of NCA 70–71

Tampere European Council (1999) 179, 181
target group audits 74
technical relationships, ECA and SAIs 140
territoriality, principle of 173
third pillar instruments, fight against fraud 156, 157–60
three H questions, Dutch Annual Report 61
three W questions, Dutch budget reform 61, 62, 63
total quality, introduction of 10–11
Training Committee (EUROSAI) 14
transfer payments, Spain 102
transparency
  external audit institutions 130–33
  NCA strategy 69
Treaties of Rome (1957) 152

Treaty of Amsterdam (1999) 22, 134,
    170, 179, 180, 181
Treaty of Brussels (1965) 152
Treaty of Brussels (1975) 134
Treaty of Brussels (1977) 22
Treaty of the European Union (1992)
    25, 134, 155–6, 158, 159, 170
Treaty of Luxembourg (1979) 153
Treaty of Nice 169–71, 180
Treaty of Paris (1951) 152
Tribunal de Cuentas 20–21, 100
    audit function 110–11
    basic features 101
    coordination between
        devolved audit bodies and 119–24
        State General Intervention and
            118–19
    evolution and present structure
        108–10

jurisdictional function 111–12
relations with
    parliament 112–13
    State General Intervention 101–2

United Kingdom, public audit
    characteristics 30–38
    devolved audit institutions 42–4
    government accounting system
        44–5
    organization 16–17
    see also National Audit Office
United States, single audit 186–7

value for money, UK auditing process
    46–9, 51
vertical group, ECA 135

'Wise Men', committee of 164